Daube On Roman Law

STUDIES IN COMPARATIVE LEGAL HISTORY

Daube On Roman Law

Collected Works of David Daube
Volume 5

Edited by

Calum Carmichael and Laurent Mayali

The Robbins Collection *Berkeley*

Robbins Collection Publications
School of Law (Boalt Hall)
University of California at Berkeley
Berkeley, California 94720
(510) 642-5094 fax: (510) 642-8325
www.law.berkeley.edu/robbins

ISBN: 978-1-882239-21-4   *Daube On Roman Law*

ISBN: 1-882239-01-6
978-1-882239-01-6   Collected Works of David Daube

Library of Congress Catalog Card number: 92-61641

Contents

The Scales of Justice   1

Analyzes in various cultural contexts the scale as an image of justice.
Modern jurisprudential attitudes are hostile to the black and white
model of the law inherent in the notion of the scales of justice.

Compromise   21

The evolution of the verb "to compromise": from the ancient concept
of a promise to arbitrate to both a preliminary and final arrangement
attained by simple negotiation as well as arbitration. The Jansenists
played a major role in the verb also acquiring its modern pejorative
sense "to hurt."

Pecco Ergo Sum   27

1) The verb "to be" is etymologically related to "sooth" (truth) and "to
sin." Truth is often about something negative, hence often about wrongdoing. 2) The *lex Salica* of the Franks applies the term *sunne*, truth, reality, to the specific situation where there is a solid reason to disregard a
summons to a trial. "That which is," *sunne*, here refers not to an offender
but stands for the circumstance justifying absence from the trial. The
same word can often refer to unlike things in unlike fields. *Sunne* may
be a remote descendant of the similar use of the term *morbus sonticus*,
"true" illness, in the XII Tables (fifth century B.C.).

The *lex Fufia Caninia* limited the number of slaves that could be freed in a will. A legend transmitted by Ausonius about a Delphic Oracle's answer as to who was first among the Seven Sages contributes to the dodge attempting to circumvent the statute: the names of the manumitted slaves were written in a circle. The underlying notion, that a circle has neither beginning nor end, may also have influenced the role of the round table in the legend of King Arthur.

1) Discusses attributes of legal expression (intelligibility, brevity, and accuracy) in terms of their impact on the reader, especially where meaning is obfuscated or hidden despite ideals of clarity. 2) How an interpreter chooses to comment on an authoritative work of law or literature produces surprisingly different types of commentaries. Writers created the popular literary genre, the Cento, by taking lines and half-lines from the works of Homer and Virgil, which were regarded as containing all wisdom, and stitching them together. Pleasure lay in the reader recognizing the original context of the line or half-line and admiring the new application.

Ancient legal authorities, Paul and Sabinus, disagreed about whether a view of an illustrious poet could be used as a legal argument. Might Homer be interpreted as supporting the proposition that money was essential in sale?

Foreword

Laurent Mayali

Lenel, Kunkel, and Daube. These three scholars represent more than a century of Roman law studies. During this period, Europe witnessed unprecedented tragedies that redrew its borders, ripped up its social fabric, perverted its political institutions, and threatened the core values of its civilization. Each of these scholars faced, in their own time, the consequences of these man-made cataclysms without compromising the moral values that shaped their intellectual pursuits. Such moral fortitude gave their scholarship its unique character. It also influenced their idea of law as the measure of human actions. It almost sounds a truism to state that a scholar's personal commitments are never too far from his scholarly output. Yet we should not consider this obvious relationship as a substitute for sorting out erudition from ideology, nor separating scholarship from propaganda, nor judgment from prejudice. As a matter of fact, in the eyes of these scholars, the study of Roman law was not a substitute for legal expertise and political ethics, nor was it an attempt to impress an idealized legal model on their contemporaries. Their interest in Roman law reflected a personal commitment to scholarship as members of academia and as active participants in the debates that defined political institutions and social order.

A student of Lenel and Kunkel, Daube expanded on their intellectual legacy while marking out his own original path. Having absorbed Lenel's penetrating scrutiny of the legal sources and Kunkel's grasp of Roman social culture, Daube challenged us to look past the nature and content of legal provisions right into people's attempts to reconcile private interests with public order and individual beliefs with common values. Much has been written about his intellectual curiosity. His flair for finding meaningful connections between distinct legal rules and their cultural tradition shed new light on the structure and function of the language of law. It is thus not surprising that Daube chose to study legal concepts or normative patterns that revealed as much about legal reasoning as about human acumen. Concern for the inherent logical structure of the rules did not preclude him from taking into consideration their concrete effect and their symbolic function. This intellectual stance assumed its full meaning when compared with the more dogmatic approach that had previously dominated German legal science. In that work, various references to legal terminology conjured up classifications of abstracts concepts and doctrinal interpretations that seemed disconnected from the social issues they purported to address. The Pandectist school's elaborate versions of Roman legal principles had offered an historical, albeit extreme, illustration of this intellectual compulsion, leading to the distinct technical character of German codification. Furthermore, in many countries, an overly confident trust in legal positivism's set of classifications led to a vision of the legal system that nurtured the germs of its eventual demise.

Daube's methodological choices are evident in the larger studies as well as in the smaller pieces that are collected in this volume. A study begins often with a candid question. The informal tone of the ensuing argumentation underscores the collegial nature of the whole enterprise. Arguments unfold as part of a discussion that considers the readers as participants in the intellectual interchange. We are not expected to confine ourselves to being passive recipients of the authoritative demonstration. This method applies also to his presentation of legal rules. They are never dissociated from the actors and the community for which they were intended.

Let us consider, for instance, the study of the *senatus consultum macedonianum* in this volume. It would seem at first that to know whether Macedo killed his father would not add much to the meaning and scope of the *senatus consultum* prohibiting the repayment of loans made to *filiifamilias*. Yet, asking this apparently simple question allows Daube to place the legislation in a context that opens up a broader window into Roman legal reasoning and the social structure that constituted its basic reference. Driving a thriftless man to parricide was an unintended consequence of a tradition that no longer served its purpose. By the time of the *senatus consultum*, more cracks surfaced on the Roman patriarchal edifice. Safeguarding family fortunes might have warranted keeping adult men who could otherwise have been active members of their community in a condition of legal and financial dependency, but it did not bode well for the society's future. "So far Macedo" observes Daube "does not seem to have a chance. The sources declare him guilty of a heinous crime." Before adding his voice to the chorus of jurists and historians who, over a period of several centuries, attempted to evaluate the extent of Macedo's guilt, Daube directs his attention to the precise wording of the ambiguous senatorial decree.

In this interval—between the written sources' account and their social implications, intended or unintended—resides for Daube the significance of the legal rule. To find "What actually went on" is what matters most. For this purpose, no ingenious interpretation nor ideological construct should supplant in the scholar's mind the comparative assessment of the text's diverse readings. In his view, social ideology and academic preconceptions quickly reveal their limits. Their one-sided inferences only "shed light on the character of the various participants" since "scholarly attitudes vary to an astonishing degree in different periods, countries and persons."

What happened then in Macedo's case? Did the deal between the conniving son and a predatory usurer prove to be fatal to the unsuspecting father? Or, should we agree with some scholars and conclude that the whole affair never reached such a dramatic climax? Could it be instead that the multiplication of usurious loans was the offense that caused the senators' alarm and not the eventual attempt on the father's life? And if this was really the case, should the *paterfamilias* be shielded from the claims of his son's creditors? There is little doubt that the moneylender's aggressive practices would strain the father-son relationship within the sacrosanct order of the Roman family. The answers to all these questions reveal a more complex state of affairs. Untangling its various twists, Daube correlates the lawmakers' intentions and the rationale of the legal institutions "with the social and economic data determining them and determined by them."

With this task in mind, Daube challenges all prior scholarly interpretations by methodically comparing their conjectures with the textual evidence. By the end of this comparative process, one conclusion appears to be more likely: Macedo, pressured by his creditor, did murder his father. But this conclusion is, as we noted earlier, only one part of the overarching story. The point made by Daube here does not simply question people's misplaced inclinations but illustrates the very nature of a legal provision that is built more on the expectation of likelihood than the assurance of the truth.

Characteristically, in solving the *senatus consultum macedonianum*'s puzzle Daube presents a more complex picture of the Roman legal system—a picture that not only takes into account the legal interpretation and enforcement of rules but also describes the overarching normative design of Roman juridical culture. Whether correcting a faulty translation of Diogenes Laertius or providing political context to an absolutist maxim, Daube always takes into consideration the diverse legal options that could present themselves in the society of that time. Furthermore, his pointed remarks on the changing nature of scholarship raise the much debated issue of the historical significance of Roman law studies in legal education and research. In a time when, in various countries, law school curricula no longer make place for the study of Roman law, invoking as justification its presumed irrelevance in today's legal world, Daube's work provides a convincing example to the contrary of both methodology and substance.

It is clear that much of the current skepticism about the relevance of Roman law in today's society results from the Romanists' choice to distance themselves from the more positivistic or ideologically oriented conceptions of the *Rechtsstaat*. This decision was vindicated by the necessity to break away from the most salient doctrinal failures of twentieth-century nationalist legal systems. It led however to the unintended consequence of separating Roman jurisprudence from contemporary legal debates and consigning it to the more antiquarian role of a historical curiosity. As Daube convincingly shows, there is certainly more to Roman law studies than an academic version of Hollywood's peplum film genre. But the gulf is by now so well established that any attempt to restore Roman law's jurisprudential significance appears either an artificial update of a long lost tradition or as a nostalgic reference to an idealized legal past. The latter is perhaps nowhere more apparent than in the various attempts to reinvent European history and its common legal legacy in light of the European Union's legal challenges.

Daube does not ignore these apparently conflicting contingencies. He chooses instead to harmonize them in a comparative perspective that captures both the historical tradition and the legal essence of the Roman rules. Macedo's crime is no longer an historical anecdote nor is it reduced to a category of offense in the Roman criminal system. The apparent ease with which he achieves such results does not come readily to most current scholarship in legal history.

On one hand, historians' recent enthusiasm for legal history has renewed interest in its social purpose. It has also brought fresh perspectives to the study of Roman law. But a limited discussion of legal concepts and institutions does not reflect the full measure of law's symbolic and real function in Roman society during the diverse periods of its history. On the other hand, there is no longer any valid justification for the use of a positivist and a historical classification inherited from last century's legal doctrines. Daube's work presents us with an effective alternative. He challenges us to combine the comparative assessments of the historical, social and legal values of law's rules into a coherent legal historical model without disregarding the close reading of textual sources.

Acknowledgements

"The Scales of Justice" was published in *Juridical Review* 63 (1951), 109–129; "Compromise" was published in *Juridical Review* 95 (n.s. 28) (1983), 188–192; "The Self-Understood in Legal History" was published in *Juridical Review* 85 (n.s. 18) (1973), 126–134.

"Pecco Ergo Sum" was published in *Rechtshistorisches Journal* 4 (1985), 137–143; "Standing in for Jack Coons" was published in *Rechtshistorisches Journal* 7 (1988), 179–183; "What Price Equality? Some Historical Reflections" was published in *Rechtshistorisches Journal* 5 (1986), 185–208.

"A Corrupt Judge Sets the Pace" was published in *Gedächtnisschrift für Wolfgang Kunkel* (Frankfurt am Main: Vittorio Klostermann, 1984), 37–52.

"Money and Justiciability" was published in *Zeitschrift der Savigny-Stiftung für Rechtsgeschichte, Romanistische Abteilung* 96 (1979), 1–16; "Did Macedo Murder His Father?" was published in *Zeitschrift der Savigny-Stiftung für Rechtsgeschichte, Romanistische Abteilung* 65 (1947), 261–311. Reprinted by permission.

"Fashions and Idiosyncrasies in the Exposition of the Roman Law of Property" was published in *Theories of Property*, eds. A. Parel and T. Flanagan (Waterloo, Ontario: Published for the Calgary Institute for the Humanities by Wilfrid Laurier University Press, 1979), 35–50. Reprinted by permission.

"The Marriage of Justinian and Theodora. Legal and Theological Reflections" was published in *Catholic University of American Law Review* 16 (1967), 380–399.

Abbreviations

BLL	*Biblical Law and Literature.* Collected Works of David Daube vol. 3. Ed. Calum Carmichael. Berkeley, 2003.
CLJ	*Cambridge Law Review*
Ethics	*Ethics and Other Writings.* Collected Works of Davide Daube vol. 4. Ed. Calum Carmichael. Berkeley, 2009.
JJS	*Journal of Jewish Studies*
JR	*Juridical Review*
JSS	*Journal of Semitic Studies*
JTS	*Journal of Theological Studies*
LQR	*Law Quarterly Review*
NTJ	*New Testament Juadaism.* Collected Works of David Daube vol. 2. Ed. Calum Carmichael. Berkeley, 2000.
TL	*Talmudic Law.* Collected Works of David Daube vol. 1. Ed. Calum Carmichael. Berkeley, 1992.
TLL	*Thesaurus linguae Latinae*
ZRG	*Zeitschrift der Savigny-Stiftung für Rechtsgeschichte*
RA	*Romanistische Abteilung*

Introduction

Calum Carmichael

David Daube began his study of Roman law in the Germany of the late 1920s with Otto Lenel, pioneer of the modern study of the discipline. Living close to Lenel's home in Freiburg im Breisgau, Daube would visit him there and also attend seminars at the University of Freiburg in which Lenel participated after his retirement. Daube viewed their close relationship as decisive in his own scholarly career. Through Lenel Daube partakes of a scholarly pedigree in an unbroken line of jurists that stretches over a thousand years. Beginning with the jurist Irnerius, who at the end of the eleventh century revived the study of Roman law in Bologna, the *Arbor Leneliana* (a generational tree of scholars preeminent in the field of civil law), includes some of the most famous names in European legal history. To be sure, as Laurent Mayali, Daube's successor as Director of the Robbins Collection at the School of Law, University of California at Berkeley, reminded me, Irnerius and his successors, the glossators, lacked philological and historical awareness, knew no Greek, and understood Latin but poorly. Daube's approach was more in the tradition of the legal humanists such as Guillaume Budé and Jacques Cujas in France, Andrea Alciato in Italy and France, and Ulrich Zasius, a professor of Law in Freiburg. (Zasius has a street in Freiburg named after him, as does Cujas in Paris.) These humanists did indeed transform the study of Roman law in the sixteenth century with their philological erudition, clear legal thinking, and historical perspective.

Daube continued his study of the subject at the University of Göttingen under Wolfgang Kunkel who was only seven years older than Daube. Eventually, because of the looming threat posed by National Socialism in Germany, with Lenel's assistance Daube left for England. Beginning in 1933 Daube pursued his Roman law studies at the University of Cambridge under the direction of William Warwick Buckland, the foremost Romanist in Britain. Like Lenel, Buckland was well on in years when Daube met him.

The impact of geography on Daube's life cannot be overestimated. Over a time span of approximately thirty years in each place, he lived first in Germany, then in Britain, and latterly in the United States. As an Orthodox Jew in Germany and an alien in both the United Kingdom and the United States, he enjoyed the role of the outsider. Referring to the biblical figure of Moses as an Egyptian, he writes: "In fact, often a fringe figure—not a total foreigner but neither from the unexciting or no longer dependable cultural core—has the best chance of being hailed as redeemer. Napoléon, from Corsica, Hitler, from Austria, and, incidentally, surrounded by *Auslandsdeutsche*: Darré was born in the Argentines, Hess in Egypt, Rosenberg in Estonia, and Göring settled in Sweden after World War I."[1] Daube had no great inclination to engage in public life, much less did he strive to be a redeemer of any kind. However, his marked, perhaps even cultivated foreignness, combined with an acute awareness of language used in all the sectors of society in which he enthusiastically mixed, proved a formidable strength.

The aim of this volume is to select items from Daube's work on Roman law that convey the distinctiveness of his mind and exemplify his distinction as the foremost humanist of the law. What makes his work on Roman law different from the work of others in the field is that, like the sixteenth-century French Renaissance writer Michel Montaigne, Daube possessed the capacity to be "a contemporary for all times." No matter what period of history Daube inquired into he had an uncanny instinct for

---

1. "Sons and Strangers," *Biblical Law and Literature*, Collected Works of David Daube, vol. 3, ed. Calum Carmichael (Berkeley, 2003), 157; also Institute of Jewish Law, Boston University School of Law (1984), 1.

uncovering unexpected insights that root us in that time and have universal application.

During Daube's residence in the United States, at the University of California, Berkeley, he frequently quoted in his publications items from the *San Francisco Chronicle*. In the spirit of the Hungarian Nobel Laureate, Albert Szent-Györgyi, Daube sought to see what everyone sees but think what no one has thought. Present or past problems were for him opportunities for discovery. As he sometimes modestly posited in the description of his course offerings at Berkeley, he thought it should be possible to say something new about the past and also think that it may have some relevance to the present. But as a confidant and colleague at the Berkeley Law School, Kathleen Vanden Heuvel, emphasized, Daube went further. In order to comprehend disturbing new ideas and new technology, it is crucial that we turn to the past and use whatever history has to offer by way of illumination. We have first "to capture change and bring it into the realm of shared understanding."[2]

Students picked up on this quest. An article about him in *The Oakland Tribune*, 4 December, 1986, had the byline: "Renowned professor teaches law for all time." The item includes students' comments about how, unlike other academic colleagues, "instead of being aloof and intellectual, he surprises his pupils and peers alike with his warm unorthodoxy and rambunctious mind." He is "an artist, a mental gymnast, who sees the law not as a series of cases built upon precedents, but as a reflection of human nature that repeats itself time after time, from pre-biblical days to the present." His class is "about who we are today. And how do we know what we're like? By looking at the way we were 2,000 years ago." Other students speak of him as "an original observer, "a crafty analyst," of how he always strives to take "conventional or accepted wisdom and shatter it apart."

In presenting Daube's work on Roman law, Laurent Mayali and I had anticipated that Alan Rodger, a student of Daube's from Oxford days, would participate in the venture. Alas, to our great sorrow, we learned of

---

2. Kathleen Vanden Heuvel, "Professor David Daube," *California Law Review* 87 (1999), 1052.

his untimely death.[3] Rodger had given the Cameron McKenna lecture in 2001 at the University of Aberdeen in Scotland—Daube had been Professor of Jurisprudence there in the 1950s—which Rodger entitled "Law for All Times: The Work and Contribution of David Daube." The topic was the one vividly commented on by the Berkeley students: how Daube's work did indeed contribute to an understanding of law at all times and how, as Rodger never failed to assert, Daube "was, quite simply, unbelievably clever." He highlighted Daube's ability to read a text probing deeply what it was saying and what it was not saying. Seeking in his own work as a judge to uncover meaning that had been missing from previous treatment of pertinent legislation, he constantly felt that Daube looked over his shoulder to see to it that he was reading the statute carefully. He urged practitioners of law to recognize that assiduous reading of documents and the onerous task of applying critical thinking to them could achieve so much.[4]

In responding to what occurs in the world at large, Daube suggested, all of us tend to pigeon-hole issues into categories of thought and belief that we have already consciously or unconsciously acquired. But for him, truthfulness to life is what counts and makes for lasting interest. By and large, he was not greatly interested in general matters that engage so many scholars. They speak of "a Roman patrician," "a nineteenth-century liberal," "the Apostles," and "the Rabbis," but such terms are used as if real people in real life are meant when, in fact, they represent abstractions.

Daube's bent was to focus on a telling detail as illustrated in some of

3. Among the many obituary notices that appeared world-wide, the following from the *Oxford Alumni Magazine* communicated in brief outline the following information: "Alan Ferguson Rodger, Baron Rodger of Earlsferry, QC, PC, FBA, FRSE, Justice of the Supreme Court of the United Kingdom, died on 26 June 2011, aged 66. He studied for an Oxford DPhil on Roman law and was then a fellow and tutor at New College. He left in 1972 to practice as an advocate in Edinburgh. In 1992 he became Lord Advocate, and was made a life peer. From 1996 to 2001, he was Lord President of the Court of Session. He became a Lord of Appeal in Ordinary in 2001, and a Justice of the Supreme Court on its creation in 2009. From 2008 he was High Steward of the University. He was unmarried."

4. See Alan Rodger, "David Daube (8. 2. 1909–24. 2. 1999)," *ZRG, RA* 118 (2001), xiv–lii. For his Aberdeen lecture, see "Law for All Times: The Work and Contribution of David Daube," in *Law for All Times. Essays in Memory of David Daube*, Roman Legal Tradition 2, ed. Ernest Metzger (Lawrence, Kansas, 2004), 3–23.

his literary insights. A remarkable feature of probably the greatest novel ever written, Cervantes' *Don Quixote*, is that throughout this story about a knight-errant the author, a survivor of the battle of Lepanto in 1571, does not portray a single mortally wounded person. For Daube, a discussion of this one feature in a tale devoted to the profession of soldiery illuminated the work as much as any literary theory could ever do. He reckoned that Cervantes' Christian belief informed his position. That equally universalistic work, the Book of Jonah, also exhibited an intense interest in destruction and violence, yet as in *Don Quixote* not one person is killed: "And should not I [God] spare Nineveh, that great city, wherein are more than six-score thousand persons that cannot discern between their right hand and their left hand; and also much cattle?" (Jonah 4:11). The biblical author generously views human creatureliness and lack of insight as mitigating accountability. Tolstoy's *Anna Karenina* ends with Karenina committing suicide. For Christians the act wipes out any merits of the person and spells damnation. Should there be, however, last minute repentance the wrongdoer receives forgiveness and salvation. Tolstoy, communicating from the perspective of Russian Orthodox belief, movingly takes up this teaching. As the train begins to roll over her, Karenina realizes her error and prays for forgiveness. Tolstoy's ending is hopeful. Readers, Daube noted, scarcely take in this detail.

Daube's attraction to surprising or unexpected details in the legal sources characterizes his work on Roman law. From early on in his studies he looked into Justinian's search for legal principles (sixth century A.D.). The much earlier classical sources (30 B.C. to 230 A.D.) formulated few such principles and the even earlier pre-classical jurists (200 to 30 B.C.) tended simply to lay down easy rules. The post-classical sources (post third-century) inclined to systematize. Attracted to the work of the classical jurists, Daube saw them as alert to the dangers of moving too readily toward principles and toward systematization. These jurists preferred to look for continuous evolution in the law. They went from case to case but stopped short of generalizing across cases. They took the obvious for granted and avoided any compulsion to pursue the later process of what Daube called "completomania" where "near-synonyms are heaped two, five, ten,

on top of one another" ("give and bequeath," "pierce, break, damage").[5]
Characterized by care, deliberation and, most of all, attention to context,
the classical jurists were acutely aware of law's complex operation. Justinian, on the other hand, introduced generalizing principles and one way in
which he did so was to omit context and consequently, if unintentionally,
mislead.

W hy was the earlier approach to law so much more engaging to a
mind like Daube's? For him, to generalize is invariably to omit and what is
lost in the generalization is often what is most interesting. He would have
been in full agreement with Machiavelli: "If anything pleases or teaches in
history, it is that which is described in detail."[6] An article in this volume,
"Fraud No. 3," demonstrates how a Justinianic legal principle, which to
this day still plays a prime role in property law in different legal systems,
by its generalization inadvertently conceals its singular origin in a certain
kind of misconduct. In the essay, Daube highlights Rodger's discussion of
the rule.

> Alan Rodger has just gone into one of those maxims in the Digest
> which were much narrower in their native context: "Things are not
> deemed to be given which do not become the property of the recipi-
> ent at the time they are given." Paul [Julius Paulus], he shows, was
> discussing the *actio aquae pluviae arcendae* available where, as a
> result of a construction on your neighbor's land, yours was exposed to
> rainwater coming from there. In classical law, your remedy was stron-
> ger so long as he who erected the construction still owned the land.
> Hence, if he made a gift of it to someone [so that legal action might be
> avoided], it was important to determine whether ownership had fully
> passed: it is this specific situation Paul has in mind."[7]

Rodger acknowledged his indebtedness to Daube's work, especially
to an article, "Zur Palingenesie einiger Klassikerfragmente," *Zeitschrift*

---

5. "The Influence of Interpretation on Writing," 260 below.
6. See Benedetto Croce, *History as the Story of Liberty* (Indianapolis, 2000), 343.
7. Digest 50.17.167 pr., Paul XLIX *ad edictum*; see A. F. Rodger, "Roman Gifts
and Rain-Water," *Law Quarterly Review* 100 (1984), 77–85. See "Fraud No. 3," 249
below.

der Savigny-Stiftung für Rechstgeschichte 76 (1959), 149–264, which he considered to be one of Daube's most brilliant and which discussed the very topic Rodger took up. For Rodger, and all who came under Daube's influence, Benedetto Croce's remark is pertinent: "What can be more delightful or more restful than a loyal confidence in the person and the teaching of a master?"[8]

Daube's insights are readily available in the articles chosen for this volume. He notes that the maxim about the Emperor being above the law, "Princeps legibus solutus," so significant in history, eventually came to be understood as advocating political absolutism and was very much used this way in the Middle Ages. Yet originally the maxim meant only exemption from some rules (mainly to do with disabilities of the unmarried and the childless). Justinian had formulated the maxim in a way that led to the all encompassing view so that even in some circles today to argue that its original meaning was of the narrow kind might be considered harmful, even hostile. In "A Corrupt Judge Sets the Pace" he mischievously points out that corrupt judges can be a source of law. Bribing them can sometimes produce brilliant decisions for reasons that Daube claims are obvious. The topic raises the larger issue of what motivates all of us to do our best work, the inspiration possibly being quite vulgar. In "The Marriage of Justinian and Theodora" an exotic idea that we might think too far out to be of much account outside of a religious context, the notion of new birth, proves to be powerfully at work in some legal developments. Looking at the topic of "The Influence of Interpretation on Writing," Daube notes that the sanctity attributed to long-established texts can result in the strangest of notions about where wisdom is to be found. Affirming "The Preponderance of Intestacy at Rome," he corrects a misunderstanding about who made wills and illustrates how law, like a distorting mirror, often makes the large small and the small large. The phenomenon also shows up in the use of language: no word existed in ancient Rome, not even in the classical period, for those, the vast majority, who did not make a will. In line with what he writes about in "The Self-Understood in Legal History," Daube

---

8. *My Philosophy: and Other Essays on the Moral and Political Problems of Our Time* (London, 1949), 19.

once told an audience that he lacked the courage to stand before them for an hour and not say a word. He was addressing the hugely significant role of silence in the law and also in language. Unwritten rules play a fundamental role in any legal system and no words exist, for instance, for those who do not murder, steal, or tell lies.

Illuminating comments, often tangential to the main topic of the discussion, come as asides. In "The Scales of Justice," Daube remarks:

> There is a fair amount of evidence that the starting-point of legal philosophy was criminal law. This is, of course, less immediately clear from the work of a man like Plato, who is representative of mature analysis. But it is criminal law problems that are put in the Oresteia, where Aeschylus attempts to harmonize religion and law. The Old Testament prophets proceed in the same way.

It is, finally, apt and revealing of Daube's contribution to Roman law, to take stock of his assessment of the work of Buckland, his own teacher at Cambridge. Some six years after coming to Cambridge Daube published his thoughts.[9] Roman legal studies in the modern sense did not exist in England until 1908, claims Daube, the year when Buckland published his book on *The Roman Law of Slavery*. A succession of books followed and his contributions to the leading journals established Buckland as the pre-eminent scholar of Roman law. Noting how generous Buckland was in finding time to advance the interests of students and colleagues, Daube comments: "how many students have been made into lawyers by him; how many colleagues, since the time when 'Mr. Buckland kept Maitland out of some blunders,' have gone to him for advice. He has, in fact, founded a school: a school of Roman law in which, as is obvious to one coming from the Continent, the best methods of English legal thinking are put to use."

What exactly were Buckland's interests? He had no inclination to study the remote past of Roman law with its "loose and scattered rules" and he gave little attention to criminal law because "it does not show (and in his opinion criminal law neither need nor ought to show) a great deal of subtle elaboration." More substantively, Buckland rejected the view that

---

9. *"Nocere* and *Noxa,"* in the *Cambridge Law Journal* 7 (1939), 23–54.

classical private law is a logical edifice, one created without regard to everyday requirements. Its lasting value is best appreciated by observing how "exact legal reasoning and common sense are combined in an unequalled manner." Being skilled in jurisprudence, in logic and in rhetoric, and enjoying the support of the community, the Roman jurists created a coherent system of law but, "being broad-minded public men, aristocratic in their attitude, dependent neither on Caesar nor on the plebs, they never forgot that law, if it is to serve its ultimate purpose, must be a living force, flexible and progressive."

Like Buckland, Daube also took his inspiration from the classical jurists and his description of Buckland applies just as much to himself:

> Professor Buckland is a true historian: and it is precisely for this reason that he has always refused to erect into an absolute dogma any one of the different methods at the disposal of the modern critic. He does, of course, use them. But he uses them with care, leaving the sources to speak the last word. He teaches that, in history, to simplify is to do violence to the documents which reflect ideas too manifold to admit of schematic treatment.... No less significant is the way he describes the fundamental concepts of Roman law, and how they work, with all their ramifications and fine inconsistencies; no less significant his weighing against each other, in tracing the development of a particular institution, the forces of tradition and reform, system and practical necessity, milieu and personality; no less significant his reserve in estimating the role played in Roman legal growth by Greek and oriental law, and in dating such importations as there exist.

Daube learned from a master scholar in Buckland and produced work of comparable complexity and sophistication, but with a difference. Having an eye for those unique details in the texts that can surprise and delight, Daube demonstrated a degree of originality that to lawyer or non-lawyer is instantly recognizable.

The Scales of Justice[1]

Portia awards Shylock the penalty he claims. But in doing so, she warns him: "If thou tak'st more or less than a just pound... nay, if the scale do turn but in the estimation of a hair, thou diest." The slightest deviation from the stipulated weight will spell his doom. It will make no difference whether he cuts too much by a stone or an ounce, or, indeed, whether he cuts too much or too little. He must be absolutely right to be safe—otherwise he loses all. Such are the scales of justice.

In any academic analysis of justice, be it by Aristotle over two thousand years ago[2] or by Professor Coing in 1950,[3] stress is laid on the importance of treating different situations differently, each in accordance with its individual character; and practical obstacles alone are recognized as limiting the principle. It would seem, however, that justice as a living phenomenon contains an element that is averse to finer differentiations, quite apart from practical difficulties. That symbolism of the scales expresses a deep-rooted tendency to see no shades between black and white, to admit no degrees of right and wrong, to allow no distribution of loss and gain among several litigants, to send a party away either victorious or defeated.

The criminal law of this country still imposes capital punishment on murder no matter whether (to adapt the words of Sir Walter Scott) "it arises out of the malevolence of the heart or the error of the understanding." As for private law, when we take the *bona fide* possessor—a person who, though not in fact proprietor, honestly believes himself proprietor—Roman law and its modern descendants, including Scots law, give him the fruits drawn

[*The Juridical Review* 63 (1951): 109–129]
1. An inaugural lecture delivered at the University of Aberdeen, on April 30, 1951.
2. *Nicomachean Ethics* 5.3 ff.
3. *Grundzüge der Rechtsphilosophie*, 181 ff.

by him while in possession; this is hard on the proprietor. English law gives the fruits to the proprietor, which is hard on the *bona fide* possessor. There is apparently no system which divides the fruits between them.[4] If an object sold is accidentally destroyed before delivery, Roman law and English law put the risk on the buyer: he must pay the price, receiving nothing. According to German law, he need not pay. There is no law which says that he should pay half the price. Paton writes that where two persons suffer by the fraud of a third, "ethics may suggest that the loss should be equally divided, but this is not a very practicable rule for the law."[5] This is perfectly true, only the law inclines to an attitude of "either-or" in a far higher degree than is necessitated by practical considerations.

It is not as if this element were present only in the strict, quiritary law of the Romans or the common law, and not in the *ius gentium* or equity. Equitable rules also favour the alternative of victory or defeat—complete victory or complete defeat—though they may differ from strict rules in deciding where victory and defeat should lie. *Condictio*, the recovery of payment made in advance if the service expected becomes impossible, is often rested on natural law. Yet it is a somewhat extreme remedy. Without it, to be sure, the party who has paid incurs an unfair loss. But the principle that he may recover the whole goes rather far in the opposite direction if, for example, the other person has already spent money on this transaction.[6] There was a period in Roman law when a seller was not automatically answerable to the buyer if the latter was deprived of the thing owing to a defect in title; the buyer might have to bear all the loss. It was largely by an elaboration of the equitable, *bonae fidei* nature of sale that warranty of title became an intrinsic part of it. The resulting rule might be preferable to the

---

4. Certain relaxations of the Roman law rule may be regarded as steps in this direction.

5. *Jurisprudence* (1946), 58. He is hardly right, however, in asserting that ethics throws little light on cases like this. If ethics demands that the loss should be divided, that is no less of a solution—from the point of view of ethics—than a demand that it should fall on one of the parties.

6. Cp. below on the way the Law Reform (Frustrated Contracts) Act, 1943, deals with such problems. Professor T. B. Smith very kindly points out to the writer that, in Scots law, the common law has proved more flexible: *Cantiere San Rocco* v. *Clyde Shipbuilding Co.*, 1923 S.C. (H.L.) 105.

earlier one, but it was scarcely less rigorous. All the loss would now fall on the seller[7]—as it does in Scots and English law. A law which takes account of the error of a party entering into a contract usually does so in pursuance of equitable notions. But many systems, in declaring such a contract void or voidable, fail to make provision for the other party who was not in error and relied on performance.

It is significant that, in legal history, whereas the institution of double, triple or fourfold damages is frequent, that of half damages is extremely rare. There is something in a compromise of this kind repugnant to justice. Certainly, even so, there is much scope for adjusting damages to the individual case. We may or may not include losses suffered as a remoter consequence of the act in question; we may proceed from the interest a party has in performance of the contract (the *positives Vertragsinteresse* of German law) or from that he has in never having heard of it, i.e., in being restored to the *status quo ante* (*negatives Vertragsinteresse*). Still, while a system will readily credit its judges with sufficient discernment to determine the exact degree of care a depositee must have shown if he is to be relieved of liability for loss of the article, and the different degree of care a hirer must have shown, and the different degree again required of a commodatary, it may never give up the simple alternative between full liability and no liability; the loss must fall either on one party or the other. The power exercised by Scottish and English courts of mitigating the damages where special circumstances warrant it is by no means a feature of all modern systems. If my dog tears your trousers, without any negligence on my part, some systems make me responsible, others do not; and most waver between the two solutions, preferring now one and now the other. There are very few indeed which demand a sharing of the loss.[8] In the Scots law of reparation, if I inflict injury in self-defence, then, provided I did not go further than the occasion warranted, I shall be free from liability; if I exceeded the reasonable limits, I shall be liable, though even then there may be mitigation of damages at least. This is a flexible regulation, which will enable a court to

---

7. In Roman law, sometimes he might have to return double the price.

8. An early example, manifestly going back to an era when restitution was in kind, not in money, is Exod 21:35; cp. *Mishnah Baba Kamma* 1:4.

deal with each case as it deserves. The English rule is similar. But when
we come to German law, we find, on the one hand, that exemption from
liability is not confined to a reasonable exercise of self-defence. So long
as I had no other means of warding off an illegal attack, I am guilty of no
wrong. Thus if a boy is about to pick one of my apples and I can save it only
by shooting, I may do so.[9] On the other hand, once I overstep the boundar-
ies of the permissible, I can no longer hope for mitigation of damages. Any
action necessary to prevent an illegal aggression is justified; any other will
involve me in full liability.

A large proportion of the law of evidence is designed to bring about a
simple, one-sided verdict even where the facts actually known would seem
to call for a middle course, if not a final *non liquet*. If A and B are agreed
that A has undertaken to paint some of B's vases for a remuneration of
$10, but neither of them remembers whether ten or twenty vases were to be
painted, the rules of evidence of most systems will enable a court to decide
whether it is to be the one or the other; and which it is to be may depend on
the timing of the suit and the distribution of the roles of plaintiff and defendant. But few systems only will permit the court to say that it should be
fifteen,[10] or that no decision is possible.[11] In Scottish criminal procedure,
the verdict of "Not Proven" is recognized. In many countries it is not; and
even in Scotland, private law is not correspondingly liberal.

Gmelin, a leader of Continental sociological jurisprudence, *Interessenjurisprudenz*, which no one can suspect of undue leanings towards
strictness of law, in exhorting the judges to put the real factors of life above
logical construction, declares:[12] "In weighing conflicting interests, the interest that is better founded in reason and more worthy of protection should
be helped to achieve victory." The various interests, private and public, are
to be carefully balanced against one another—no school makes more of

9. Some authorities, however, would invoke a general, unwritten prohibition of
grossly immoral exercise of rights.
10. See, however, a group of provisions in *Mishnah Baba Metzia* 8:2 f.
11. Classical Roman law did allow *non liquet*; there were no definite rules of
evidence.
12. In *Science of Legal Method*, ed. Bruncken and Register (1917), 131, quoted by
Friedmann, *Legal Theory* (1944), 219 f.

this balancing—yet the verdict is to be acceptance of one and rejection of the rest. No doubt his language is a little unguarded, but it is interesting to note the kind of idea coming to the fore in an unguarded moment.

II.

The association of the scales with this peculiar element of justice is extremely old. It derives from Egypt, where man, after death, in the nether world, is weighed against truth. Man, represented by his heart, is placed in one dish, truth, represented by a feather, in the other. The hieroglyph for truth is a feather: the slightest turning of the scales—"but in the estimation of a hair"—will decide the issue, and the choice is between salvation and annihilation. Osiris, King of the Blessed, waits to receive the acquitted, but the hellish monster with a crocodile's head, a lion's neck and the body of a hippopotamus, is eager to devour the condemned.

From Egypt the symbol spread in various directions and it generally carried with it that extremist flavour. There is the episode from the *Iliad*,[13] where Zeus weighs the fates of Hector and Achilles, engaged in desperate single combat, to decide which is to live and which to die.[14] *Psychostasia*, the weighing of two souls one against the other, became a popular theme in Greek literature. Its foreign origin is betrayed by the fact that, at a stage of mythology prior to Homer,[15] the fates of warriors are weighed, not by Zeus, but by Hermes: he corresponds to Thot who records the judgment in the Egyptian nether world. Aeschylus wrote a tragedy entitled *Psychostasia*. Aristophanes in *The Frogs* parodies the weighing of souls. There is a throne in Pluto's palace reserved for the greatest poet. For some fifty years Aeschylus has held it, but now he is challenged by Euripides, newly arrived. So their verses are weighed in the balance. Essentially the scene

13. 22.208 ff. Cp. 8.68 ff, a weaker imitation.
14. Homer, with dramatic effect, transfers the sinking scale from the winner to the loser; Aristophanes and others are nearer the Egyptian model in this respect. Moreover, Hector's scale sinks more than just a little: it departs to Hades.
15. Though preserved in a later source, the *Aethiopis*: Gruppe, *Griechische Mythologie und Religionsgeschichte* (1906), 681, n. 6.

is closer to the Egyptian prototype than is Homer: we are shown a proper judgment of the dead in Hades. It may also be noted that, in the end, the question is not so much which of the two poets should occupy the throne as which is to live again and which to stay among the shades. For the winner of the contest may return to Athens, to avert by his advice and encouragement the doom threatening the city. If Dike and Themis, goddesses of justice, are represented with scales, so are Kairos, Nike and Nemesis, gods and goddesses of opportunity, victory and retribution. The scales symbolize things standing, or being weighed, on razor's edge:[16] the slightest deflection spells triumph or ruin.

It is curious that Rome did not really adopt the symbol. The weighing by a god of the fates of warriors, as we find it in Homer, is indeed imitated by Roman writers, Virgil among them.[17] But there is no statue of Justitia holding the scales, neither do they figure among her attributes in any literary work. It is only on some coins that she is given them, like Aequitas and Moneta, but this is a relatively late development, and the scales have reference to the correct weight of the money rather than to the nature of justice in general. Hermes with the merchant's balance also is far from early and cannot be regarded as a continuation of the ancient idea. Possibly Venus, who occasionally appears with scales, has a stronger claim to consideration, if the meaning is that she weighs the hearts of rival lovers, to admit one to paradise and consign the other to despair. The interpretation, however, is uncertain.[18] Maybe the Romans found the radicalism of the symbol unattractive where the law was concerned. It may be recalled that of the austere description of the goddess of justice by the Stoic Chrysippus, Roman philosophers were inclined to say that it was the goddess of cruelty they would portray in this manner.[19] One third-century poem celebrating the syncretistic Virgo forms an exception. She is described as "weighing

16. For the latter translation of *Iliad* 10.173, see A. B. Cook, *Zeus* (1914), 2.1.860 ff. The Virgo with the scales of astronomy no doubt contributed to the bestowing of scales on Dike, Justitia and so on; see Morris Jastrow, *Aspects of Religious Beliefs* (1911), 363 f.

17. *Aeneid* 12.725 f.

18. Though supported by a highly indecent weighing scene on a Roman tomb in the Rhineland; see F. Hettner, *Die Römische Steindenkmäler*, 186 f.

19. Gellius, 14.4.5.

in the balance life and laws."[20] This is plainly an allusion to the scales of justice; and somehow the weighing of laws or rights is again conceived as a matter of life and death.

However, the Egyptian scales travelled not only to the west but also to the east. The Persian creed has it that a deceased person's good and bad actions are weighed at the Bridge of the Separator; and according as the former or latter predominate, he may cross into paradise or must fall into the abyss below.

In the Old Testament, almost up to the end, allusions to a judgment in after-life are indeed suppressed. But the scales are there. Only it is the living that are weighed and whose hearts are probed. Man is light in the balance, mourns the Psalmist.[21] In Ezekiel's balance, the people is represented by the prophet's hair, of which God commands him to burn one part, strike with his sword another, and scatter the third.[22] Job desires to be weighed, in order to be found righteous.[23] God searches man's heart and spirit, says the author of Proverbs.[24] The most famous passage is no doubt from Daniel: "Thou art weighed in the balances and art found wanting."[25] That means utter destruction: "In that night was Belshazzar the king of the Chaldeans slain. And Darius the Median took the kingdom."

Nevertheless, the belief in a judgment of the dead may well have persisted underground. At any rate, by the time of the New Testament, as a result of Persian influence, it had become part of orthodox Pharisaic doctrine: the Apocrypha and the Talmud are full of it. On death, or on the last day, a person's good and bad deeds are weighed against each other, and a single deed may prove decisive. It is in these writings that we first meet with the notion, dear to the Middle Ages, of God—or Mary or St. Michael—freely removing some of the bad deeds or throwing an additional

20. *C.I.L.* 7 No. 759, quoted by Cook, 2.1.734, n. 3. The Latin is *"vitam iuraque pensitans."* Ought we to translate "weighing the laws, i.e., span, of life?" Cp. a reference by Macedonius Consul to the scales of the Zeus of the *Iliad*, with which he weighs πάντα νόμον βιότου, "every law of life" (*Greek Anthology*, II.380).

21. 62:10.

22. Ezek 5:1 ff.

23. Job 31:6.

24. Prov 21:2, 24:12.

25. Dan 5:27 ff. Whether *tekel* originally had a different sense is here irrelevant.

weight into the dish with the good ones. Even the motif that Satan himself
is cheated, that for example the bad deeds are taken off while he, in search
for more, is not looking, already occurs here. All this time, the scales of
justice are also applied, as in Daniel, to whole nations. In an apocalypse
of the reign of Nerva, God is asked to weigh the sins of the unhappy Israel
against those of the happy Gentile races, when he will surely resolve to
overthrow the latter and reinstate the former.[26]

It is worthy of notice that the symbol was taken up by Islam as well
as the Christian Middle Ages. On the last day, the Koran says, "whosoever
shall have wrought an atom's weight of good shall behold it, and whosoever
shall have wrought an atom's weight of evil shall behold it";[27] and again,
"as to him whose balances are heavy, his shall be a life that shall please
him well, and as to him whose balances are light, his mother shall be the
pit—and who shall teach thee what the pit is? a raging fire."[28]

In Christian legend, the weighing of the good and bad deeds plays
a great part. A usurer, whose life was one of wickedness and cruelty, is
saved because of the Aves he prayed every day: Mary throws a rosary into
the otherwise empty dish for the good deeds, and it outweighs the crimes.
In artistic representation, however, we come across something much nearer
psychostasia proper: the person awaiting judgment kneels in prayer in one
dish of the scales, while his evil actions lie in the other. How long the ancient setting of the scales survived in Christian art may be gathered from
a tapestry after a cartoon by Angelo Bronzino, of the sixteenth century,
where Innocence is rescued by Justice. The latter is holding sword and
scales. Her gesture purposely imitates the traditional gesture of Christ res-
cuing souls from hell; and her action is accompanied by that of Time who
can be seen unveiling a young girl, the figure of Truth."[29] We are almost
back in the hall of Osiris.

26. 4 Ezra 3:33 f. Of course, judgment here is in favour of the party whose scale
is the lighter.
27. 99.7 f.
28. 101.5 ff.
29. See Panofsky, *Studies in Iconology* (1939), 84.

III.

When we ask how justice comes to comprise this element of radicalism, the first point to mention is that there are many goods—among them perhaps the most important, such as good repute or a wife—the very nature of which precludes any compromise; or at least any compromise will appear unsatisfactory, if not artificial.

The original use of the scales of justice, we saw, is for settling a deceased person's fate. Of salvation, man feels that it must be complete— anything less is misery. Either he enters the kingdom of Osiris, or he is devoured by the crocodile-headed beast. Certainly most higher religions know degrees of salvation. But they are a product of reflection. In Plato's *Gorgias*,[30] Socrates recounts a legend about the judgment of the dead. In this legend, there are two roads, one to the Isles of the Blest, for the holy, and one to Tartarus, for the impious. There are two roads and no more. It is only in drawing out the moral of the story that Socrates introduces a place of custody where fitting sufferings are inflicted; and the incurably wicked alone are sent to the infernal dungeon for everlasting punishment. Zoroaster spoke of the House of Song, with eternal sunshine and happy companionship, and the House of the Lie, forever dark and lonely. In the later Avesta there are levels of heaven and levels of hell. A similar evolution, or tension, may be observed in Judaism and early Christianity. That "I have set before thee this day life and good, and death and evil" is a motif which, from Deuteronomy[31] through Jeremiah[32] to the *Teaching of the Twelve Apostles*,[33] again and again drowns any subtler distinctions. Between Lazarus in Abraham's bosom and the rich man tormented in the flame "there is a great gulf fixed."[34]

A man is alive or dead. You enjoy good repute or you do not; and not so long ago it was widely held that if an enemy besmeared your good name, the law could not right such wrong but you had to kill, or be killed by, the

30. 523 ff.
31. Deut 11:26, 30:15.
32. Jer. 21:8.
33. 1:1.
34. Luke 16:26.

offender. You cannot have a share in a wife. Solomon's judgment illustrates well the situation created by a dispute about property which you can only possess fully or not at all. He simply must discover the true mother, since a verdict to halve the child would establish only a sham balance. Such a course might be possible if it were a question of a piece of land or a sack of corn. It is a subtle feature of the story that he should discover the mother precisely by urging the impossible compromise. The practice, nowadays common in a case of divorce, of dividing several children, or even one child, between the two parents is of modern origin. There are other examples of goods placed in the sphere of the absolute in one age and that of the relative in another. The Roman law of succession had two strange rules: one that a will must cover the entire property, i.e., you could not restrict your testament to part of your belongings, leaving the rest to pass on intestacy; and another, "once an heir always an heir,"[35] i.e., once a man holds the position of heir, he cannot be divested of it. This meant, for instance, that you could not appoint an heir conditionally on his never touching whisky. Both rules go back to a time when to be heir was tantamount to being successor in the chieftaincy, the new sovereign—a dignity necessarily conferring powers over the whole estate and attaching to a person for good. When at a later date inheritance became a monetary affair, the jurists had no little difficulty in changing the law and giving effect to a partial disposal by will and to conditions like that mentioned.

It is safe to assume that cases involving those goods, which are susceptible neither of division nor, indeed, of compensation, exercised and still exercise a considerable influence on the concept of justice. In this connection, we may advert to Stoic ethics. According to the Stoics, in strictness, a man is either perfect or lost; either absolutely wise and just or absolutely foolish and wicked. If he is a hair's breadth below the highest standard, it is as if he were among the basest of the base. Here what is in general a minor, if significant, element of justice has become its dominant feature. And the explanation may well be that, fundamentally, this is a religious system, concerned with salvation—that good which you must have fully to have it

35. This apodictic form *semel heres semper heres*, however, occurs in no ancient text.

at all. It is often asked which portions of Zeno's teaching, if any, reflect his native background. Presumably this extremist attitude owes something to Eastern ideas of initiation, and a severe division between those within, the few redeemed, and those without, the mass of perdition. The terminology employed in Stoic works supports this view. Seneca says that[36] "even that which is near is still outside," and Plutarch reports that, in the opinion of the Stoics, "a man may fall asleep mad and awake wise."[37] While Plato had encouraged conversation, Zeno demanded conversion.

The Romans, we remarked, did not count the scales of justice among the essential attributes of Justitia. Nor did they greatly favour this Stoic principle. For Horace, the view that all offences of whatever kind are equally damnable is "contrary to natural feeling, tradition and expedience itself, the source of justice and equity."[38] Cicero had said much the same, not only in a philosophical treatise,[39] but also in his defence of a consul prosecuted for bribery in the election campaign.[40] No doubt the jury thought that Cato, Cicero's opponent, a great-grandson of the censor, must be a queer fellow to hold that it was the same whether you unnecessarily strangled a rooster or murdered your father. Of course, Cicero was a clever advocate as well as a thinker, and, as far as his client's conduct was concerned, he was really begging the question. For he took it for granted that bribery, in moderation, was comparable to killing a cock rather than to killing one's father. But that is a different matter. He got Murena acquitted. The influence of Stoic philosophy on Roman law would have been very much weaker than it was had the "either-or" ethics not been considerably modified, on lines first suggested by Zeno himself. It is interesting that those parts of Roman law where the unmitigated principle is applied belong to the post-classical period, when academic speculation sometimes prevailed over common sense. We do find texts containing the notion that you are answerable for the consequences if you have not acted as a *diligentissimus paterfamilias*, or with *exactissima diligentia*, i.e., if you have not

36. *Epistles* 75.9.
37. *That the Stoics make More Paradoxical Assertions than the Poets* 4.
38. *Satires* 1.3.96 ff.
39. *De finibus* 4.19.55.
40. *Pro Murena* 29.61 ff.

shown the highest conceivable degree of care, if your conduct has not been absolutely ideal. But as far as they are attributed to classical jurists, they must be looked upon as spurious.

However, even where the law deals with goods in themselves perfectly capable of being shared or made up for by other goods of a similar nature, there are narrow limits to the degree of differentiation actually feasible. This practical necessity of drawing a line must have affected speculation about justice from the earliest times. It is no doubt among the factors responsible for the drawing of the line acquiring a status in its own right, irrespective of the needs of life.

This aspect is so well known that it suffices to select a few of the more relevant considerations. A thorough adaptation of each decision to the individual case would mean giving the judge a free hand. That would be too high a price to pay: it would be the end of any law. It is easy to go too far in this direction. In Rome, under the late Republican régime of fixed, statutory punishments for the various crimes, little allowance could be made for any special circumstances of a case. In the second century A.D. greater flexibility was demanded, and the judges acquired the power of choosing a suitable penalty. But it was not long before the disadvantages of cadi justice made themselves felt, and from Constantine, the previous system of fixed punishments operated again, though on a different constitutional basis.[41] Again, in contradistinction to the XII Tables, which had subjected certain forms of insult to fixed money penalties, the *actio iniuriarum aestimatoria* made it possible to adjust the fine to the individual facts. But, significantly, a number of precautionary measures became usual, designed to prevent any excessive arbitrariness. The results were probably more satisfactory than under many a modern regulation, where the judge's discretion to assess the damages for insult is practically absolute. The dangers of the programme of the Free Law School have often been emphasized.[42] It would not do to allow the judges freely to vary the punishment of murder in accordance with the impression produced on them by the particular situation.

41. Levy, *Gesetz und Richter*, I, *Strafzumessung* (1938).
42. But it is hardly fair to say, as Friedman does (*Legal Theory*, 224), that National Socialist administration of justice was an application of it. Rather was it a travesty, and there is no set of principles which is not open to abuse.

Again, though flexibility of the law could sometimes be achieved without conceding undue freedom to the judge, there are other obstacles. Theoretically, there is no reason why many different types of murder should not be established by statute—most systems known went through a stage where murder and culpable homicide or manslaughter were not carefully distinguished; no reason why there should not be a rule dividing the fruits of a thing between owner and *bona fide* possessor, or the risk of accidental destruction of an object sold but not yet delivered between vendor and buyer, or the loss resulting from harm inflicted without intent or negligence between the agent and his victim; no reason against the unrestricted admissibility of *non liquet*. But a lawgiver moving too rashly this way might find his losses greater than his gains.

In criminal law, in particular, simplicity and general intelligibility are of the highest importance, and not bought too dearly at the cost of some rigidity. The recognition by some American States of various degrees of murder does not seem to have produced satisfactory results. It is a sound instinct which prevented the Romans, as it prevents the lawyers of this country, from elaborating criminal law in the same degree as private law.[43] As for the latter, oversubtle solutions are apt to upset the smooth running and security of commerce. A provision that an honest vendor who did not procure title should be liable only for half the loss would hamper trade. A buyer must be able to rely on title and safely dispose of the object. If you in good faith obtain a stolen thing, the law may specify conditions under which you acquire it for good, and others under which the original proprietor retains his position. In several Oriental and medieval systems, but also in modern French law, a compromise is struck: you may keep the object which you bought in good faith unless and until the original proprietor offers you the price you gave for it. There are advantages in this compromise: a buyer in good faith will never lose his money, while the original proprietor, for whom the object may have sentimental value, has a chance of redeeming it. The classical Roman jurists, however, consistently rejected this

---

43. Mommsen, in his chapter on punishments in the criminal law of the Roman Republic (*Römisches Strafrecht* [1899], 906), speaks of the "wonderful simplicity" of the system.

right of redemption, which was suggested to them by provincial authorities. It was not compatible with their clear, precise notion of ownership.[44] Similarly, the institution was eliminated from the final draft of the German Civil Code. In general, the attempt to distribute as widely as possible any loss innocently suffered would render legal relations quite unstable: every time there would be set in motion a wave going the length and breadth of the community.[45] With regard to the law of evidence, obviously, the exclusion of a verdict of *non liquet* by appropriate presumptions—except perhaps in a few closely defined, exceptional cases—prevents uncertainties intolerable in modern commerce. A wrong solution of a dispute brought about by the rules of evidence is preferable to no solution.

IV.

There is little doubt, however, that, in addition to these practical factors operative at all times, certain historical developments have contributed to the infusion into justice of an element of extremism. The prevalence at some stage of civilization of trial by battle or by ordeal must have been favorable to the idea that litigation can end only in complete triumph for one party and complete defeat for the other. In the judgment scene of the ancient Egyptian Book of the Dead, man is weighed against truth: it is not a balancing of actions and arguments, but a contest between two beings— man and truth. The picture of man's good deeds being weighed against his bad ones is much later. We find it only in Hellenistic Egypt,[46] in Persia and in regions influenced by the two. In the Greek epic, the God weighs the fates of heroes actually fighting: Achilles and Hector, Achilles and Memnon. Aristophanes, it is true, introduces the scales to settle the claims of Aeschylus and Euripides. But as the two are allowed to choose the verses they want considered, and as each time Euripides places a verse in his dish

44. Felgentraeger, *Antikes Lösungsrecht.*
45. See Paton, quoted above.
46. The significance of the change between the Book of the Dead and the Hellenistic conception is not noted by Erman, *Handbook of Egyptian Religion,* trans. Griffith (1907), 102, 230.

Aeschylus tries to think of a weightier one for his, and also as they keep insulting each other, the atmosphere is that of a duel, and the chorus is justified in likening the poets to warriors.

Up to this day, terms of combat are far commoner in descriptions of legal disputes than, say, in those of controversies between scholars. The latter may be just as heated, but the historical background is different. "In weighing conflicting interests, the better founded should be helped to achieve victory," says a spokesman of *Interessenjurisprudenz*.[47] Such a reference to victory is more than a mere manner of speaking. As is well known, where a dispute is settled outside the courts, by private arbitration or an understanding between the parties, one-sided solutions are less frequent and there is usually give and take. These ways of ending a dispute originated precisely as alternatives to the more violent method, feud or combat. The Latin term *pactum*, first used in this context, comes from *pax*.

Another historical phenomenon here to be mentioned is the tendency of early lawyers to conceive of any legal question as one of wrong-doing and its suppression. Crime and delict will always arouse greater interest than, say, contract in anyone not a specialist in the latter field, and will therefore always contribute rather more than they should to the popular concept of justice. But in early law, cases are brought under crime or delict which, in the modern view, have nothing to do with either. There is a feeling that the mere fact of your not obtaining what ought to belong to you constitutes aggression: if a person who has given you a promise does not fulfil it, the matter calls for vengeance rather than enforcement. As a corollary, it is thought that, fundamentally, the repulsion of aggression is the principal task of the law. Here is a further source of the radical leaning we are investigating.

There is a fair amount of evidence that the starting-point of legal philosophy was criminal law. This is, of course, less immediately clear from the work of a man like Plato, who is representative of mature analysis. But it is criminal law problems that are put in the *Oresteia*, where Aeschylus attempts to harmonize religion and law. The Old Testament prophets proceed in the same way. The earliest, or at least the most archaic, extant work on rhetoric, the *Rhetorica ad Alexandrum*, in its chapter on forensic pleading,

47. Gmelin, quoted above.

distinguishes between charge and defence. And it says that the defence
must do one of three things: either deny the deed, or admit it but show
that it was justified, or admit it but ascribe it to a mistake and represent
the harm which resulted as negligible. Manifestly, the author has in mind
criminal proceedings.[48] The oldest occurrence of the scales of justice is in
the underworld, as a means of deciding a capital charge.

Yet a third cause of the aversion of jurists to overmuch differentiation and compromise should not be overlooked in a discussion of historical
factors, namely, individualism—the idea that a man can look after himself, that he wants to be his own master and all he asks of others is not
to interfere with him. It has often been pointed out that this approach is
particularly pronounced in classical Roman and English common law. But
it is noticeable, in some degree, wherever private law reaches a certain
level of evolution.

Take the example of damage caused without fault. It is quite consistent with an individualist régime to exact compensation, since there has
been interference by one person with another. It is also consistent with it
to refrain from exacting compensation, since a person must put up with
accidental losses befalling him, and damage caused without fault might be
classed as accident. But to make them share the loss—in itself a perfectly
reasonable solution—would be establishing a community of interests in the
place of two separate spheres. Similarly, the position of a *bona fide* possess-
or, in actual control of the property and honestly conducting his affairs as
if it were his, may be deemed strong enough to entitle him to the fruits; or it
may not be deemed strong enough. A rule that the fruits should be divided
between him and the true proprietor, though it might produce the fairest
result, would be infringing the independence of each. If an object is sold
at an excessively low price, the law may let the sale stand, as in conformity
with the declared will of the parties, or it may treat it as void or voidable,
since it is contrary to the principle of fair exchange. It may also lay down
that the sale should be upheld—or that the buyer should have power to
uphold it—at a just price. But this solution amounts to the law making the

48. Ch. 4; Himmelschein, *Symbolae friburgenses in honorem Ottonis Lenel* (1931),
377 f.

contract for the parties. It did not enter Roman law till the post-classical epoch or even Justinian, and, while French law has adopted it, other Roman law systems like Scots law, German law and Swiss law have not.

V.

The modern development is clearly hostile to the "either-or" attitude and, within the limits of the practicable, tends to do away with the vestiges of this element. An institution like the rent tribunals goes far beyond the provisions of the *Corpus Juris* regarding sale for too low a price in imposing external terms on a private agreement. Even the almost unfettered discretion of the tribunals does not seem to have been found an insuperable objection. This is only one of many instances of the encroachment of administration and administrative methods on the judicial domain—a characteristic trend of our age.

Administration does not use the scales of justice as conceived by the ancients. The ideas of combat and of the exclusiveness and self-sufficiency of the individual's province are alien to administration. They do not here interfere with the aims of a proportionate distribution of goods and risks, and of the subtlest possible adjustment of any decision to the particular situation. The wide discretionary powers of those in charge are indeed a danger, but less so than they would be in judicial questions. In a way they carry their own remedy with them: the same freedom which may lead to misjudgment usually makes possible its rectification.

It is superfluous to dwell on the expansion of the field of administration in the past hundred years or so. We may observe it in criminal no less than in private law. The prominence of the objects of education and rehabilitation in the former and measures of socialization in the latter are all part of the same development. If we were to apply the traditional Aristotelian categories, we might say that contemporary evolution is from *iustitia commutativa* to *iustitia distributiva*. The ideal of a universal community of interests, subdivided into smaller communities, in all of which each member at any moment should occupy the position best suited to his needs, faculties and deserts is constantly gaining ground at the expense of the ideal of justice between man and man. The hope for justice between man and man is replaced by that for justice among men.

The spirit of the age is at work even in branches of the law remote from administration. Two recent Law Reform Acts illustrate this. The Law Reform (Frustrated Contracts) Act, 1943, applicable to contracts governed by English law, provides that, if a contract is discharged because performance has become impossible, no payment can be asked for and any made in advance must be restored. If this were the whole regulation, it would be typical of the "either-or" justice which avoids a compromise. In the Roman law of hire, for example, if events occurring after the conclusion of the contract made it impossible for the lessor to supply the object, the lessee was released from the obligation to pay rent and could recover anything paid in advance. Scots law agrees, and so, since the judgment of the House of Lords in the Fibrosa Case, [1942] 2 All E.R. 122, does English law, though in neither case on classical Roman grounds.[49] However, the Act in question adds that, if the party who cannot perform has already incurred expense, the court may allow him to claim or retain a fair sum; and similarly if the other party has already derived some benefit. Here, even at the price of allowing the courts a good deal of discretion, a middle course has been adopted between various older solutions. One wonders whether any claim could have been preferred by the ticketholders for a recent boat race ended by one team sinking into the depths like a stone.

The Law Reform (Contributory Negligence) Act, 1945, is no less remarkable. Roman law and common law, from different starting-points, had come to the conclusion—roughly—that a pursuer's failure to take reasonable care for his safety was a complete defence to the action. Thus a person invited into unsafe premises and suffering injury could not recover anything if by the exercise of care he might have escaped. Under the new Act—anticipated by Continental codes—the court awards damages reduced by as much as appears fair having regard to the claimant's share of responsibility. It is not accidental that similar regulations have long existed in maritime law—the rules concerning collision at sea of the Maritime

49. See Buckland, *Harvard Law Review* 46 (1884), but, as for Scots law, cp. also above note 6.

Conventions Act, 1911, may be recalled. In maritime law, the idea of a community of interests plays a dominant part from very early times. By the *lex Rhodia de iactu*, a Roman statute modelled on Rhodian sea law, it was provided that, if one freighter's cargo was thrown overboard to save the ship from peril, the loss must be shared between all.

It is not unlikely that, at some future date, principles like this will be extended to many more or less analogous situations. The law relating to damage inflicted on another's property in order to avert danger to one's own or a third party's may well undergo fundamental changes as a result of the general relaxation of rigid rules and under the influence of a fresh orientation. The doctrine of a community of interests and proportionate shares may be stressed over against that whereby there is non-interference and the loss lies where it falls. Decisions may be adjusted to the particular circumstances of the case instead of being wholly in favour of one party or the other.

Recently, at Cambridge, a statistical laboratory has for the first time been established. Something of this kind is perhaps destined to become the symbol of modern justice in the place of a simple pair of scales.

Compromise

Writers on Roman law are careful to point out[1] that, in the ancient texts, *compromittere* and *compromissum* denote not—as contemporary usage might suggest[2]—a coming to terms but only a preliminary to arbitration; more precisely, the disputants' agreement to take this route rather than go to court. They "promise together" or "mutually" to do so, maybe even to pay a penalty should they still set in motion the ordinary machinery or disobey whatever award the arbitrator will make. As late as in Justinian, the scope of the concept has barely widened. It is not surprising, however, that in the less punctilious atmosphere of common medieval speech it does widen; so that by the time we come to modern languages, it includes a final arrangement as well as a preparatory one and one reached by simple negotiation as well as arbitration.

What is puzzling is the distinctive, pejorative thrust of which the verb—"to compromise," *compromettre*, *kompromittieren* and so on—has become capable; say, "he denies favoring rent control, but the statements he made when courting the electorate are too compromising," or "the lady compromised herself by emerging from the Men's Faculty Club at 4 a.m.," or "academic freedom would be compromised by the abolition of tenure." To be sure, countless words primarily neutral or praising can be employed with regard to an evil: "he felt sold by his friends." But usually, as in this blackening of "to sell," the basic meaning is quite noticeable and the twist obvious. This is not so with the pejorative "to compromise" which, so to

[*Juridical Review* 95 (n.s. 28) (1983), 188–92]
1. See e.g. W. W. Buckland, *A Text-Book of Roman Law*, 3rd ed. by P. Stein (1963), 532.

2. Throughout this essay, recourse will be had to the recognized dictionaries such as the O.E.D.

speak, is endowed with a life of its own. We may compare it to "gratuitous" in the sense of "groundless," "absurd," pretty independent of the original "freely bestowed," "liberal."[3] In such instances, often (not always, it can happen in other ways) some major social or cultural influence is at work.

Let us inspect the particular semantic development involved. Most lexicographers assume, rightly I think, something like from "to bargain about one's case" to "to be remiss about one's case in thus exposing it to risk" to "to expose anything to bad risk in any manner." The prime mover, then, is the notion that it is culpable not to stand on one's rights; and the question is whether we can discover a setting where sustained, grave censure of this conduct would be so strong as to lead not just to a sporadic derogatory use but to the decided turn before us. The Talmudic Rabbis do debate how far it is laudable, how far reprehensible, to settle amicably,[4] yet none of the Hebrew or Aramaic equivalents of "to settle" spawns a pejorative of the kind of "to compromise." Nor am I aware of a parallel anywhere else. We must look out for something rather unique.

Date and place furnish the clue. There is no trace of the transmuted signification either in the Latin sources or in the English or Romance of the Middle Ages.[5] It comes in, with a vengeance, around 1600 in France, while in England, except for a single, problematic appearance (on which see below), it is naturalized only towards the close of the century, and in Germany much later yet.[6] Evidently, it is a product of the climate of Jansenism, with its rigorous anti-Jesuit stance. This school condemned not simply immorality—everybody did that—but more specifically a pragmatic give-and-take attitude to fundamental values. For example, the Jesuits were tolerant to heathen rituals so long as the natives would consent to baptism. This was anathema to the Jansenists.

---

3. See my *Roman Law* (1969), 118 ff., and "'Suffrage' and 'Precedent', 'Mercy' and 'Grace'," in *Tijdschrift Voor Rechtsgeschiedenis* 47 (1979), 243 ff.

4. See M. Elon, "Compromise," in *Encyclopaedia Judaica* 5 (1972), 857 ff.

5. Nothing in F. Godefroy, *Dictionnaire de l'Ancienne Langue Française* 2 (1883), 214; nothing in *Middle English Dictionary*, ed. Kurath and S. M. Kuhn, Vol. C (1959), 476.

6. Nothing in H. Paul, *Deutsches Wörterbuch*, 5th ed. by W. Betz (1966), or 7th (sic) ed. by A. Schirmer (1960).

It is this root of the pejorative which explains why, to this day, there is an aura of unpleasing ambiguity about it. Also why it is normally confined to matters deemed of general concern: dignity, honour, religion, ethics, public welfare. "My living would be compromised by the abolition of tenure" would be more affected than the illustration offered above, indeed, it would sound self-important, claiming too much. The prominence of reputation in this province also stems from the Jansenist beginning. A big complaint was that Jesuitic casuistry brought the Church into disrespect.[7] If women are perhaps the most constant victims, we must remember that the Jesuits were accused of being lax, and allowing laxity, where ladies of rank might be useful to their overriding, ultimate goals.

(I have the impression that the *Ullstein Lexikon der deutschen Sprache*[8] postulates a direct impact of a passage from the Digest. Under Roman law, once you had undertaken to the parties to arbitrate between them, you could not back out since—so the Digest tells us[9]—you might misuse the material they submitted to you in expectation of a verdict. This idea of the arbitrator as a potentially dangerous *Mitwisser*, confidant, seems to be regarded by the *Lexikon* as accounting for the frequent reference of the pejorative to the revelation of secrets. I greatly doubt it. It is a remote text. Moreover, it is not in the least critical of the non-official method, whether the parties totally work things out by themselves or whether they choose arbitration; on the contrary, the tone is helpful. The reason the pejorative not seldom has to do with disclosure is precisely its tie with reputation just considered: the image presented outside is by its nature singularly imperilled through the inside being shown up as different.)

The adoption of the pejorative into English may have been furthered by puritanism. Still, the latter was far less intensely engaged than Jansenism in the combating of undue compliance. Certainly, when German followed suit, the old battles played no part.

Above I spoke of the distinctive, pejorative, thrust of which the verb

---

7.   In Jewish terminology, *ḥillul hashshem*, "profanation of the name"; see my lecture "Limitations on Self-Sacrifice in Jewish Law and Tradition," in *Theology* 72 (1969), 294 ff. [*TL*, 47–54].

8.   Ed. R. Köster (1969), 513.

9.   4.8.3.1., Ulpian XIII *ad edictum*, probably spurious.

has become capable. I advisedly said "the verb." Whereas for a meeting half-way Latin has the noun *compromissum*, English "a compromise," French *compromis* and German *Kompromiss* (actually, German has not taken over the verb in this primary area), there is—with two provisos to follow presently—no noun for the pejorative. "The disputants reached a compromise" is alright, but not "academic freedom would incur a compromise by the abolition of tenure." What this means is that the activities covered by the pejorative have not, linguistically, attained the status of an institution, they are still mere activities, not yet pressed into an abstract.[10] In French, it is true, the process may be under way: *compromission* (of which my friend Walter Pakter reminds me), though rarely heard, is gaining recognition as signifying "surrender of principle."[11] The second reservation, as to *mettre en compromis*, has definite historical relevance. This standard legal phrase, "to submit a case to negotiation or arbitration," already prior to the rise of the pejorative outlined so far is met in transferred applications. Littré[12] quotes Montaigne, holding that to explain, excuse, interpret himself would be *mettre ma conscience en compromis* like a *plaider pour elle*. This is still very near the basis: "to submit my conscience to other people's judgment." Note the juristic expressions, culminating in "to plead." But a palpable approximation to the pejorative occurs in the rendering of Plutarch's teaching[13] that it would be absurd to commit dishonesty and thereby *mettre en compromis* our own name and virtue in order to aid someone else in enriching himself: "to expose high values to risk." Presumably, this sort of use helped to pave the way for the Jansenist take-off.[14]

It is interesting that the isolated English occurrence of the pejorative in the early seventeenth century to which I alluded above—1603, to be precise—is found in P. Holland's translation of this passage, clearly imi-

---

10. Cf. my remarks on the action noun in *Roman Law*, 11 ff.

11. See The *New Cassell's French Dictionary*, rev. D. Girard (1962), French-English, 174.

12. See E. Littré, *Dictionnaire de la Langue Française* 1 (1875), 706.

13. *On Compliancy* 17, in *Moralia* 535D.

14. I shall not go into *mettre quelque chose en compromis à quelqu'un*, "to dispute something to somebody," which can figure outside the legal domain; as when J. Amyot, *Agesilaus*, writes that the hero considered attacking the Persian king in order *lui mettre en compromis ses richesses et ses délices*.

tating the French translators.[15] He does acknowledge his indebtedness to them in the title. He is plainly conscious of his boldness, writing "to hazard and put to compromise (as it were) our own reputation and virtue for another man." First, he feels compelled to add the parenthesis: the reader cannot be expected to be familiar with the transferred sense. Secondly, to make doubly sure to be understood, he starts with "to hazard." The Greek has only one verb here, *apheidein*, "to make light of." He gives two, an ordinary one and the neologism. Exactly, by the way, as Shakespeare does in *Titus Andronicus*, where he shows off with the then newly-resurrected sense of "suffrage" as "vote" and takes the precaution of placing a well-known term in front: "Give me your voices and your suffrages."[16] That Holland's innovation had little effect on regular English is hardly a matter for wonder.

Addendum. The mention of arbitration may serve as an excuse for pointing out that Latin or medieval *arbitrarius* never signifies "despotic." Both in English—"arbitrary"—and in French—*arbitraire*—this becomes one of the established meanings in the struggles of the second third of the seventeenth century. Rushworth seems to be among the first English representatives of it.

15. Noticed by the *New (Oxford) English Dictionary* 2, ed. J. A. H. Murray (1893), 746. The reference is to P. Holland, *The Philosophie, commonly called the Morals, written by the learned philosopher Plutarch of Chaeronea, translated out of Greek into English, and conferred with Latin and French* (1603), 174. The main French scholar behind it is J. Amyot.

16. Act 1, Scene 1, 218; see my article in *Tijdschrift voor Rechtsgeschiedenis* 47 (1979), 243.

Pecco Ergo Sum

Nowadays, "to sin" and *sündigen* are virtually confined to religion, denoting an affront to divine authority. To be sure, even a Marxist may denounce "sinful waste"; and in a Freiburg Konditorei you hear ladies not churchgoing describe their consumption of Torte as *sündhaft*. But these are trivial fall-outs. The limitation dates from rather early: the Oxford Dictionary offers no deviations. It does, however, point out that, in Old English, the word included wrongdoing of any kind,[1] and illustrations are cited in Anglo-Saxon lexica—e.g. from the Beowulf: "Then there was *synn and sacu* (wrongdoing and strife) between Swedes and Gaetes."[2] C. T. Onions[3] lists these initial meanings: wrongdoing, offence, enmity. A. R. Borden:[4] sin, crime, enmity, injury, mischief, feud, guilt. Presumably, it was its prominent role in Scripture which narrowed its compass.

Its etymology is interesting. It is related to "sooth," which signifies truth. How come? "Sooth" itself—along with a number of synonyms in dead languages, *sanna* in Old Nordic, *sunjis* in Gothic—has the same root as Latin *sum* and German *sein*, to be. Quite reasonable: there is obvious affinity between the true and that which is. In Greek, too, *etos*, true, derives from *esti*, to be.[5] But how can to be develop into to offend? (I am speaking of to offend in general, since this scope precedes the specifically theological one.) The, to me, most plausible answer given focuses on the basic emotions in the face of mischief: at first, the question who is the real culprit,

[*Rechtshistorisches Journal* 4 (1985), 137–143]
1. See W. A. Craigie, in J. A. H. Murray, *A New English Dictionary* (1919), 9:69: In OE there are examples of the original, general sense offence, wrongdoing, misdeed.
2. See J. Bosworth, *An Anglo-Saxon Dictionary*, ed. T. N. Toller (1882), 963.
3. *The Oxford Dictionary of English Etymology* (1966), 828.
4. *A Comprehensive Old-English Dictionary* (1982), 1285.
5. See J. B. Hofmann, *Etymologisches Wörterbuch des Griechischen* (1950), 97.

and then, the conclusion that it is so-and-so. Latin *sons* means guilty. It is plainly an old participle of *sum*, hence, literally, the one who is. The semantic steps, then, accounting for *sons*, "to sin" and *sündigen* are: "the one who is," "the one actually counting," "the malefactor." Roughly, this is the sequence adopted by E. Klein.[6]

The exceptional impresses us more than the routine, and within the exceptional the unpleasant, possibly, more than the pleasant.[7] It is not surprising, therefore, to find the label "the real one" attached to the peace-breaker. Imperfect variants of this evolution abound. The Latin *facinus*, deed, from *facere*, to do, more often than not refers to a misdeed, the German *Täter*, doer, to the *Übeltäter*, evil-doer. By "the realities of life" we understand the opposite of the agreeable vision; and "the truth about the late President" is apt to be nasty.[8] A Whodunit, despite the enormous range of both to do and it, is concerned with a crime. Perhaps the most striking analogy, however, to the main case under discussion is provided by the game of tag, *Haschen* or *Nachlaufen* in polished German, *Fangerles* in Südbaden. The bogy to run from since his touch will transfer his devilry into you "is it." The German designation is even more pregnant: it does without the it. When you join an ongoing game and want the bogy pointed out to you, you ask, not *Wer ist es?* or *Wer ist's?*, Who is it?, but simply *Wer ist?*, Who is? When the bogy manages to touch a guy, he calls out, not *Du bist es* or *Du bist's*, You are it, but simply *Du bist*, You are.[9] An absolute identification of to be with to act the outlaw. That so exact a replica of the

6. *A Comprehensive Etymological Dictionary of the English Language*, (1967), 2:1447: "that which is," "really true," "he whose guilt has been doubtless established."

7. See David Daube *The Sudden in the Scriptures* (1964), and *Ancient Jewish Law* (1981), 124 ff. [*NTJ* 683–743 and 226].

8. [Ed. Truth is most found with awful, bitter, brutal, harsh, inconvenient, naked, sad, simple, terrible, uncomfortable and unpalatable. Home truths are most often hard, inconvenient, painful, uncomfortable, unpalatable or unpleasant. See Chris Tribble, *Guardian Weekly*, 8 November, 2011, who writes a column on uses of words in the newspaper.]

9. My friend Hanna Hohmann to whom I showed this paper reminds me of the counting-out-rhyme by means of which, at the start of the game, "the one who is" is determined: *Eins zwei drei, und du mußt sei*. By a lucky coincidence it is easily renderable as a verse in English: "One two three, and you must be."

growth of "to sin" and *sündigen* should occur in a children's pastime is significant, but I shall not linger. Nor shall I go beyond a distant nod to the *ani hu, ego eimi*, "I am," of the Divine or Messianic Presence in the Passover eve service and the gospels.[10]

Something must be said about the *lex Salica*'s application of *sunne*, that which is, truth, reality, in the sense of a solid datum preventing attendance at a trial.[11] (An addendum to the *lex* enumerates fire, disease, death in the family, king's business).[12] For instance: "If somebody is summoned and does not come, *si eum sunnis non detenuerit*, if *sunnis* has not detained him, he shall be fined 15 shillings."[13] This usage is easy to comprehend. From time immemorial, an excuse for non-compliance with such an order will be accepted or rejected according as it is serious or flimsy. By and by, the former quality takes the place of the valid reason itself: condemnation unless truth, substance, has held him back. No doubt, the term ends up very differently in this context than in that of an injury, considered above, where the injurer "is it." Here "that which is" stands for the authentic circumstance justifying absence. But this is nothing to boggle at: the words referring to unlike things in unlike fields are legion—"gratuitous" either freely bestowed or baseless, "to compromise" either to settle or to hurt.

However, in a study published in the fifties,[14] Th. Frings turns around the orthodox understanding: *sunne*, he argues, shifts not from truth, substance, to a convincing cause of staying away but from the latter to the former. Actually, he makes it into the linchpin of his proposition that there is a primeval Germanic, if not Indo-European, *Notstand des Seins*, "necessity inherent in being," less literally, "duress, compulsion, of existence." It is this philosophical-spiritual concept which, in his opinion, comes out in *sunne* signifying an outside interference with one's obligation, in *sons*, "to sin" and *sündigen* signifying a shortcoming before God, also, ultimately, in Latin *sum*, German *sein* and English "sooth" signifying sheer, imposed

---

10. See my *He That Cometh* (1966), 11 [*NTJ* 435].

11. See H. Geffcken, *Lex Salica* (1898), 1, 45, 47, 49, 51, 77, 79, 83, 108, 330, K. A. Eckhardt, *Lex Salica, 100 Titel-Text* (1953), 104 f., 204 f., 211 f., 214 f., 220 f., 306.

12. Capitulare 6.1; see below, towards the end.

13. *Lex Salica* 1.1.

14. *Beiträge zur Geschichte der Deutschen Sprache und Literatur* (1959), 81: 416 ff.

being or reality. Hence, to repeat, the process by which *sunne* attains its force is the reverse from that so far assumed: not first "truth," then "a true impediment," but first "existential impediment," then "true information about it." We must replace, he urges, F. Kluge's interpretation of the noun as "a truthful recognized obstacle in the way of appearing at court" (*das auf Wahrheit beruhende rechtsgültige Hindernis, vor Gericht zu erscheinen*) by the opposite: "an existential impediment, which becomes the truthful information about it" (*ein existenter Notstand, eine darauf beruhende Mitteilung, die wahr ist*).[15] The 1963 edition of Kluge, s.v. *Sünde*,[16] accepts the reassessment: the starting-point is *Notstand des Seins*, which basic notion finds its legal function as *sunne* in the *lex Salica*, its religious one as *Sünde* in the missionary realm. Curiously, as yet no consequences have been drawn s.v. *sein*;[17] no trace, as yet, of Fring's doctrine that *sein*, "to be," carries the idea in question to its logical extreme, representing existence itself as a *Notstand des Seins*, a state that is thrust on you.

Frings buttresses his thesis with material from many tongues and, as one would expect, the essay is fascinating from beginning to end. Certainly, not a few of his observations will stand the test of time. There are, however, weaknesses. For one thing, if *sunne* were expressive of that tremendous system he postulates, its very narrow, technical range would be inexplicable. It is not only restricted to law nor only, within law, to procedure; even within procedure, it occupies a tiny corner, the disregard of a summons. I shall concentrate on a fundamental flaw: his failure to take note of the relief granted by the XII Tables[18] if a person summoned is afflicted with *morbus sonticus*, "a true, grave sickness." The *lex Salica*'s *sunne* cannot be separated from this, no matter whether it is, as I believe, a remote descendant or just an independent parallel.

It almost looks as if his oversight were universal. I find no mention of the XII Tables in J. Grimm's chapter on approved alibis though he is

15. Op. cit., 425.
16. *Etymologisches Wörterbuch der Deutschen Sprache*, 19th ed. by W. Mitzka (1963), 765.
17. Op cit., 700 f.
18. II 2.

familiar, of course, with the epithet *causae sonticae*.[19] Nothing in Brunner-Schwerin.[20] Nothing in J. Balon's more recent monumental treatises.[21] If my impression is correct, it seems to follow that, even yet, *Germanisten* and *Romanisten* do not talk to one another. Anyhow, here, in the fifth century B.C., we meet *sonticus* envisaging exactly the same problem as *sunne*. It is an adjective from *sum*. As the participle *sons* is set apart for the specialised "guilty," the more elaborate *sonticus* serves for "definitely being," "overwhelmingly real," so as to call for exceptional treatment. (Comparable pairs spring up down to our day).[22] From first to last this is its value. It marks off the weighty from the trifling or even the ordinary. Aelius Stilo, Cicero's teacher, got it right: *certus cum iusta causa*, "certain, affording a legitimate dispensation."[23]

The legal life of the decemviral phrase over the next thousand years is remarkably well documented. Five reasons may be singled out. (1) The humane aspect of the concession appealed to the imagination of the cultural elite, who loved debating it.[24] (2) There was continuous need for juristic scrutiny. For example, the illness, it was explained, must incapacitate you from any mode of conducting your case.[25] Even the medics found employment, recommending a means of smoking out—quite literally: *suffitus*—a pretended coma or delirium.[26] (3) The excuse was extended to other par-

---

19. *Deutsche Rechtsalterthümer*, 4th ed. by A. Heusler and R. Hübner (1899), 2: 479 ff.

20. H. Brunner, *Deutsche Rechtsgeschichte*, 2nd ed., new rev. by C.V. Schwerin (1928), 2: 447 f.

21. *Lex Iurisdictio* (1960), 43, 291, *Traité de Droit Salique* (1965), 20, 23 f., 90 f.

22. In English, "politic" is now chiefly confined to scheming, replaced by the later "political" in talk about governing. The former's original width survives in "body politic" and, above all, in combinations with "politico-."

23. Festus, *De significatione verborum* 290, s.v. *sonticus*. In *Pauli Excerpta* 291, *sonticus* is defined as *iustus*.

24. Gellius, *Attic Nights* 20.1.11, 25 ff.

25. Digest 50.16.133, Javolenus XIV *ex Cassio*. Followed by 42.1.60, Julian V *digestorum*. Venuleius in 21.1.65.1, V *actionum*, also on the authority of Cassius, stresses the chronic nature of the malady, which accords with Festus, *Pauli excerpta* 111, s.v. *insons*.

26. Pliny, *Natural History* 36.19.34.142. Same method will unmask a fake virgin.

ticipants in litigation—such as the judge[27]—and indeed to G.I.s when a
levy took place.[28] (4) It was examined why the law at times takes account of
mere *morbus*, at times only of *morbus sonticus*.[29] The XII Tables themselves
lay down that a conveyance is to be furnished if the person summoned is
hampered by *morbus*, an ordinary ailment, or by his advanced years.[30]
(5) Already the XII Tables put a prior appointment in a process with a
foreigner on the same level as *morbus sonticus*. In course of time, further
exemptions were added,[31] some—like burial of a near of kin or blockade
by ill-wishers, storms or floods—closer to *morbus sonticus*,[32] some—like
an overriding public duty, say, in high office—closer to the date with a foreigner. The attribute *sonticus*, it is worth noting, always remains attached
to the former group: philologists and lawyers never see in it anything but a
severely noxious quality,[33] and Festus, in fact, in so many words characterizes the heading *causa sontica* as an offspring of *morbus sonticus*.[34]

This finding is underlined by the *sonticus*-texts outside the legal orbit.
They never stray far from the model. Naevius's line "You must have *sontica
causa* for which to ruin the woman" is adduced by Festus in his paragraph
on *morbus sonticus*.[35] Surely, we are meant to think of love-sickness: "You
must be utterly struck down by your passion to act thus." Over a hundred
years later, for Novius, the plethora of slaves around an oldster is a symbol

27. *Lex Ursonensis* 95.19 ff., Digest 5.1.46, Paul II *quaestionum*, 2.11.2.3, Ulpian
LXXIV *ad edictum.*

28. Gellius, *Attic Nights* 16.4.4.

29. Digest 21.4.5, Ulpian I *ad edictum aedilium curulium.*

30. II 2, a discourse on which by Sextus Caecilius is preserved in Gellius, *Attic
Nights* 20.1.26 f.

31. *Lex Julia municipalis* 116 ff., *Lex Ursonensis* 95.19 ff., Gellius, *Attic Nights*
16.4.4, Digest 2.11.2.3, Ulpian LXXIV *ad edictum,* 42.4.6.1, Paul LVII *ad edictum,* Code
2.50.4, Gordianus.

32. Festus, *De significatione verborum* 344, s.v. *sontica causa,* belongs here. If
there was mention of enemies and natural threats the word *timidus* may be a leftover of a
reminder that a cowardly overestimate of a danger will not do: cp. Digest 4.2.5, Ulpian XI
ad edictum, 4.2.6, Gaius IV *ad edictum provinciale.*

33. The relevant passages appear in the foregoing footnotes: Festus 111, 290, 344,
Gellius 20.1.27, Digest 21.2.65, 50.16.113.

34. *De significatione verborum* 344.

35. *De significatione verborum* 290, s.v. *sonticus, Pauli Excerpta* 291.

of *senium sonticum*, "grave old age," old age making a paraplegic of you.[36] There may actually be involved here an, at the time, readily perceived allusion to the discussion mentioned above concerning *morbus* and *morbus sonticus*. The former, we saw, is coupled in the XII Tables with *aevitas*, "old age." To introduce a *sonticus* old age, analogous to a *sonticus* illness, would be applauded as elegant learning. Lastly, Tibullus begs a lady no longer to refuse herself to the beautiful young Marathus: his present yellow color, he assures her, comes not from *causa sontica*—obviously the *morbus sonticus* of the code—but from excessive, mournful longing.[37]

As for the *lex Salica*, we may safely assume that *sunne* by this time embraces a fair number of exculpations. Their accumulation no doubt contributed to the role attained by the noun. Once you go beyond just one or two defences, it is natural for the decisive ingredient common to them, "substance," "gravity," to be elevated into an overall designation: this is what, in sum, is required. I have already voiced my feeling that the choice of *sunne* is inspired by *sonticus*, to which I now add that, very likely, the Roman pattern determines the bulk of the rules respecting disregard of a summons.

One pointer in my favor is that, in the *lex Salica* proper, *sunne* does not yet cover the king's business, corresponding to the Roman public duty. It is still limited, like *sonticus*, to the noxious, as is clear from the formulation:[38] *si eum sunnis non detenuerit aut certa ratio dominica*, "if *sunnis* has not detained him or (*sic*) a definite royal affair." A few generations later, in the *Capitularia*,[39] the latter has merged with the rest. I am persuaded, incidentally, that by admitting Roman influence on these statutes in general, we shall be in a better position to appreciate the manifold genuinely Germanic elements incorporated.[40]

36. *Gallinaria*, in O. Ribbeck, *Scaenicae Romanorum Poesis Fragmenta* (1898), 2:314 f.

37. *Elegies* 1.8.51.

38. 50.4.

39. 6.1.

40. To which, provisionally, I would assign the plight of him whose house has burnt down and who has not yet found a safe place for the objects he managed to salvage: Capitulare 6.1.

However, even on the supposition of no Roman input whatever, the precedent of *morbus sonticus* cannot be brushed aside. There is too much resemblance to construe *sunne* along different lines. The alternative to a genealogical link is a virtually identical semantic transmutation—improbable, I think, in this case but not unheard of.[41] The upshot, then, is that, for the moment, we had better stay with the pedestrian, traditional view: the primary meaning is "truth," "material truth," which, in connection with missing a date in court, turns into a more concrete nuance, "true, material obstacle."[42]

41. Above I adverted to the two meanings of "gratuitous": graciously given and wanton. The latter grew out of the former in Hebrew (*ḥinnam*) as well as Latin (*gratuitus*), in similar conditions, independently; see my article in *Tijdschrift voor Rechtsgeschiedenis*, 47 (1979), 243 ff.

42. Through the mediation of my friend Dieter Nörr, the foregoing reflections were submitted to Dr. Harald Siems, whose knowledge of the Germanic sources and their background far surpasses mine. I fully agree with him that we have no texts showing how ideas connected with *morbus sonticus* would penetrate into Northern Gaul by the early sixth century. That is indeed why I do admit the possibility of an independent parallel development (Just so, Count Almaviva in Act II of *The Marriage of Figaro* admits that his wife may not have entertained Cherubino.) Hopefully, Dr. Siems' comments will point the way to a more conclusive treatment of the subject. —He just let me have the welcome news that they are to appear, in an expanded form, in the forthcoming issue of the Savigny-Zeitschrift ["Bemerkungen zu sunnis und morbus sonticus. Zum Problem des Fortwirkens römischen Rechts im Frühen Mittelalter," *ZRG, RA* 103 (1986), 409–446].

A Corrupt Judge Sets the Pace

I.

A "grandpupil" of Kunkel's, Alan Watson, has in the past decade produced several works on the relation of a community and its laws. In *Legal Transplants* he impresses on us the extent and relevance of the borrowing of laws by one people from another, and in *Society and Legal Change* he comes near revealing the DNA responsible for a system's growth. The following pages are devoted to a recombinant—a perversion of the normal, objectionable in one way, useful in another.

Religion has for millennia taught us what psychoanalysis confirms, that—by the standards of traditional morality—no judge is truly upright: "for the imagination of man's heart is evil from his youth."[1] Any verdict is tainted by personal aspirations which, in turn, are a product of a variety of factors, many of them of a dubious nature. The same, of course, *mutatis mutandis* goes for the opinions of scholars, both in the arts and in the sciences. Nevertheless, we can distinguish between inevitable fallibility of a general kind and conscious, crass misconduct; say, between, on the one hand, a judge who, disinclined to rock the boat in which he occupies a comfortable seat, tends to go along with the establishment or one who, forever smarting under parental tyranny experienced as a child, likes to act the rebel and, on the other hand, one who accepts cash from a party. I am concerned with the latter.

[*Gedächtnißchrift für Wolfgang Kunkel*, ed. D. Nörr and D. Simon (Frankfurt am Main: 1984), 37–52]
1. Gen 8:21.

To be sure, the line is not always easy to draw. A vague hope of future promotion presumably falls into the first, tolerated category; if a definite hint is dropped by the government that a certain decision will be rewarded or penalized, that makes it different. Where were we to place the presidents of some English parliamentary tribunals of the post-war years once a soothing report seemed to be a reliable presage of higher office? Another reservation may be in order: I am not here saying anything about how the two categories would emerge from a comparative ethical or social evaluation. Let us proceed from them as given. By corrupt I mean the taking of a bribe, the favouring of a claimant with whom one has an affair, the sentencing of an accused because he has spoken ill of one, and the like.

My thesis is that there are important advances due to wicked judges. Legal skill—or medical, musical, boxing, academic—does not depend on integrity; and if, as Johnson notes,[2] it concentrates a man's mind to know that he will be hanged in a fortnight, other emotions like greed, vengefulness, love may have the same effect. Yet over and above these, a dishonest judge has a special incentive to excel. In the vast majority of cases, he must keep his motives hidden—when his best chance of success lies in coming up with a sparkling result. But even where the public knows or suspects them—for example, his daughter's prospective engagement to the son of the party in whose favour he pronounces—in the face of first-rate quality criticism is likely to be muted.

That we do not hear much about this, I think highly fruitful, source of progress should not surprise. As just mentioned, mostly, the culprit and his accomplices do their best to cover up. Nor have writers on law and its evolution been keen on finding out, preferring a dignified march from precedent to precedent. The reflections of a Rabbi of the second century A.D. on the wonders a *douceur* will do to the brain are an exception.[3] Authorities on other branches of culture show a similar penchant, except that they do sometimes admit war to be, regrettably, a great begetter of pioneering devices. Still, this stimulus is not considered half as bad as an unsavory, private one: the research officer of

---

2. Letter to Boswell, 19 September 1777, in *Boswell's Life of Johnson* 3.167.

3. *Babylonian Ketuboth* 105b; see my "Recht aus Unrecht," *Festschrift für Ernst von Caemmerer*, ed. H. C. Ficker, D. König, H. F. Kreuzer, H. C. Leser, W. Frhr. Marschall von Bieberstein, P. Schlechtriem (1978), 14 f. [*TL*, 15–21].

a firm designs a superior machine for a rival firm that promises him a director-ship. But who knows?, the wheel may have been invented this way.

– My interest in the subject was triggered years ago by a relevant epi-sode of the early Empire. However, as it can be appreciated only by an adept in Roman law, I postponed publication in the hope that, by keeping my eyes open, I might discover a less technical illustration with which to pair it off. I phantasized of an ancient code laying down that the estate of a man who left no son must go to his uncle; one day a judge removed the in-equity by declaring that "son" signified progeny of either sex; and it could be demonstrated that, at the time, he planned to marry a lady who was her rich, old father's only child. By great good luck I have come upon a case pretty much of this nature, to be presented under II, together with a few references to mythology, romance etc.; and as for the Roman law texts—under III—they are certainly in order in a memorial volume dedicated to my beloved and revered teacher in that field. Under IV I append a papal verdict though it hardly constitutes wrongdoing according to my definition.

Before closing this section, however, I shall recapitulate a Talmu-dic instance discussed in a recent paper of mine.[4] Rabbi Gamaliel II and his sister (grandchildren of Paul's teacher)[5] wished to show up a Jewish-Christian judge living nearby and enjoying a reputation for correctitude. They approached him concerning their inheritance. She asked for half of it, despite the Biblical regulation entitling a daughter only in the absence of a son;[6] and since her request was accompanied by the gift of a golden lamp, it was granted. Daringly, brilliantly, the judge explained that the Mosaic dispensation was replaced by a new one which provided for equality of the sexes.[7] However, he reversed himself the following day, on receiving from the brother a Libyan ass, more valuable than the lamp. Once again, his ar-gumentation was superb: he had studied further and had found that the new dispensation itself confirmed the earlier norms, by declaring that it was not designed to destroy them but to supplement them.[8] The two conspira-

4. "Recht aus Unrecht," 15 ff. [*TL*, 15–21].
5. Acts 22:3
6. Num 27:8
7. Gal 3:28
8. Matt 5:17

tors now had their fun with him. The lady remarked, "should not your light
shine forth like a lamp?" while Gamaliel quipped, "An ass has knocked
it over." On that occasion, then, a judge was exposed notwithstanding his
extraordinary ability, because the litigants were in collusion against him.

I I.

In primitive usage, punishment of a ruler—a king, a father, a husband—by
doing harm to his subjects—the people, the children, the wives— is common.[9] (It is not so uncommon today.) We find it especially where the ruler's
offence itself consists in interfering with another ruler's subjects; say, one
father is responsible for another's loss of a child. Here, in turn to deprive
the culprit of a child may look like justice. Hammurabi lays down that if I
build a house for you incompetently and your son perishes by its collapse,
my son is to be killed.[10] Similarly, according to pre-Biblical Hebrew custom, if my ox gores your son to death, given certain conditions the ox and
my son are to pay with their lives. The Bible, however, combats the putting
to death of a blameless person, ordaining that it is the ox and myself who
are liable to capital punishment.[11]

Irish law, too, once knew the kind of retaliation just outlined; and
the sources tell us of a trial where the terrible practice was rejected and
the innocent victim spared—the judge being his father. In the first half of
the seventh century, Domnall, King of Ireland, received Congal, Prince of
Ulster, in fosterage. A bee of the king's stung the prince in the eye, which
was lost. The Ulstermen demanded an eye of the king's son in forfeit. The
king himself was in charge of the case; and while decreeing that the entire
swarm be destroyed in order to be sure to do away with the guilty animal,
he refused to have his son's eye plucked out.[12]

---

9. See my *Studies in Biblical Law* (1947, rpt. 1969), 160 ff. [*BLL*, 476–95].
10. Code of Hammurabi 230.
11. Exod 21:29, 31.
12. See C. Marstrander, *Ériu* 5 (1911), 235, M. Dillon, *The Cycles of the Kings*
(1946), 66.

There are several versions of the anecdote,[13] some differences being explicable by changes in the law concerning just this problem and related ones. One account imputes to Domnall a degree of instrumentality in the disaster: he sent back to Ulster the nurse who brought Congal and gave him one of his own people, and it was her neglect which allowed the bee's attack. But there is no need to go into details: manifestly, we have before us a judgment breaking new ground—and corrupt.

The historicity of the event, it might perhaps be objected, is not assured. But if made up, it still testifies to what people, going by their experience, felt to be likely. In fact, it would be instructive systematically to inspect the behavior of imaginary judges in fiction, theology and so on, surely to a considerable extent modelled on their flesh-and-blood counterparts.

Here it suffices to recall the magnificent achievement of Shakespeare's Portia, whose happiness depends on the defeat of the Jew, and the freedom with which God and the gods, when judging, take presents, have favorites and sit in their own cause. The last-mentioned feature is not readily amended even by advanced religions: it harmonizes too well with paternal authority that knows no separation of powers. Yet Job almost raises the problem. It is certainly seen by the Rabbi quoted above on the energizing property of a bribe. He is alive generally to the precariousness of judicial office; and he advises never to act as a single judge, "for there is no single judge save One."[14] His reverence, it seems, is tinged with an element of complaint: it is on record[15] that a statement from some fifty years before in which God is described as "a single judge" was deemed subversive by the then orthodoxy. Richard Stookey with whom I discussed the matter reminds me of the "stern rule of necessity" in English and American law, bidding even a biased judge act if no other of the required standing is available.[16]

13. See Marstrander, 228 f.; Dillon, 61 f.
14. *Mishnah Aboth* 4:8.
15. *Mekhilta on Exodus* 14:29, citing Job 23:13.
16. See K. C. Davis, *Administrative Law Treatise*, 2 (1958), 162 ff., *Administrative Law Text*, 3rd. ed. (1972), 251 ff.—Since that conversation, the investigation of the Supreme Court of California has rendered this rule highly topical.

III.

Here is my specimen from *condictio*. As the leading experts inform us,[17] one of the major areas covered by it is payment made on the understanding that the recipient do for it something which turns out to be from the outset impossible. A simple example: you hand me a sum on the terms that I release my slave Stichus, but we are unaware that he has just died. The end with a view to which you pay me at no moment has any substance, so I am not justified in holding on. You have *condictio* "of what was given for a purpose," *ob rem dati*, or in terminology preferred by Justinian, *condictio* "for lack of a valid ground," *sine causa*.

No doubt such is the law by the end of the classical period. But it was reached gradually; and several decisions preserved in the sources, though today looking like applications of the principle and represented as such in modern literature, when first enunciated constituted steps on the road toward it. At least in one of them, the judge's self-interest appears to have played an enormous part.

Digest 12.4.3.5, Ulpian XXVI *ad edictum*

> If a free man who, unconscious of his status, served me as a slave gave me money in order that I should release him and I did so, the question arises whether, subsequently proved to have been free all the time, he has *condictio* against me. And Julian in book XI of his *Digesta* writes that the released man is entitled to recovery. Neratius, too, in his book of *Membranae*, relates that the actor Paris successfully reclaimed before a judge from Nero's daughter Domitia the 10 *aurei* which he had given her for his freedom, and that it was not inquired whether Domitia had accepted the money knowing that he was free.[18]

17. See F. Schwarz, *Die Grundlage der Condictio im klassichen romischen Recht* (1952), 135 ff., 248 ff., 256 f.

18. Si liber homo qui bona fide serviebat mihi pecuniam dederit ut eum manumittam et fecero, postea liber probatus an mihi condicere possit quaeritur; et Julianus libro undecimo digestorum scribit competere manumisso repetitionem. Neratius etiam libro membranarum refert Paridem pantomimum a Domitia Neronis filia decem quae ei pro libertate dederat repetisse per iudicem, nec fuisse quaesitum an Domitia sciens liberum accepisset.

Once the wide doctrine set out above is established, the situation considered by Ulpian creates little difficulty: a *bona fide serviens* pays me on the understanding that I manumit him, the operation is from the outset impracticable since he is free already, hence *condictio*.[19] So obvious does this outcome seem to modern authorities that they look on the final words of the paragraph, referring to the possibility of my having known the truth throughout, as a superfluous appendage: why should anyone think that my state of mind matters? It is a good thing that the distinct phrasing of this clause as part of Neratius's notice (accusative and infinitive) and its excellent, concise Latin save it from being thrown out as an interpolation. F. Schwarz tries to make sense of it by explaining[20] that it may concern a point not really belonging to the preceding main exposition: somebody contemplated an *actio doli* if I had known, but as this action is subsidiary, given only in the absence of other remedies, it was rejected—*condictio* was good enough.

This approach, however, is unhistorical. As for the final portion, it is hard to believe that, with *condictio* lying, *actio doli* was ever tried on; still harder that, if it was, Neratius deemed it worth reporting and Ulpian re-reporting. The passage in fact contains not the remotest allusion to this action. It does not go off at a tangent; on the contrary, it plainly continues the preceding discussion. It is not even a separate sentence but carries straight on with *nec*, "and not": "and that it was not enquired." This presentation should be respected: the argument must have to do with the principal topic—the circumstances in which *condictio* is or is not available.

Going on to the body of the text. For Ulpian, we may take it, the matter is no longer doubtful. But in Julian's time, at least a vestige of a problem still existed. The solemn quotation of his view indicates that it was he who finally settled it. Already Neratius, slightly older, probably inclined the same way. He recorded an actual trial in which the judge took this stand, pronouncing against the putative master, or rather mistress, and doing so— here comes the curious punchline—without bothering to find out whether she had acted in bad faith.

---

19. See W. W. Buckland, *The Roman Law of Slavery* (1908; rpt. 1970), 674.
20. Op. cit., 249.

The following picture emerges. From relatively early, if I am paid by a *serviens* for his release when I know that he is free, he will recover. I am guilty, if not of theft, of behavior very close to it. We may recall the debates of the jurists in connection with theft about accepting payment as due when one knows it is not;[21] and it is not accidental that the expression "to accept, knowing," *sciens accipere*, occurs there[22] as well as here. A *condictio* for the victim of my fraud is in order—whether we class it as *furtiva*, as *ob turpem rem dati* or simply as *ob rem dati*.

By contrast, if I am ignorant of the man's status, prior to the suit adverted to by Neratius, he had no claim. With hindsight, we can now say that all requirements for *condictio ob rem dati* are fulfilled. But it took time for this construction to be adopted. Why? What distinguishes this case from that offered above as a model: you pay me in order that I manumit Stichus of whose death we have not yet heard?

For one thing, at least I exert myself, do what I can, go through the procedure of manumitting him. Again, this pseudo-manumission is not quite devoid of legal effects. Up to then, for instance, wages earned by him when hiring himself out to a third party went to me.[23] Henceforth, as he is no longer a *bona fide serviens*, whatever he makes is his. Most important, however, is the factual change in his position that results. Before, however wrongly, he counted as a slave, had to live the life of a slave; from now, he counts as free, he cannot be beaten up, he may choose a wife, he has property at his disposal. This transformation, it should be noted, comes about directly on my supposed grant of freedom to him. There must always elapse some time—it may be years—between this moment and that when this grant is shown to have been illusory, made to one free already.

In the model case, where you pay me in order to procure my slave Stichus's freedom but he is dead, it does not come to any effort on my part and no benefit of any sort accrues to you. It is surely understandable why the arrangement between the *serviens* and me, very dissimilar in these respects, was not at first put on the same level. Not, that is, until the judge

21. See W. W. Buckland, *A Text-Book of Roman Law*, 3rd ed. by P. Stein (1963), 577, H. F. Jolowicz, *Digest XLVII.2 De Furtis* (1940), XXV ff.

22. E.g. Digest 13.1.18, Scaevola IV *quaestionum*.

23. See Buckland op. cit., 278 f.

mentioned in the fragment realized that, essentially, here also the object for the sake of which the money passes never has any substance: the *serviens* being free, conferment of freedom is from the beginning out of the question.

The particular dispute, between a famous actor and the sister of the Emperor's father, was something of a *cause célèbre*. Tacitus comments on it.[24] (He correctly speaks of "aunt," *amita*; it has long been seen that "daughter," *filia*, in the Digest is a slip.) We may assume that the novel analysis implicit in the decision at once attracted the attention of the legal world. As observed above, at the latest from Julian on it was orthodox doctrine, and nowadays it requires an effort to reconstruct a stage without it. Yet the breakthrough was achieved from fear of the stick or desire for the carrot or both.

Paris, a freedman of Domitia's, was among Nero's favorites: "a promoter of imperial late-night debauch."[25] She, on the other hand, was definitely not in his good books; not too long after the events here of interest he had her poisoned.[26] From Tacitus we learn[27] that, at Nero's behest, a court found him to have been erroneously regarded as her slave: he was really of free birth. The court, that is, put up with fake testimony—say, that he was kidnapped from his parents as a child and sold. This, while giving him advantages of various kinds, deprived her of the position of a patron: he had not, it was held, in the past been her slave, only her *bona fide serviens*, so he was not her freedman. (It is true that, possibly, the rights of a patron who has taken money for the manumission are in any case curtailed.)[28] Not content with this windfall, he proceeded to demand back what he had paid her for his manumission. Obviously, the judge was well advised to come down on his side. His verdict, considerably refining the system of *condictio*, was corrupt.

24. Tacitus, *Annals* 13.27.

25. Tacitus, *Annals* 13.20, *solitus alioquin id temporis luxus principis intendere*; see also 13.22.

26. Suetonius, *Lives of the Caesars*, *Nero* 34.5, Dio Cassius, *Roman History*, Epit. 62.17.1.

27. Tacitus, *Annals* 13.27; see my article in *Natural Law Forum* 12 (1967), 59 f.

28. The texts are complicated—e.g. Digest 38.1.32, Modestinus VI *pandectarum*; 38.2.3.4, Ulpian XLI *ad edictum*, Code 6.4.1 pr., Severus and Antoninus, A.D. 204; see Buckland, *The Roman Law of Slavery*, 640 ff.

It may be asked why she let it come to a legal battle instead of, gentlepersonlike, returning to Paris the 10 *aurei* he so badly wanted; after all, it would make no inroad into her extraordinary wealth. First, she loved litigating even about less than vital amounts, and perhaps particularly against close relations and acquaintances. On an earlier occasion her second husband Crispus Passienus, a famous orator, represented her against her brother, equally rich. In his peroration, in order to make matters less tense, he said: "There is nothing either of you would miss less than what you are contending about."[29] Secondly, she was a miser generally. When she reproved the orator Junius Bassus—who was presumably pleading against her in a lawsuit—for alleging that she was in the habit of selling old shoes, he countered: "I swear I never said this; what I said was, that you are in the habit of buying them."[30] Thirdly, right to the last, to go by Suetonius,[31] she underestimated the lengths to which Nero would go in his egotistic designs. Fourthly and most weightily, as the law stood on the eve of her contest, she had a watertight case and anyone she consulted would advise her so. She did not reckon with the powerful combination in a judge of selfishness and ingenuity.

Some authorities think[32] that a single judgment delivered at Nero's command found both that Paris was freeborn—this part was deferring to fake evidence—and that he was entitled to a refund—an inevitable conclusion from part one. We have seen that, at the time, the conclusion was anything but inevitable. Whether it was or not, a two-pronged verdict is most improbable. Not that it would affect the thesis here submitted. Still, for a full understanding of the case it is useful to look at the question.

A major point to bear in mind is that the formula for a matter of status and that for recovery of a payment are totally different. It is hard, therefore, to imagine one verdict covering the two issues. It is just conceivable, perhaps, that Paris brought a *condictio* only, and that the award implicitly settled the problem of his provenance in his favour. But there is no hint at

---

29. Quintilian, *Elements of Rhetoric* 6.1.50.
30. Quintilian, *Elements of Rhetoric* 6.3.74.
31. Suetonius, *Nero* 34.
32. E.g. E. Wüst, "Paris," in Pauly-Wissowa, *Realencyclopädie der Classischen Altertumswissenschaft* 18:4 (1949), 1536 f.

the admissibility of such a procedure anywhere in the sources.

The prevalent view rightly assumes two trials.[33] In addition to general considerations, the references to the affair both in the Digest and in Tacitus decisively speak for this alternative. In the Digest, Ulpian proposes to inquire whether a *bona fide serviens*, "proved to have been free all the time, can reclaim his payment."[34] This clearly envisages two distinct stages: first, establishment of status, then, the question of *condictio*.

Tacitus writes: "And not long after, the freedman Paris was snatched from Nero's aunt as by the civil law, not without discredit to the emperor by whose order a judgment of free birth had been brought about."[35]

"And not long after" refers to the dispute between those senators who felt it was necessary to legislate to curb the growing impudence of freedmen towards their patrons and those who felt it was not. Nero sided with the latter and no decrees were passed. "And not long after," Tacitus charges, he himself assisted a freedman in precisely the kind of conduct the advocates of stricter controls had in mind. For Tacitus, of course, Paris remained a freedman despite the court's enforced pronouncement to the contrary.

What interests here is that the statement manages in the tersest style to bring out the two successive phases of the scheme. First came the establishment of Paris's elevated origin, so that he had never in truth been Domitia's slave. The pluperfect—"it had been brought about"—tells us that it occurred before the next step, in the perfect—"he was snatched from her." By "he" is meant the sum she had received in Paris's stead. Tacitus's readers still knew enough about the scandal to understand such shorthand information.

A few more features of the *aperçu* may be worth mentioning. According to it, the Emperor directly influenced the initial, basic decision: "by whose order a judgment of free birth had been brought about." The judge in the *condictio* may well have taken his cue without an express warning. At any rate, Tacitus sees the *condictio* as the chief blow to Domitia, illustrating the degree of audacity of which freedmen could be capable. The first

---

33. E.g. A.-J. Boyé, *Mélanges H. Lévy-Bruhl* (1959), 32.

34. *Liber probatus, an mihi condicere possit.*

35. Tacitus, *Annals* 13.27: *Nec multo post ereptus amitae libertus Paris quasi iure civili, non sine infamia principis, cuius iussu perpetratum ingenuitatis iudicium erat.*

suit had resulted in her losing the rights of a patron, bad enough (though, as pointed out above, they were perhaps somewhat abridged). But it is the second, extorting the 10 *aurei* from her, which constituted the final rip-off, *eripere*. (It is fascinating how the Latin term is reincarnated in the hippie one.) Accordingly, it is the second of which he remarks that, following upon the first, it brought the Emperor into disgrace, *infamia*.

It is the second to which he attaches the characterisation "as by the civil law." *Ius civile* here signifies "the law gained by subtle, learned, juristic interpretation." The expression can be laudatory, as when we hear that "this discussion and this unwritten law created by the jurists is called the civil law"[36] or that "in our state what counts is either through law, i.e. statute, or it is the civil law proper, unwritten and consisting solely in the interpretation of the jurists."[37] But it can also be pejorative, as when a right of way is drawn up with the proviso that "fraud and the civil law shall be remote from all this."[38] Significantly, another similar arrangement stipulates that "fraud and jurist shall be remote":[39] "civil law" and "jurist" are interchangeable, the former being the product of the latter—and either may be distrusted as given to trickery. Tacitus, then, a contemporary of Neratius, is emphasizing the misuse of legal acumen in the *condictio* decision: *quasi iure civili*. The words would be less pregnant in connection with the preliminary finding concerning status. That was a straightforward, crude miscarriage of justice, with no finesse about it. "As by law," *quasi iure*, might be said of it. (In Livy,[40] the man fraudulently claiming to be Virginia's master declares that

36. Digest 1.2.2.5, Pomponius *singulari enchiridii*: *Haec disputatio et hoc ius quod sine scripto venit compositum a prudentibus... appellatur ius civile.*

37. Digest 1.2.2.12, Pomponius *singulari enchiridii*: *Ita in civitate nostra aut iure, id est lege, constituitur, aut est proprium ius civile quod sine scripto in sola prudentium interpretatione consistit.* In paragraphs 6 and 8 the phrase is used in the same sense; also, for instance, in Digest 50.17.202, Javolenus XI *epistularum*. See my comment in *ZRG, RA* 76, (1959), 208 f.

38. *Corpus Inscriptionum Latinarum* VI.2, 8862: *Ab iis omnibus dolus males abesto et ius civile.*

39. *Corpus Inscriptionum Latinarum* VI.12, 133: *Dolus malus abesto et iurisconsultus.* See C. G. Bruns, *Fontes Iuris Romani Antiqui*, 7th ed. by O. Gradenwitz (1909), 340.

40. Livy 3.44.8.

he will proceed "by law, not by force," *iure non vi*.) Anyhow, the fact is that "as by the civil law" is not applied to it by Tacitus.

V. Arangio-Ruiz misunderstands the passage.[41] He takes the view that Domitia released Paris informally, which made him into a freedman under the *lex Junia Norbana*, with the rights of a Latin only, not of a full citizen;[42] and the outrageous judgment which, as Tacitus reports, was ordered by Nero found that the manumission had been *vindicta*, so Paris became a freedman with full citizenship. However, this conflicts with both accounts of the matter. The reason, in the Digest, he wins his *condictio* is that, owing to a previous judgment, he must be considered freeborn. A judgment that he was released *vindicta*, and not merely informally, would not have supported the *condictio* at all; on the contrary, he would have received full value for his payment. As for Tacitus, *ingenuitatis iudicium* means "judgment of free birth." There is no way in which to convert this into "judgment of formal manumission."

The turnabout which, I am contending, took place in the handling of a payment for his freedom by a free man serving as a slave—from non-recoverability (except if the recipient acted with *dolus*) to recoverability—is confirmed by an analogous development respecting a slave become free on his master's death but believed to be only a *statuliber*, freed by testament on condition of making a payment.

Digest 12.4.3.7, Ulpian XXVI *ad edictum*:

> If a slave whom the testament had declared to have to pay the heir 10 *aurei* and to be free received freedom unconditionally in a codicil and, ignorant of the latter, pays the heir 10 *aurei*, can he recover? And Celsus relates that his father was of opinion that he could not recover; but Celsus himself, prompted by natural equity, believes that the money can be recovered. This is the better view.[43]

---

41. *La Parola del Passato* 3 (1948), 143. How far (if at all) his error vitiates the major propositions of his article may be left open.

42. See Buckland, *A Text-Book of Roman Law*, 78, 93 f.

43. Sed si servus qui testamento heredi iussus erat decem dare et liber esse codicillis pure libertatem accepit et id ignorans dederit heredi decem, an repetere possit? Et refert patrem suum Celsum existimasse repetere eum non posse; sed ipse Celsus naturali aequitate motto putat repeti posse. Quae sententia verior est.

We have seen that, by Ulpian's time, if I make you a payment for which you are to do something which turns out to be from the outset impossible, I may bring a *condictio ob rem dati*. Just so, by this time, I may bring a *condictio* if I comply with a testamentary provision which confers a right on me conditionally on my making a payment to the heir, yet the right cannot materialize. Say, there is a will appointing you heir and adding that, if I give you a certain sum, the library belonging to the estate shall be mine; I do give you the money, but now the will proves to be forged. I have *condictio* "for what was given in fulfilment of a condition," *condicionis implendae causa dati*, or we might say, "for what was given because of a condition," *ob condicionem dati*; Justinian tends to assign it to the same comprehensive heading as *condictio ob rem*, namely, *condictio* "for lack of a valid ground," *sine causa*.[44] However, in this case, too, it is a mistake to place the final doctrine at the beginning, thus covering up the step-by-step evolution towards it. The younger Celsus's dissent from the elder is one such step, virtually parallel to the innovation achieved in Paris's action.

Under the rule prevalent by Ulpian's time, nobody could question the availability of *condictio*. The slave is unconditionally released by the codicil. That, for the moment, the parties are unaware of the existence of the document does not, of course, alter this datum. Accordingly, the clause in the original will, releasing him conditionally, is ineffective, the payment he makes in accordance with it leads to no right for him—so it must be refunded.

F. Pringsheim[45] regards the words "prompted by natural equity" as spurious; his argument is that the elder Celsus's refusal of *condictio* is so "odd and striking"[46] that the son did not need natural equity to arrive at the correct solution. In fact, the explanations of the father's opinion to be found in the literature all take for granted his proceeding from the rounded doctrine of the *Corpus Juris*—and are correspondingly tortuous. The most

---

44. Digest 12.4.2, Hermogenianus II *iuris epitomarum*, 12.6.53, Proculus VII *epistularum*, 12.6.65.3, Paul XVII *ad Plautium*; see Schwarz op. cit., 163 ff., 251 ff., 259 ff.

45. *ZRG, RA* 52 (1932), 141 f.

46. *Eigenartig und auffallend.*

popular one is A. Pernice's,[47] approved by Pringsheim[48] and more or less followed by Schwarz:[49] Celsus father divided the testamentary ordinance "to pay and to be free" into two separate ones; the codicillary, unconditional release did not cancel direction no. 1, to pay, it merely reiterated direction no. 2, to be free. Had the codicil superseded both parts, Celsus senior would have admitted *condictio* no less than Celsus junior—who does assume revocation of both. Basically, P. Frezza takes the same line,[50] adding a detail which Schwarz rejects: Celsus father adhered to the *verba*, the letter of the will, Celsus son stressed *voluntas*, the testator's intention. But none of this has any textual support, be it in this fragment, be it in others.

Things are simpler: prior to Celsus son, though the codicil bestows freedom without payment, cancelling the conditional testamentary "he shall pay and be free," payment made under the testament before the codicil is discovered cannot (save if the heir has knowledge of the codicil) be claimed back. The model *condictio* "for what was given in fulfilment of a condition" submitted above is as follows: a man is left a library on condition that he pay the heir a certain sum, he does pay, then the will turns out to be forged. Of the elements distinguishing the present case, it suffices to mention two. First, the would-be recoverer from the heir was a slave of the testator's, and a testator is normally the heir's father. This alone may well render *condictio* less acceptable. The second point is very close to what we found to be crucial in the early jurists' approach to payment by a *bona fide serviens* for his manumission: factually, it is the putative *statuliber*'s payment under the testament, not the codicil, which sets him up as definitively freed. The interval between payment and emergence of the codicil may indeed be brief, but it may also be quite long. He does not, as far as his life situation is concerned, pay the heir in vain: he does get something. It needed considerable acumen to analyze more rigorously and conclude that, whatever change his payment may produce in raw reality, *au fond* its purpose is to qualify for a right that cannot come about since

47. *Labeo* 3.1 (1892), 413.
48. Op. cit., 142.
49. Op. cit., 253 f.
50. *Mélanges F. De Visscher* 1 (*Revue Internationale des Droits de l'Antiquité* 2) (1949), 297 f.

it is already there, by virtue of the codicil—hence *condictio*. One could imagine—though, admittedly, it is far from certain—that Celsus son, for whom the great goal of his craft was "the good and the equitable,"[51] did invoke natural equity in this context. Rightly or wrongly, he is elsewhere represented as resting on "the good and the equitable" another progressive decision in the field of *condictio*.[52]

From the wording it looks as if, while the elder Celsus was consulted about an actual suit, the younger Celsus had pondered the matter in theory only. The former, as the latter reports, held that "he (the freedman) could not recover" *repetere eum non posse*: this sounds like a reference to a live claimant. The latter is said by Ulpian to hold that "the money can be recovered," "there is recovery," *repeti posse*, a more detached formulation. It has been suggested[53] that the father did not write at all.

However this may be, as a contemporary of Neratius, he must have expressed his old-fashioned view regarding the putative *statuliber*'s payment quite a few years after Paris versus Domitia had pioneered a different answer in connection with payment by a *bona fide serviens*. There is nothing strange in this. The transfer of new criteria from one case to another is far from automatic. Moreover, people vary in receptiveness: he may have been particularly cautious—*non constat* that some of his confrères did not switch faster than he. Very speculatively, one might think of a further, special reason for his reserve. He seems to have been intensely opposed to despotism;[54] and he may have disliked following in the footsteps of a judge whose innovation, however masterly, sprang from a contemptible desire to please Nero. The son, though generally, it appears, sharing the father's convictions,[55] felt that equity must be deferred to no matter how the insight into it was gained.

---

51. *Ius est ars boni et aequi*: Digest 1.1.1 pr., Ulpian I *institutionum*; cp. 45.1.91.3, Paul XVII *ad Plautium*. See P. Stein, *Law Quarterly Review* 77 (1961), 247, and *Regulae Juris* (1966), 102.

52. Digest 12.1.32, Celsus V *digestorum*.

53. See P. Krüger, *Geschichte der Quellen und Literatur des Römischen Rechts*, 2nd ed. (1912), 170.

54. Dio Cassius 67.13; see W. Kunkel, *Herkunft und soziale Stellung der römischen Juristen* (1952), 137 f.

55. See my essay in *Die moderne Demokratie und ihr Recht, Festschrift für G. Leibholz* (1966), 1.320.

It remains to glance at a ruling by Diocletian and Maximian, comparable to that here analyzed.[56] Their help was sought by A's heirs as they reclaimed from B a slave woman transferred by their father, who had wrongly believed his daughter to be a slave of B's. By then, indeed, the principle whose origins were so disgraceful had been fully worked out. Hence there was no longer the slightest doubt that, if A conveyed the slave woman on the understanding that B would manumit his daughter, the *condictio* must succeed—*causa dandi non secuta*, "the purpose of the transfer not being attained". The only reservation made by the emperors concerns the possibility that A might have acted *donandi animo*, "with intent to make a free gift," independent of a specific counter-service—say, in order to render B more amenable to further negotiations. In that case, no *condictio*: a gift once made cannot be revoked merely on account of an error as to the situation.

IV.

My friend John T. Noonan, whom I told of my preparing this study, draws my attention to an article in which he discusses a judgment of Urban II, pope from 1088 to 1099.[57] Towards the beginning of his reign, at the instance of Jourdain I, Prince of Capua, he annulled the marriage of the latter's daughter to Renaud Ridel, Duke of Gaeta, on the ground that, at the time, Jourdain had acted under duress, his wife and family had deplored the match and their daughter, an infant, had offered what resistance she could. The pope, Noonan holds, definitely changed the existing law, in the direction of treating a bride's consent as a *conditio sine qua non* of a valid union. His motives, however, were far from pure: he was politically obliged to, and needing the support of, Jourdain, while Ridel belonged to the enemy camp.

On balance, the decision does not qualify for inclusion in the present inquiry. For one thing, it is not corrupt in the vulgar sense: the party

56. Code 4.6.6, of A. D. 293; see Buckland, *Slavery in Roman Law*, 644.
57. *Viator* 4 (1973), 419 f.

favored is not a close relation of the judge's, there is no money bribe, there is no direct promise or threat. The bias is of a kind met in many, if not most, cases involving important persons or issues, and a fair number of modern scholars are alert to its role. True, it is rather extreme on this occasion.

For another thing, Urban may not have been so innovative after all. Certainly, he was conscious that, to the unlearned, his attitude must appear strange, but it was dictated, he explained, by Church legislation and Roman law. According to Noonan, this argument was specious since "he gave no citations to any such authority." But he did: Church legislation and Roman law, he declared, rejected marriage lacking consent "as is demonstrated below," *ut infra ostenditur.* So he appended the texts—lost to us for the simple reason that Gratian, our main transmitter of this verdict, quotes the substantive part only, without the documentation.[58]

In one respect, the decision was even more playing up to Jourdain than one might gather from Noonan's account. He writes: "The marriage, the pope added, could still be made good if the girl, her mother and her relatives were willing." What the pope said was that it could still be made good "if the Prince, with the agreement of the daughter, the mother and the relatives, wished to complete what had been begun," *si princeps cum filiae, matris et parentelae assensu id quod ceptum est perficere voluerit.*

---

58. *Corpus Iuris Canonici*, 2nd ed. by E. Friedberg, pt. 1, *Decretum Magistri Gratiani* (1879; rpt. 1959), P.2 C.31 Q.2 C.1, 1113.

The Self-Understood in Legal History[1]

By self-understood I mean something so much taken for granted that you do not bother to reflect on it or even refer to it. Now I am not going to discuss the assumptions of this kind which we legal historians make in our work; for instance, that men want to get on in life, that petty fraud is despicable, that a scholar can achieve a modicum of objectivity. To pursue this aspect of my theme would mean to construct a complete epistemology.

My business will be to say something about what the jurists of the past treat in this way. Even within this compass I shall further narrow down my subject by not inquiring into their general beliefs about the nature of the individual, society, the world. I shall restrict myself to actual rules of law which, because of their absolute familiarity, are passed over in silence when others are set forth; or to put it in roughly equivalent terms, rules which are not, when it might be expected, elevated, or demoted, from— custom to *ius scriptum*—and the latter, for my purpose, includes private collections or expositions as well as legislation.[2]

The sort of thing I have in mind is illustrated in fairly recent times at All Souls College (if I may advert to the law of a group within the state). The

[*Juridical Review* 85 (n.s. 18) (1973), 126–34]

1. Lecture delivered before the Munich Faculty of Law on the occasion of the 500-years' jubilee of the University. The German version may be found in "Das Selbstverständliche in der Rechtsgeschichte," *ZRG, RA* 90 (1973), 1–13. I should like to thank the editors for consenting to the present publication.

2. Cf. my remarks in "Zur Palingenesie einiger Klassikerfragmente," *ZRG, RA* 76 (1951), 165–66. See also K. Engisch, "Der rechtsfreie Raum," *Zeitschrift für die gesamte Staatswissenschaft* 108 (1952), 385 f. In "The Preponderance of Intestacy at Rome," *Tulane Law Review* 39 (1965), 254–55 [below, 190], I call attention to a linguistic evolution which has much in common with the legal one I am discussing in this lecture: "Basically, language gives an inverted reflection of reality; it is a laughing mirror in which the small appears large and the large small."

very first paragraph of its statutes runs: "The College shall consist of the Warden and such number of Fellows as is in these Statutes provided. No woman shall become a member of the College."[3] The clause about women, paradoxically, is among the latest additions to the statutes; it is not found in the pre-twentieth-century versions. But not because women were then eligible. On the contrary: their rejection was so much a matter of course no one thought of formalizing it. That was done when, at the beginning of this century, the danger of female dons first appeared on the horizon. One day, with further advance of molecular biology and brain transplants, yet another clause will be appended to keep out monkeys. At the moment, as their participation in academic life does not enter consciousness even to a minimal extent, they are contemplated by no rules express or tacit.[4]

Some legislators or recorders of law have no intention of covering the ground. Ancient ones in particular, not suffering from what Beseler called completomania, are apt to communicate only the really needful: the settlement of doubts and reforms. Hence it may be precisely the most basic rules for which we look in vain.

Neither the XII Tables nor the Mishpatim—the archaic assembly of provisions in Exodus—set out the grounds of slavery: birth, capture in war. In both works, it is only incidentally, in the course of regulating theft—an offence which at the time called for a restatement—that the possibility of a thief becoming enslaved is noted.[5] For that matter, the Mishpatim, where they *ex professo* go into theft, tackle only theft of a beast (and of a person, if we reckon 21:16 among them[6]), with its peculiar difficulties of proof.[7] Double restitution if an inanimate object is stolen comes up incidentally in their section on deposit.[8] But it is omitted from the *sedes materiae*: the author is not motivated to lay down what no one questions.

---

3.   See *Private Manual for All Souls College* (Oxford, 1958), 2.
4.   At least psychologically; there is a considerable difference between a practice like the exclusion of women and one like the exclusion of animals; though it is probably arguable that, in strict logic, the latter just like the former implies a tacit, customary norm.
5.   XII Tables VIII 14; Exod 22:2.
6.   The form of Exod 21:12, 15, 16 and 17 differs from the usual one.
7.   See my *Studies in Biblical Law* (1947; rpt. 1969, 2004), 89 f. [*BLL*, 338–40]; B. Jackson, *Theft in Early Jewish Law* (1972), 41 f.
8.   Exod 22:6. See Jackson, *Theft*, at 100 f.

Another remarkable example occurs in the field of damage to property. Neither of the two collections contains a rule about direct damage by a *paterfamilias*, except that the XII Tables, at the same time as imposing a fine of 300 coins on breaking a free person's bone, impose one of 150 if the victim is a slave.[9] Yet the XII Tables do deal with a man's liability for damage done by his slaves or cattle, and the goring ox and *pastus pecoris* do appear in the Mishpatim.[10] It is sometimes held that the directions regarding the simple case happen to be lost. But the coincidence is too striking. We should have to assume a conspiracy between Rome and Palestine—and a whole series of other systems I am not here quoting—compared with which that alleged by Mr. Garrison would be mere child's play. Better to put up with the situation as it presents itself. The simple case is not considered: it goes without saying. Even the *lex Aquilia*, some hundred and fifty years after the XII Tables, though concerned with direct damage by a *paterfamilias*, treats only (if we discount later re-interpretations) of damage to animate objects, slaves and cattle, which involves special complications[11]; just as the widest Biblical ordinance, in Leviticus,[12] treats only of the killing of cattle. Philo in his *Special Laws*[13] still does not break through to a plain demand of compensation in the simple case. By contrast, the Greek law respecting *blabe* was straightforward and comprehensive already by Plato's time.[14]

Still, the phenomenon is met not only in codes and surveys not aiming at exhaustiveness, but also, though in a less degree, where this objective is indeed pursued; be it that the thoroughly accustomed is overlooked, be it that it is felt to be just too platitudinous for mention. According to the Proculians, if I make a new thing—a chair, a vessel—with your raw material—your wood, your gold—I become owner. The non-application of this principle if I am a worker in your factory is so self-evident that Gaius does

9.   XII Tables VIII 3.

10.   XII Tables XII 2; VIII 6, 7; Exod 21:28–36, 22:5.

11.   See my observations in "On the Use of the Term *damnum*," in *Studi in onore di Siro Solazzi* (1948), 93–156.

12.   Lev 24:21.

13.   Philo, *De specialibus legibus* 3.26–30 (144–68), 4.5–6 (20–29).

14.   See J. H. Lipsius, *Das Attische Recht and Rechtsverfahren*, 2.2 (1912), 652 f.

not trouble about it.[15] A slightly later work based on his *Res Cottidianae* does say that, to become owner, I must have made the new thing *meo nomine*, on my behalf.[16] The BGB, the German civil code, follows in Gaius's footsteps.[17] In the second commission a proposal to insert this requirement was rejected. It was declared *selbstverständlich*, manifest, that he who has the thing made is the true maker: *herstellen lassen* equals *herstellen*.[18] The authorized German version of Pius XI's encyclical *Quadragesimo Anno*,[19] incidentally, contains a remarkable deviation from the Latin. The encyclical emphasizes that production is a ground of acquisition only in well-defined circumstances; but only the German says that this restriction applies "naturally." Latin: *Industria vero quae ab homine proprio nomine exerceatur, cuiusque ope nova species aut augmentum rei accesserit, ea una est quae hos fructus laboranti addicit.* German: *Was sodann die Arbeit betrifft, so besitzt natürlich nur diejenige, die der Mensch im eigenen Namen ausübt und soweit sie eine Umgestaltung oder Wertsteigerung an ihrem Gegenstand hervorbringt, eigentumschaffende Kraft.* The adverb *natürlich* is represented neither in the Latin nor, for instance, in the English rendering:[20] "The only form of labor, however, which gives the workingman a title to its fruits is that which a man exercises as his own master, and by which some new form or new value is produced."

Unfortunately, a norm may be missing from a source for reasons other than its obviousness. The commonest one is indeed, as one would expect, that it does not exist.[21] This explains, for instance, why the XII

15. Gaius 2.79.

16. D 41.1.7.7, Gaius II *rerum cott.*

17. Para. 250.

18. See *Protokolle der Kommission für die zweite Lesung des Entwurfs des Bürgerlichen Gesetzbuchs*, 3 (Berlin, 1899), 242 f.; J. Biermann, *Kommentar zum Bürgerlichen Gesetzbuch*, 3rd ed., 3 (Berlin, 1914), 229. German jurisdiction has made use of the absence of an express reference to *meo nomine* and has established subtle differentiations, so that in some exceptional cases the requirement does in fact lapse.

19. *Unseres Heiligen Vaters Pius XI. Rundschreiben über die gesellschaftliche Ordnung* (Freiburg, 1931), 43.

20. The Missionary Society of St. Paul the Apostle in the State of New York, ed., *Five Great Encyclicals* (1939), 139.

21. As for a stand taken by Aristotle, see below note 43.

Tables and the Mishpatim—and also Justinian and later Old Testament portions—include no penalty for verbal insults in private or air pollution. Again, the missing norm may not belong to law proper in a certain culture, as when the chastisement of an adulteress is left to her family. At Rome, while she figures in criminal statutes only from Augustus, sanctions within the household or circle are far older—however lax the second half of the Republic may have become.[22] Similarly, as for Hebrew civilization, narratives like that of Tamar in Genesis and Samson's wife in Judges show that she might be put to death by husband, father, father-in-law or clan long before Deuteronomy names this as the appropriate, official punishment.[23] Given these alternatives—and there are more—we must always weigh up a good many factors before coming to a decision; and now and then we may end up with a *non liquet*.

Let me present a small selection. There is no pronouncement in the XII Tables on repayment of an informal loan. (*Nexum* is a very different matter.) At one time I inclined to see this accounted for by *ça va sans dire*. But I have changed my mind. There is no pronouncement because the law in fact keeps out. In that epoch, *mutuum*, literally the mutual, here the mutual service[24]—I lend you money or seedcorn when you need it and you at an opportune moment return it or lend me what I need—belongs to the area of gift trade,[25] not brought before the courts. A modern parallel would be dinner parties: Professor and Mrs. X, having been entertained by Professor and Mrs. Y, are expected to invite them back to a similar evening. Social pressure will indeed be strong, but there is—as yet[26]—no legal claim. When, in the third century B.C., *mutuum* is rendered actionable, this marks a breakdown in the gift trade. It is significant that the money loan becomes actionable first: it moves from the personal to the commercial

22. See T. Mommsen, *Römisches Strafrecht* (1899), 688 f.

23. Gen 38:24; Judg 15:6; Deut 22:22.

24. See W. Kunkel, *Römisches Privatrecht: auf Grund des Werkes von P. Jörs*, 3rd ed. (1949), 220.

25. On which see M. Mauss, *Essai sur le don* (1925); C. S. Belshaw, *Traditional Exchange and Modern Markets* (1965), 11 f.

26. This is only half-jocular. Certain privileges in regard to expense accounts and taxation are signs of a progressive commercialization of hospitality.

before the loan of objects, just as in present-day Western law monetary tips and gratifications enter the legal, compulsory orbit before other presents. This sort of development is at the root, too, of the distinction in Roman law between an agreement to let somebody have an object for money, sale, which finds early legal recognition, and an agreement to let somebody have an object for an object, exchange (*permutatio*, from the same root as *mutuum*), without recognition as late as in the *Corpus Juris*. (Interestingly, in the nineteenth century, the idea of mutual—in mutualism, the mutual societies etc.—again attaches itself to a more spontaneous way of managing economic life, above all, the avoidance of monetary transactions. This is particularly so in France, but it extends much further.) It is in connection with the money loan that Biblical law has first to condemn interest;[27] for the loan of victuals, the condemnation becomes necessary at a later stage only.[28] The impossibility in mature Roman law of bringing interest under the contract of *mutuum* is a remnant of the gift trade period. The prominence of the verb *dare*, to give, to make a gift, in *condictio*—the action used for *mutuum*—and the fact that the action states no legal cause are largely attributable to this background. The upshot, then, is that, however plausible it may seem at first sight to explain the absence of *mutuum* from the XII Tables on the same ground as that of direct damage, this would be an error. Repayment is not enforceable.

A contrast is provided by the Biblical law of incest. The earliest list of punishments, in Leviticus 20, starts by prescribing the death penalty for intercourse with the step-mother.[29] It is totally silent on the mother, as also on the daughter. Moreover, the oldest section of this list is silent on the sister from the same mother, though she must have been prohibited from a remote age. She does emerge in a secondary section, in a paragraph the point of which is to interdict—on pain of *kareth*, commonly understood as obliteration of a family by God[30]—the sister from the same father; it opens, "And if a man take his sister, his father's daughter or his mother's

---

27. Exod 22:24.

28. Lev 25:35–37; Deut 23:20–21.

29. Lev 20:11. See my *Studies in Biblical Law*, at 77 f.

30. See my "Über die Umbildung biblischem Rechtsgutes," in *Symbolae Friburgenses in honorem O. Lenel* (1933), 249 f. [*BLL*, 776–81]

daughter."[31] Here there is no doubt that the cases in question are omitted because everybody knows. It might perhaps be argued that they are still the internal affair of the family; but this solution is unconvincing considering the paragraphs about stepmother and daughter-in-law.[32] Or that they are so terrible that the lawgiver feels they must not be put in words. But this would only add an extra feature to the situation—the rules would still be so anchored as to require no promulgation.

How careful we have to be not to draw hasty analogies becomes clear when we go on to the grandmother, equally left unmentioned in this or indeed any other Old Testament catalogue of forbidden degrees. The reason is surely not that the taboo is taken for granted but that the liaison does not occur. Even in the ancient Orient, by the time a man is fifteen, his grandmother will be around fifty; and while for a woman of today this means the beginning of a good, lively decade,[33] her counterpart then might pack up. (This would not be true, incidentally, of a man; and we do come across a warning against intercourse with the granddaughter, Lev 18:10.) Doubtless, as soon as the interpreters of Scripture set to work, building up a full system, the grandmother was included among the kin to be avoided; she is so included in the Tannaitic sources.[34] Epstein takes a different line. From her non-appearance in the Biblical texts he infers that she was permitted in that epoch. I cannot believe it. He has the greatest difficulty in explaining why the Zadokite sect (interest in which has been greatly revived by Qumran), while it charges the Pharisees with wrongfully allowing marriage with an uncle, does not reproach them for the more objectionable one with a grandmother; and he postulates a legislative act by the Pharisees making the grandmother ineligible, an act which just preceded the quarrel with the Zadokites. There is no trace of it—the whole construction is untenable.[35]

The pre-Augustan Roman material on relations debarred from inter-

---

31. Lev 20:17.

32. Lev 20:11, 12.

33. Or of three, as proved by that beautiful film *Harold and Maude* (1971).

34. *Mishnah Yebamoth* 2:4, *Babylonian Yebamoth* 21a.

35. See L. M. Epstein, *Marriage Laws in the Bible and the Talmud* (Cambridge, Mass., 1942), 232, 236, 254 f.; my criticism in "Texts and Interpretations in Roman and Jewish Law," *Jewish Journal of Sociology* 3 (1961), 3, 26 [*TL*, 181].

course is essentially not too different. It is very meager, and Mommsen[36] must rely chiefly on reasonable speculation. It was superfluous to enunciate these rules. Plutarch contains a revealing passage. "Formerly," he writes,[37] "men did not marry cognates"—meaning no one at all identifiable as cognate, which included the sixth degree in the sideline—"just as even now they do not marry their aunts or nieces." The abstention from mother, daughter and sister is too natural to illustrate his point; it cannot serve as a contemporary parallel to those rigid ancient barriers; he needs restrictions felt to be imposed by the laws, aunts and nieces. I accept S. A. Naber's emendation of "sisters" into "nieces."[38] Even without it, my argument stands: no reference to mother and daughter, the most settled taboos.

The more fundamental an institution—fundamental in the sense of embedded in the fabric of society—the more apt it is to be accepted without ado and to remain unformulated. This is a major cause (not, admittedly, the only one) of the resistance of constitutional law to codification, a characteristic by no means limited to antiquity: think of Britain. (Israel is in this as in many respects rather *sui generis*.) I have already remarked on there being no enumeration of the modes of enslavement in the XII Tables or the Mishpatim. Neither do they tell us that a child follows the status of the father.[39] Neither anything about the composition of or election to the governing bodies of the state. Eduard Fraenkel used to say—and he was only half-joking—that Mommsen's *Römisches Staatsrecht* was the greatest work ever written on a non-existent subject. This is to proceed from an extremely narrow definition of law. It cannot, however, be denied that

36. See Mommsen, above note 22, at 682 f.
37. Plutarch, *Moralia* 265D (*Quaestiones Romanae* 6).
38. Of *adelphas* into *adelphidas*, see F. C. Babbitt, ed., *Plutarch: Moralia* [Loeb Classical Library], 4 (1936), 16 n. 2.
39. [Editor's note: Daube had wrongly written that the child followed the status of the mother (partly true in later Jewish law). When I drew attention to the error, he wrote: "Yes, in 'Self-Understood,' the sentence you quote is faulty. It should be 'status of mother or father' or perhaps, 'status of this or that parent.' My forgetting about the father results from the fact that this paragraph is written mainly with an eye on Roman Law, more precisely, early Roman Law where the child of a Roman and alien is a citizen if the mother is one. Testimony to the danger of telescoping."]

the bulk of Roman or Hebrew constitutional law is unwritten and must be deduced from its operation.

Two problems. One arises when a system, hitherto satisfied with a good deal of custom, decides—generally or for a particular branch—to acknowledge solely rules expressly set forth as such: *nulla poena sine lege, nulla actio sine lege* or the like. At Rome, at that stage, the gaps were filled by legislation, such as the *leges Silia* and *Calpurnia* introducing *condictio* or the *lex Aquilia* about damage to property. To the Jews, this method was available only in a very limited degree since no later legislation could attain the status of the Biblical. They had to manage by means of an extensive interpretation—often very forced—of what the Pentateuch offered them. Thus the punishment of stoning for incest with the mother was arrived at by finding in the text of Leviticus a clause or two justifying a taking over of the punishment imposed on incest with the stepmother.[40] Direct damage by a *paterfamilias* was dealt with largely by interpreting in a suitable manner the provisions concerning the goring ox: a fantastically topsyturvy procedure, the ox, the indirect case, furnishing the model for when I break a window.[41] The Samaritans, who—understandably—rejected most of the flexible Rabbinic modes of interpretation, found the going hard indeed, the old texts becoming less and less adequate. But I shall not here give details.[42]

The second problem I have in mind is this, that rules not spelled out inevitably, by definition, tend to escape scrutiny. This is a matter of great moment, especially if among them are many of the most ordinary everyday ones and many of the most far-reaching ones, both kinds profoundly affecting communal behavior. The Pythagoreans taught that the revolving spheres produce a music which human ears are so accustomed to that they do not hear it.[43] It is a testimony to the ultimate optimism of this school that it believes that, if we could hear it (as Pythagoras himself did and also

40. *Babylonian Sanhedrin* 53a f.

41. In *Mishnah Baba Kamma* 1:4, 2:6, for instance, man is declared legally equivalent to an ox known to be dangerous.

42. See my paper cited above note 35, at 21 f.

43. See W. K. C. Guthrie, *A History of Greek Philosophy* 1 (1962), 295 f. Aristotle (*De caelo* 2.9.290b) maintains that we do not hear it because it does not exist.

Scipio, though he only in a dream), the sound would be marvelous; *dulcis* Cicero calls it.[44] Unless you are an arch-conservative, however, like my friend John Barton, who affirms that all change is for the worse, you will wonder whether an unveiling of the hidden rules would cause nothing but joy and content.

Perhaps I may conclude by pointing out that there is a huge difference between what is self-understood and what a writer explicitly introduces as such. Actually, it is a sound working principle to prick up one's ears when coming upon an assurance like "obviously," "it is clear that." It is often assertiveness making up for lack of substance. This goes for classical literature as well as contemporary.

Gaius, who flourished under Hadrian, contrasts the statutory force of senatusconsults and that of imperial decrees.[45] The former, he informs us, had at one time been questioned; the latter, never, *nec umquam dubitatum est*. "The lady doth protest too much, methinks."[46] Why? He is far too great an expert to be unfamiliar with the growth of the Emperor's legislative power. But he badly wants to raise it above any conceivable criticism. So he represents it as undisputed from the beginning, eager to drown lingering doubts, in himself as well as others. I do not concur with Professor Honoré's suggestion that the wording is chosen in a spirit of irony.[47] For one thing, that would have been far too dangerous. Motivation of the type I ascribe to Gaius is perennial. The Preamble to the 1960 Republican Constitution of

---

44.   Cicero, *De republica* 6.18 (*Somnium Scipionis*) 5. A little further on, however, in 6.19, he says it would overpower us, just as the sun is too much for our eyes if we look straight into it. Maybe we are here in touch with a variant of the tradition met in Plutarch, *Moralia* 745E (*Quaestiones conviviales* 9.14.6) (see Guthrie, *History of Greek Philosophy*, at 297 n. 3, with an interesting reference to Shakespeare's *Merchant of Venice* 5.1.64 f.), that our deafness to the spheres is due, not to familiarity, but to our earthly imperfection. In passing—while according to Aristotle the Pythagoreans compare the coppersmith who no longer notices the din around him, Cicero compares the inhabitants of Catadupa who pay no attention to the roaring cataracts of the Nile. Is there a little snobbism behind this change?

45.   Gaius 1.5.

46.   *Hamlet* 3.2.242.

47.   See A. Honoré, *Gaius* (1962), 118 f.

Ghana opens:[48] "We the People of Ghana, by our Representatives gathered in this our Constituent Assembly, In exercise of our undoubted right to appoint for ourselves the means whereby we shall be governed..."

48. See A. J. Peaslee, *Constitutions of Nations* 1, 3rd ed. (The Hague, 1965), 213.

Standing in for Jack Coons[1]

I propose to make two recondite points concerning Roman contract, one of them linguistic,[2] the other socio-economic,[3] and then to recall you from slumber or gloom by the low-down on Humpty Dumpty.[4]

I.

In what counts as the heyday of the system, the period of the Principate, contracts are divided into four classes based on modes of inception. (1) Contracts coming about through the physical thing involved, *re*. If I am lending you money, for example, your obligation to repay arises from my giving you the coins. Or in an arrangement for safekeeping, your obligation to look after my Picasso while I serve in the army and to return it on my discharge arises from my handing you the picture. (2) Contracts coming about through certain words, *verbis*. For example, Do you promise to weed my

---

[Selection from *Rechtshistorisches Journal* 7 (1988), 179–190. For the final two sections see *Ethics* 39–44.]

1. Professor John E. Coons, whose lectures on Contracts attracts and provides stimulus to a lively class, occasionally gives a colleague the opportunity to meet them. I had my day on November 13, 1987, and enjoyed it no end. Here is more or less what I said.

2. See my articles in *LQR* 52 (1936), 259; *CLJ* 6 (1938), 398 ff.; *JTS* 45 (1944), 182 f. [*NTJ* 177–85]; *Studi Solazzi* (1948), 139 ff.; *Philosophy and Public Affairs* 1 (1972), 394 ff., rpt. *Suicide and Life-Threatening Behavior* 7 (1977), 139 ff. [*Ethics* 72 ff.]; *Theories of Property*, ed. A. Parel and T. Flannigan (1979), 38 f. [below, 89 ff.].

3. See my articles in *ZRG, RA* 90 (1973), 6 ff. (English trans. *JR* 18 [1973], 129 ff.) [above, 53–63]; 96 [1979], 1 ff. [below, 71–87].

4. See my article in *Oxford Magazine* (1956), 272, 274. The explanation there given "they widened and deepened the existing ditch" is only half-correct. I am grateful to Professor Coons for pointing out to me that the reference to widening makes no sense.

garden? I promise. (3) Contracts coming about through certain entries in account books, *literis.* (4) Contracts coming about through accord, *consensus.* In sale, for example, once we are agreed that you are to get my bicycle for ten *aurei,* you can sue for delivery of the object and I for the price. Or in mandate, once we are agreed that you will acquire a Hebrew-speaking slave for me during your forthcoming visit to Jerusalem, I can hold you to it and you can compel me to reimburse you for what you laid out.

Now obviously, accord, *consensus,* is a decisive element also in the first three classes, contracts by means of the thing, words, entries. Why does it receive recognition only in class four, sale, mandate and so on? The major reason lies in a feature met in the development of all languages, a basic sequence in the history of human experience: the abstract or general goes on unremarked for very long where the concrete or specific monopolizes attention, blocks the view. In the first three classes, a striking external datum stands at the beginning: the coins or the Picasso, *res,* the formal undertaking, *verba,* the document, *literae.* Nothing remotely as impressive or consistent in sale or mandate. They may be concluded in whatever fashion you choose, from a solemn handshake to a grudging "Alright, then," from an epistolary approval to a mere nod. It is here, then, that the jurists first become aware of the concurrence of wills as the creative factor.

Naturally, in time, they realize its encompassing function and, by the Dominate, all contracts are consensual, with those previously domineering components—thing, words, entries—put in their place as subsidiary requirements. This never-ceasing process of unfolding, by the way, plays a major role in the "death of contract" sponsored by today's analytical avant-garde. But I shall not digress.

Here are two illustrations from delict. In the section of the XII Tables on assault, retaliation is threatened if you maim a person's limb, a heavy fine if you fracture a person's bone and a moderate fine if you slap a person's face or kick his shin. The third offence is called *iniuria,* "unlawfulness." Clearly, the first two are also instances of unlawfulness, indeed, worse ones. But the abstract, general essence is kept from entering consciousness by the obtrusive, immediate and well-defined spectacle. To put it more simply, imagine a victim of assault in 500 B.C. going to court. In the first two cases he will say, "Look, I am minus my left leg" or "Look, my jaw is broken." In the third case, of a slap or kick, he has nothing dramatic to show and there is more variation between the exact complaints comprised by it, hence access to the nature of the deed is much easier and he charges *iniuria*, "unlawfulness." It is only around the end of the Republic that the scope of this designation is grasped and the maimed limb and broken bone are subsumed under it.

An identical route is traceable for the fundamental concept of "loss" in the field of damage to property. A third-century B.C. statute devotes two chapters to this delict. One lays down that a man who kills another man's slave or beast must pay its value, the other that a man who "causes loss" to another man by harming his slave or beast must pay according to the state of the affair at the end of thirty days. The term "loss" is confined to the second case; why? Originally, if you kill, this plain, solid result dominates the thinking, no need to penetrate into subtler regions behind it. Whereas if you merely wound, everything is fluid. A wound may range from trifling to fatal; indeed, it may look one way to begin with and turn out the other in the end. Again, there may be expenses for a temporary substitute, medical fees and so forth. The comprehensive idea "loss," then, first comes to the fore in this context, where it is not hidden behind a clear-cut reality. Later, pretty soon in fact, it is taken over into the first case as well—when it has been learnt that even here the outer phenomenon may not be all: the slave killed may have been one of a famous pair of actors, the killing of the ox may have delayed the plowing. So the wider notion "loss" is useful here too, and it ends up as the overarching standard of restitution.

Perhaps the most amazing Roman law specimen of this evolution is the distinction between corporeal assets, i.e. tangible objects, and incorporeal assets, i.e. rights. The latter include an easement to walk across neighboring land, a claim for a sum of money or for delivery of a horse and so forth. What is not included is the principal right, ownership: this falls under corporeal assets, tangible objects. The explanation: where I am owner, the basic situation is always the same, and always interest centers on the concrete, specific piece of land or the car or the dog. My relation to it, therefore, can be sufficiently indicated without digging further. Even today, "This house is mine" is heard more frequently than "The ownership of this house is mine." It is in more variable, complicated, diffuse situations—I raise one of the countless demands possible in the name of one of the several contracts or delicts, or by virtue of an easement I, with no title to your land, may walk across it even though you, with title, object— that recourse is had to the abstract, general: to incorporeal assets, rights. Justinian still continues the primitive inexactitude, which indeed lingers on till fairly recent times.

Outside the law, an observation by Hermann Fränkel belongs here.[5] The Greek word for "time," χρόνος, to begin with, denotes, not the time during which anything of interest happens—since here, the happening stands in the foreground—but the interval between one meal, battle, flood, and another. It is when confronted with time bared that people start being sensitive to this dimension—gradually discovering its pervasiveness. English must have traveled the same path, which has left plenty of vestiges. Time in the *Winter's Tale* addresses the public half-way through the play to account for the sixteen years without action; he is not needed, and hardly remembered, so long as the stage is crowded. Even in modern speech, "time flies" when something fully engaging our mind goes on (are you with me?); and "I shall have time this evening" does not envisage an extraordinary astronomical duration—as when Joshua bade sun and moon stand still[6]—it speaks of time in its archaic sense, time unoccupied.

Contemporary usage indeed suggests that "space," Latin *spatium,* matured along similar lines, from empty space, a gap, a hole, to an omnipresent condition. "No space here" means "no unfilled space here;" "space exploration"—"exploration of uninhabited expanse." The adjective "spacious" implies freedom, openness. In a crossword of the *San Francisco Chronicle* of October 29 the clue was "interval of time" and the solution "space"—plainly unobstructed. (Don't worry: I shall not drift into spacetime.) It pleased me when, looking around a little in preparation for this lecture, I came upon fairly direct evidence of this genesis of the concept. Etymologically, it stems from the root that produced Greek σπάνις, "lack," "unsatisfied want."[7] Confirming that man's initiation to "space" is effected

---

5. See *Zeitschrift fur Ästhetik* (1931), Beilageheft 98 f.
6. Josh 10:12 ff.
7. See C. T. Lewis and C. Short, *Latin Dictionary* (1962), 1735.

by the vacuous, the void—maybe the infinity of a vast plain or the sea. The insight that "space" is no less thriving in a packed cafe of the Latin Quarter or in my chaotic little office requires an enormous deal of further reflection, represents a far more sophisticated stage. The Hebrew for "space," I may interject, is *ḥalal*, literally "hollow," "cavity."

Of course, in daily life, we are primarily concerned with the specific, so even though a general word is available, it may—indeed, in vivid, narrative style should—be reserved for exceptional occasions. Let me give one illustration from my inquiry into the terminology of suicide. The Bible—the canonical portion, leaving aside Apocrypha and Pseudepigrapha—records few suicides only. Nevertheless it is scarcely accidental that these texts contain no overall description like "to kill oneself," "to take one's own life." The blind Samson, mocked by the Philistine crowd in their temple, "took hold of the pillars and the house fell upon all the people;"[8] Saul "fell upon his sword," as did his armorbearer;[9] Ahithophel "strangled himself;"[10] Judas "hanged himself."[11] Yet an overall description does appear twice—of suicide intended but not completed. The jailor of Peter and Silas, in the belief that they escaped during an earthquake, "drew his sword and was about to do away with himself." Here it would not be enough to mention the outer act: he might be getting ready for pursuit. We have to be informed of his design, and once that is the focus, it is natural to introduce the comprehensive verb and not be satisfied with "and was about to fall upon it." Actually, Paul, who intervenes to save him, uses even more comprehensive phrasing, meant to banish any self-destructive impulses: he says not "don't do away with yourself" but "do yourself no harm."[12] In the Fourth Gospel, as Jesus proclaims that where he goes the Jews opposing him cannot follow, the latter are taken aback: "He will not kill himself?" They are helplessly groping at what, by and large, he may have in mind; no particular mode is named at all, the actual realization is

8. Judg 16:29 f.
9. 1 Sam 31:4 f.
10. 2 Sam 17:23.
11. Matt 27:5.
12. Acts 16:26 ff.

left quite open.[13] More open, in fact, than might be guessed at first sight. Leading commentators hold—correctly, I incline to believe—that the Jews are depicted as unwittingly prophesying (like Caiaphas):[14] Jesus will truly kill himself, though in a very different sense from what they are thinking of, he will lay down his life for his flock.

Incidentally, if John can represent Jesus' sacrificial death as self-killing, in however roundabout a fashion, this greatly strengthens the likelihood that the New Testament no more than the Old shares the horror of suicide which subsequently, on and off, obtained hold over large sections of Christendom. It may be added that in the prison scene just quoted, Paul with no word condemns the jailor's resolution as sinful.

13. John 7:34 ff.
14. John 11:48 ff. See my *Appeasement or Resistance* (1987), 89 [*NTJ* 100].

Money and Justiciability*

I.

Here are some observations on how transactions originally belonging to the gift area of fellowship, "Gemeinschaft," tend to assume the more rigid, legalistic characteristics of partnership, "Gesellschaft," when money enters. Let us begin by looking at the Old Testament, and first at some narratives.

It should be noted at the outset that even in the absence of money the temperature may be below zero, as when Jacob gets Esau to part with his birthright for a red dish.[1] The former's successive arrangements with Laban,[2] none of them involving money, are among the many cases with elements of both fellowship and partnership.

How misleading it would be to make too much of the use or non-use of money is shown by the vocabulary: the same verb *makhar* is applied to barter, transfer of one thing for another, and to sale, transfer of a thing for money (Esau "sold" his birthright),[3] by a number of minor data, such as the complaint of Leah and Rachel that their father "devoured their silver."[4] Jacob served for his wives instead of handing over cash; and the increase in his employer's herds due to his efficiency is here described as "money"—

[*Zeitschrift der Savigny-Stiftung für Rechtsgeschichte, Romanistische Abteilung* 96 (1979), 1–16]
    * To my friend Ernst Bammel.
    1. Gen 25:29 ff. See my *Studies in Biblical Law* (1947; rpt. 1969), 193 ff. [*BLL*, 244 ff.]
    2. Genesis 29 ff.
    3. See *Studies*, 196 [*BLL*, 246]
    4. Gen 31:15.

Laban, his daughters feel, ought to have shared it with them and not kept it all for himself.

Still, caution need not become paralysis. The early story of Naboth's vineyard does point to a basic difference in aura between barter and sale.[5] Ahab's proposal is: "I will give you for it a better vineyard, or if it is good in your eyes I will give you the worth of it in silver." He receives a no; and when the queen inquires why he is vexed he replies: "Because I spoke to Naboth, Give me your vineyard for silver, or if you wish I will give you another vineyard for it." Evidently, the choices are here switched around. In the end she informs him of Naboth's execution: "Take possession of the vineyard which he refused to give you for silver, for he is dead." By now, money alone figures.

I have found nothing on these changes in any commentary. Yet they are significant. The king starts by suggesting a swap between friends—though even this opening, by mentioning the superior quality of the vineyard he will supply, tries to rouse the profit motive in Naboth. The alternative offer of money directly holds out to the latter the possibility of making a good, cold deal. In telling Jezebel, Ahab puts first his readiness to pay. This, when he broods on the rebuff and, even more, when he describes it to his hard-nosed wife, is what counts: he subjected himself to the rigors of the market—what more could he have done? The amicable trading, being a lesser concession, comes second. The queen, finally, omits the non-monetary exchange altogether. No trace of joviality is left: Naboth thought himself too good to do business—he got what he deserved.

It may be objected that this gradation is too subtle to be consciously built up by the narrator. However, on this basis, it would testify all the more strongly to the then prevalent relation between the two transactions; for it would represent a deep-rooted, unreflected mode of seeing their respective roles. I shall leave the matter open.

There is immense room for complications; maybe, indeed, we should not look for "pure" instances. When Abraham arrives in Egypt, he introduces Sarah as his sister, suppressing the fact that she is his wife.[6] Pharaoh

5. I Kings 21.
6. Gen 12:11 ff. See my *Sin, Ignorance and Forgiveness in the Bible* (1960), 7 ff. [*BLL*, 378–380].

takes her into his harem and "entreated him well for her sake, and he had sheep and oxen and he asses and manservants and maidservants and she asses and camels." To some extent, this is gift trade; and an intrusion of money would no doubt change the atmosphere. Nevertheless Abraham being a complete isolate and Pharaoh in any case having full control, we can hardly speak of fellowship.

The patriarch's purchase of a burial place[7] illustrates a transitional stage, with considerable remnants of gift trade. While he sojourns among the Hittites, Sarah dies and he approaches them for a grave. They bid him choose the best, acknowledging his powerful position—"you are a mighty Prince among us"—which, though he is an alien, makes him into something of a fellow. So he goes on to ask them to persuade one Ephron to let him have "for full silver" a cave at the edge of a field of his. Owning no hereditary Hittite ground, he cannot tender land for land, he must employ money—and the impact of this means of exchange is subtly noticeable: "for full silver" presupposes an exact rating that would be less appropriate to barter. Ephron replies, "Not so," immediately making over gratis the entire field. This is the ritual of gift commerce: an offer for free in the knowledge that consideration will be forthcoming. To this day, in quite a few corners, the charade persists. Now it is Abraham's turn to demur: he begs Ephron to accept "the silver of the field." Whereupon Ephron quotes a sum: "The field is worth four hundred shekels of silver—between me and you what is this? bury therefore your dead." Even this specific valuation is accompanied by a denial of any mercenary concern; and we shall come back to the phrase "between me and you" as expressing the idealist, personal aspect.[8] How phony it is comes out in the next verse: "And Abraham hearkened unto Ephron and weighed the silver which he had named, four hundred shekels of silver, current with the merchant." "He hearkened"— so that is what it is really at. Needless to say, the payment is not declined.

The negotiations between David and Araunah are similar. They are recorded twice in Samuel and Chronicles.[9] To go by the former, David is

7. Gen 23:3 ff.
8. See below.
9. 2 Sam 24:18 ff.; 1 Chron 21:15 ff.

advised by a prophet to acquire Araunah's threshing floor and erect an altar there. Araunah at once donates not only the land but also sacrificial animals and wood. In this case it is the present holder who is the underdog, a Jebusite in Hebrew-dominated territory, and who is none the less treated with respect. Possibly the puzzling clause "all this did Araunah the king give to the king," is intended to stress their equality in this deal—somewhat corresponding to "you are a mighty prince among us." As a rule the passage is emended, and that may indeed be the preferable course. The offer sounds rather more genuine than Ephron's: a notable difference is that Araunah is not induced to mention a figure. Moreover, while David insists on paying a price—"fifty shekels of silver"—he feels called on to produce a reason. It is a remarkable one: he will not offer to God what he obtained gratuitously. The meanness of a gift at somebody else's expense is emphasized in another narrative about him: there, he is actually likened to a rich man who, when entertaining a guest, "spared to take of his own flock but took the poor man's lamb."[10]

Of the deviations in Chronicles, three may be listed. The difficult verse about the king giving to the king does not appear. The "fifty shekels of silver" have become "six hundred shekels of gold." Above all the Chronicler seems to have spotted the affinity with Abraham's purchase:[11] he twice introduces the words "for full silver", once as David first tells Araunah (Ornan in Chronicles) what he wants and again as he turns down the liberality.

I shall dispense with a detailed inquiry into how far the presentation of the two agreements with Hittites and Jebusites is geared towards foreign policy. For the purpose in hand, it is enough to realize that when you claim an area to be lawfully yours, there will scarcely be a stronger argument than that you obtained it from the owner for good money.

The Purim saga reminds us of the wide variety of circumstances in which the gesture of a gift may cover up a firm monetary arrangement.[12]

---

10. 2 Sam 12:4. See my and B. Jackson's forthcoming *Ancient Jewish Law*, section The King [unpublished, but see "Nathan's Parable," *Novum Testamentum* 24 (1982), 275–288 (*BLL*, 715–725)].

11. See W. Rudolph *Chronikbücher* (1955), 147.

12. Esth 3:9 f., 7:4, 10:1 f. See my remarks in *JQR* 37 (1946), 139–147. [*BLL*, 797–801] .

Haman engages that if the king will allow him to wipe out the Jews, the treasury will be enriched by as much as ten thousand talents. The king graciously yields all proceeds to the petitioner: "The silver is given to you and the people." The renunciation, however, is entirely pro forma and, later on, Esther realistically says: "We have been sold (*makhar*) to be destroyed." In fact, what she demonstrates is that Haman, pursuing his personal vendetta, lured the king into a bad bargain. If a putting down of the Jews were advisable at all, this would surely be more profitable to the treasury to have them sold into slavery than to have them killed. But even a once-for-all expropriation is a less wise course than a sharing in their enterprises by means of taxation. Basically, it is by the same pleas that, throughout the Middle Ages, Jews tried to dissuade host governments from exterminating them.

The reports about a prophet's honorarium are revealing. Balak[13] assures Balaam that "he will greatly honor him" if he will curse Israel. It would be unseemly to lure a revered seer with the prospect of a material gift in so many words. But Balaam rightly takes the king as referring to "silver and gold"—which probably includes both objects and money. He does not refuse but he vows to act only as God will bid him even should he thereby forfeit his reward. God tells him to bless Israel, he obeys and thus does leave "kept from honor."

Naaman,[14] indebted to Elisha for his cure, urges him to accept "a blessing"—once again a euphemism for a material gift of money and objects; money and garments, to be precise. Elisha steadfastly declines, a self-denial not without a missionary purpose. His conduct foreshadows Simeon ben Shatah's "preferring to hear the Arab say, Blessed is the God of the Jews, to all gain of this world."[15] He inflicts fearful punishment on his servant for running after Naaman and swindling a gift out of him. An interesting feature of the servant's approach to Naaman is that he says his master would like a donation for two young disciples. Then as today, a tip for a subordinate may be a way out where you yourself must remain aloof.

---

13. Num 22:17 ff., 24:11 ff. See "my Ancient Hebrew Fables" (1973), 14 ff. [*BLL*, 704–705]

14. 2 Kgs 5:8 ff.

15. *Jerusalem Baba Metzia* 8c. See my *The New Testament and Rabbinic Judaism* (1956; rpt. 1973), 338 f, 359 f. [*NTJ*, 563–565, 581–582]

(A multi-millionaire politician who wants to rope in a talented struggling university professor sends the latter's children to a good school.) Already the life of Abraham furnishes an example.[16]

Belshazzar[17] proclaims that whoever can interpret the writing on the wall "shall be clothed with scarlet and a gold chain and shall be the third ruler in the kingdom." Scarlet and chain, valuable as they are, are not money: in this milieu, the latter may be too common for an eminent sage while the former (and the elevation to high rank) emphasize his closeness to the throne. Daniel, to whom the king repeats the announcement personally, is unmoved even by the refined inducements: "Let your gifts be to yourself and give your rewards to another; yet I will read the writing." The phraseology "let your gifts be to yourself" is reminiscent of Ahasverus's insincere, "the silver is given to you and the people." We may rate Daniel ninety percent authentic. Not one hundred: he does accept everything after expounding the message.

II.

To pass on to the laws, the prohibition of usury merits attention.[18] We first meet it in Exodus, where it has regard solely to a money loan: "if you lend silver to my people, to the poor that is with you." The reason is that, by this epoch, usury has not yet reached other loans.

If I may expand—the provision itself is manifestly not concerned with a major loan to a tycoon. The borrower is expressly characterized as poor. We may also note that the preceding section is directed against oppression of helpless folks like widows, and that the ordinance here discussed, after condemning usury, goes on to oppose the excessive harshness of pressure pledge: a lender to whom the borrower has pawned his wrapper should return it for the nights, so the man need not freeze. This is clearly not the

---

16. Gen 14:23.
17. Dan 5:7 ff.
18. Exod 22:24; Lev 25:25 ff.; Deut 23:20 f. See my lecture, "Das Selbstverständliche in der Rechtsgeschichte," *ZRG, RA* 90 (1973), 1–13; English translation, "The Self-Understood in Legal History," *JR* 85 (1973), 130 [above, 57–58].

fail-safe pledge like a string of pearls, a good horse or a field, by realizing which a creditor can recoup himself if he is not repaid. The wrapper is worthless but, as its owner badly needs it, he will do his utmost to redeem it: pressure pledge is appropriate where the debtor is indigent. Transactions between capitalists, then, we can leave on one side.

As for a small loan, that is originally a friendly service, often between neighbors.[19] Gradually, however, when made by a well-to-do person to a needy one, it becomes less relaxed—and this happens in money loans before, say, in loans of a jar or of seedcorn. It is in the former that such practices as usury—or pressure pledge—will first come up.

The ordinance applies to one who lends "to my people": there is nothing against taking usury from outsiders. *Au fond*, by taking it from an outsider, you turn him into an outsider, you replace warm fellowship by cold partnership—or worse. At the time of Exodus, this development, well under way in money loans, need not yet be combated more generally.

When we come to Leviticus, a warning against enforcing an extra when lending food has been added: "your silver you shall not give upon usury, and upon increase you shall not give your victuals." Finally, Deuteronomy reckons with an even wider extension of the evil: "you shall not lend upon usury to your brother, usury of silver, usury of victuals, usury of anything that is lent upon usury." If the prior ruling of Exodus were lost, the very form of this one would enable us to reconstruct the process, usury of money evidently representing the starting-point, usury of food the next phase and usury of anything an ultimate sweep. It may be added that, in attacks on greedy lenders outside the Pentateuch, whereas the money loan is invariably included, the loan of other objects is not:[20] the latter always remains far less dominated by the business spirit.

I refrain from taking up offerings and their regulations. Not because there is nothing to be learnt but because there is too much. An investigation of the gift trade between man and gods or God, coeval with religion, assuming innumerable shades, patterned after and in turn drawn on by earthly commerce—not to mention its very own peculiarities—would

19. E.g. 2 Kgs 4:3.
20. Ps 15:5.

swamp this paper. (Aristophanes' *Birds* alone might fill a book.) In another essay,[21] adverting to the paradoxical duty of happy generosity, I quote God's instruction to Moses: "Speak unto the children of Israel, that they bring me an offering; from every man whose heart makes him willing shall you take my offering."[22] Many Roman inscriptions recording the fulfilment of a vow contain the abbreviation *L.M.*: the person performed *libens merito*, "willingly, duly.") The intrusion of money is of import here just as in other provinces. The earliest Biblical example is: "The children of Israel shall give every man a ransom for his soul unto the Lord, that there be no plague among them, half a shekel. The rich shall not give more and the poor shall not give less."[23] The *quid pro quo* is no less in evidence in cases where the deity receives beasts or valuables. But the emphasis on rigid equality is surely bound up with the use of the undifferentiated medium.

Who knows?—the fateful Greek speculations concerning the equality of men may owe something initially to insights first reached in connection with money. The adoption of coins especially, in the seventh century B.C., with its tremendous social consequences, must have stirred up intense probing: here was a substance which could stand for any other (almost), into which any other (almost) was convertible. It would not be surprising if ideas about it had contributed to those about the make-up of the world as a whole and mankind in particular.

III.

There is ample Roman material for comparison.[24] Regarding sale and barter, we find a gulf dividing an agreement to let somebody have an object for money from one to let somebody have an object for an object. Whereas the former enjoys recognition from around 200 B.C.,[25] the latter is without

---

21. "'Suffrage' and 'Precedent', 'Mercy' and 'Grace,'" *Tijdschrift voor Rechtsge-schiedenis* 47 (1979), 244.
22. Exod 25:2.
23. Exod 30:12 ff.
24. See "The Self-Understood in Legal History," above.
25. See A. Watson, *The Law of Obligations in the Later Roman Republic* (1965), 40 f.

an action as late as in the *Corpus Juris*. In the Principate, an attempt by the Sabinians to subsume barter under sale fails.[26] From some time in the classical or postclassical epoch, once one side has in fact transferred his property to the other, he can compel the latter to follow suit. This development, important though it is, does not remove the inactionability of an agreement to trade.

The decisive argument of the Proculians is that, in sale, the two parties have different duties (the vendor's referring to delivery, title and qualities of the thing, the buyer's to payment), in barter, the same (each being responsible for a thing). But, at best, this explains why, once consensual sale is fully worked out, barter does not fit into it. It does not explain at all why consensual barter should not be acknowledged in its own right as early as sale, let alone its lack of enforceability—even secondary, praetorian one—throughout the ensuing centuries. This phenomenon is the result of the essentially intimate nature of moneyless barter as opposed to the distant aura in money-geared sale. Even at present, as a rule, an arrangement to swap records, cameras, houses (or partners) is more private and less law-oriented than one to transfer any of these possessions for money.

Similar considerations apply to hire. Here also, unless one side will give money, the courts are not interested. If I undertake to put my slave philosopher at your disposal for two years, at so and so many dollars a year, it is hire. By contrast, if I am going to let you use him for your letting me use your slave cook, or for your making over to me a copy of Catullus it is not—there is no action. Just as in the case of sale, the Sabinians advocate a reform but are defeated (though, where you agree to make me owner of your Catullus, it cannot even be said that the duties of the two parties are the same). Justinian still *au fond* adheres to the old regulation.[27] In the absence of money, fellowship prevails, with no need for outside directive. Money leads to partnership and justiciability.

For a long time the practitioners of liberal arts are indeed unable to exact remuneration of any kind; they are above hire. By and large, needless

26. On the disputants' appeal to Homer, see my note, "The Three Quotations from Homer in Digest 18.1.1.1," *CLJ* 10 (1949), 213 ff. [below, 278–281].
27. See A. Watson op. cit., 101 ff.

to say, this means not something for nothing but gift commerce: in recognition of your doctor's favor, you send him a present of a horse or a sack of coins. One designation of this, *honor* or *honorarium*, recalls Balaak's wish "greatly to honor" the prophet he engages.[28] From around A.D. 200, a money reward promised can be claimed, though even now not by a normal action but by *cognitio extraordinaria*.

Some jobs are so sensitive that even a present is out of order. A plebiscite of 204 B.C. lays down that an advocate may not accept one for appearing in court—at least till the case is over; my impression is that afterwards he may.[29] The wording implies a noteworthy distinction, He may not take *pecuniam donumve*, "money or gift,", and similarly, in reporting a later revival of the prohibition by the senate, Tacitus speaks of *merces aut dona*, "fee or gifts." A horse, it is felt, is a token of devotion, but a sack of coins is businesslike payment.

This perception recurs again and again. When you manumit your slave, you may make him promise *donum*, *munus*, *operas*, "special gifts, conventional gifts (as for New Year), work," but not money.[30] The charter for Urso in Spain (now Osuna) of 44 B.C. makes it a crime for an official, when contracting out public land, to accept *donum*, *munus*, *mercedem aliudve quid*, "a gift, a service, a fee or anything else"[31]—a fee in money being listed separately from gift proper. Another paragraph forbids a candidate for a magistrary, or a supporter, with dishonest intent to hold a banquet or to show his generosity by *donum*, *munus aliudve quid*, "a gift, a service or anything else."[32] Here money is not mentioned: so gross a method is presumably rare in a small town campaign of this period. At a pinch, it would be caught by "anything else."

The notion of money as unsuitable for a true gift is by no means confined to ancient Rome. It is shared by other civilizations of antiquity and still alive in ours. Naturally, there are variations in intensity and coverage.

28. See above.
29. Tacitus, *Annals* 11.5., 13.5.
30. See W. W. Buckland, *A Text-Book of Roman Law*, 3rd ed. by Peter Stein (1963), 89, M. Kaser, *Festschrift Fritz Schulz* (1951), 2.40 ff.
31. *Lex Ursonensis* ch. 33, tab. 3, col. 1.1.22.
32. *Lex Ursonensis* ch. 132, tab. 4, col. 3.11.25, 29.

To this person you cannot give cash but you can send a cheque—more respectful not only because normally associated with major affairs but also because a bit removed from the actual sordid coins or notes. A new ten-dollar bill is superior to ten old one-dollar ones. I have witnessed changes in my own lifetime; and though I do my best to be with it, deep down I am still a bit uncomfortable when youngsters prefer dough for a birthday to a lovingly (and, I do see, often foolishly) chosen object.

When we go on to loan, Roman law distinguishes between that of an individual object—a garment, a horse—which is to be handed back after use, *commodatum*, and that of money or other fungibles—wheat, oranges—where, at the agreed time, it is not the identical coins, grains, or oranges that need to be restored but objects of the same quantity and quality, *mutuum*. The first thing to note is that the former becomes actionable—so that a commodator can sue for return on the ground of this transaction—only in the last century of the Republic.[33]

Certainly, even before then, a person anxious to safeguard himself may refuse to lend unless return is promised by *stipulatio*, a separate contract; and now and then, the owner's *vindicatio* or an action on the ground of theft will help. But this does not alter the main fact that for a long time, *commodatum* as such is without legal protection: this relieving a person's temporary need for a specific thing you happen to have is very slow to shed the traces of its origin in fellowship.

We must not forget that the latter has its own sanctions—via conscience, shame, fear of forfeiting good will, social pressure. Even at present, I suspect, reliance on these is strong in *commodatum*, and an action for the return of a book or umbrella lent is a rare occurrence.

What about *mutuum*? It too grows up outside the law. At one time, I thought the XII Tables were silent about it because its enforceability went without saying. This was a mistake.

No doubt, even in that era, a lender of money or wheat is not necessarily without a remedy. There is the ceremonial *nexum*, giving considerable power over a defaulter. Apart from this, just as in the case of *commodatum*, if it is important to have an action—say, it is a major commercial

33. See A. Watson, op. cit., 167 ff.

affair—a separate *stipulatio* can always do the trick. Occasionally, failure to repay may be treated as a kind of theft. Still, *mutuum* itself does not at this stage ground an action.

The literal meaning of the term is "the mutual."[34] The arrangement starts as a mutual service between people with close daily ties: I lend you a little when you need it and you at an opportune moment pay me back or lend me what I need. Nothing here for the courts though, to be sure, there are the fellowship constraints just mentioned. When, in the third century B.C., the *lex Silia* does establish an action, *condictio*, this marks a breakdown in the gift trade. What is directly pertinent to my thesis is that this statute is confined to money loans. The loan of other fungibles is not subsumed under *condictio* till the *lex Calpurnia*, in the following century.[35] Minor varieties of the latter loan—the loan of cigarettes, for example (or of chewing gum, in deference to the anti-smoking lobby)—still often retain the primeval attributes.

As is well known, the *condictio* asserts a claim without naming its basis. One reason (I am not excluding others) is that, at the time of its introduction, it is not yet natural to think of an ordinary, informal loan as a proper obligation. Again, from the outset, the verb *dare*, "to give," is prominent in this action: plaintiff declares that defendant ought to *dare* to him and, to succeed, must show a previous *dare* by himself to defendant. While *dare* covers any transfer of ownership, its special connection with gift is quite likely a factor in its choice.

The most conspicuous feature, however, due to *mutuum*'s provenance is the impossibility even in the mature system of bringing interest into it; any interest has to be arranged by a separate contract. In course of time, exceptions are creeping in. But, in principle, *mutuum* is gratuitous as late as Justinian, who lays down an exception for loans by bankers.[36]

It may be well to point out that even if, on whatever grounds, *mutuum* is held to have been binding prior to the *leges Silia* and *Calpurnia* and

---

34. See W. Kunkel. *Römisches Privatrecht auf Grund des Werkes von P. Jörs*, 3rd ed. (1949), 220.
35. Gaius 4.19.
36. *Novella* 136.4.

these are seen as merely amending the procedure,[37] my chief contention is scarcely affected: the modernization of enforcement commences with money loans. The overall trend is clear: first, actionability (or improved actionability) of a monetary loan, next, actionability (or improved actionability) of a loan of other fungibles, last, actionability of a loan of an individual object.

A linguistic aside. *Vendere*, "to sell," frankly displays its venal nature, *commodatum*, "loan of an individual object," equally clearly stresses regard for the other person's convenience. If water is to be "lent," *commodare*, even to a foe, surely, within the city, a pretty girl must not refuse to "lend" assistance of a certain kind to a guy: Plautus.[38] "To accommodate" with reference to a money loan is less than 200 years old, of American origin.[39] I shall not detail its history. It has long been used by lenders to suggest that they have the borrowers' welfare at heart—sales talk.

The legal texts on "barter" commonly speak of *permutare* and *permutatio*. Plautus uses *mutare* and *commutare*,[40] and once already *mutatio*.[41] (A man whose son is a prisoner in enemy hands hopes that, as he himself is holding a young enemy soldier, it will come to an exchange between him and his fellow-father. Exchange of prisoners fairly early became a prominent item in peace and truce pacts.)[42] The root is the same as in *mutuum*, "loan of fungibles," and, for that matter, as in *munus*, "service," *communis*, "common," and Sicilian Greek *moitos*, equivalent of *charis*, "grace," "favor," all indicative of togetherness. The fanciful Roman etymology of *mutuum*—so named because *ex meo tuum fit*, "mine becomes yours"[43]—still

37. See e.g. F. de Zulueta, *The Institutes of Gaius* II (1953), 146: "It was actionable from the time of *Ll. Silia* and *Calpurnia* and probably much earlier."

38. Plautus, *The Rope* 2.4.21 f., 433 f.

39. See *A Supplement to the Oxford English Dictionary*, ed. R. W. Burchfield (1972), 1.12.

40. A purist distinction between *permutare* and *commutare* is set out by Festus, *De verborum significatu* 214.

41. Plautus, *The Captives* 2.3.6.366. On the relation of verb and noun, see my *Roman Law* (1969), 11 ff.

42. Cicero, *De officiis* 1.13.39, *commutare*; Livy, *Ab urbe condita* 22.23, *permutare*; Periochae 18, *commutare*, 19, *commutatio*; Gellius, *Attic Nights* 6.18.2 ff., 7.3.1, *permutare, permutatio*. See C. Phillipson, *The International Law and Custom of Ancient Greece and Rome* (1911), 2: 262 ff.

43. E.g. Gaius 3.90. Nonius Marcellus, *De differentia similium significationum* 439.

preserves an afterglow, more noticeable, interestingly, in the grammarian Nonius than in juristic quotations. For him, *mutuum*, without interest, is more honorable than *fenus* because *sub amico affectu fiat meum tuum usu temporis necessarii*, "from friendly sentiment mine becomes yours for the time of necessity." It should also be pointed out that the nuance of reciprocity characterizes the corresponding Sanskrit.[44]

In fact, the idea of good neighborliness sticks to "mutual," "mutuality" and so on with extraordinary tenacity. Though the words can be attached to hostile deeds—"mutual slaughter"—as well as friendly ones—"mutual support"—yet when they appear by themselves, when "the mutual" or "mutuality" as such is being thought of, mostly, optimistically, the positive aspect is to the fore. In the nineteenth century—over two thousand years after the XII Tables—expressions like "mutualism" and "mutual societies" are resorted to as implying a more spontaneous management of economic life and, above all, the avoidance of monetary transactions. This is particularly so in France, but it extends much further. There is no such potentiality in, say, the phrases "one another" or "each other": they are quite neutral.

In Hebrew, an idiom like "between me and you, *beni ubhenekha*, what is this?", met in the negotiations about Sarah's sepulchre,[45] makes one feel that *ben* or some derivative might have acquired the meaning "mutual." It did not, however, happen. What we do find is the sense of "middle," "mean." On the other hand, two Biblical terms for "one another" and "each other" do essentially presuppose positive, personal relations: *'ish—'aḥiv*, "a man—his brother" (feminine *'ishsha—'aḥothah*, "a woman—her sister"), *'ish—re'ehu*, "a man—his neighbor." (Admittedly, they are employed also with reference to inanimate things, or perhaps better, what nowadays at least would be classed as such.)[46] In modern Hebrew, the neutral *ze—ze*, "this one—that one," predominates.

---

44. See *Thesaurus Linguae Latinae* 8 (1936), 196, 1722.
45. See above, 73.
46. E.g., Exod 25:20, "The faces of the cherubims (in the tabernacle) shall be one to another," *'ish 'el 'aḥiv*, 26:3., "The five curtains shall be coupled together one to another," *'ishsha 'el 'aḥothah*, Gen 15:10, "Abraham cut them (three sacrificial animals) in the midst and laid each cut one over against the other," *'ish ligrath re'ehu*.

I V.

Among the most distinctive traits of the classical Roman suit is *condemnatio pecuniaria*: whatever the claim, judgment against a defendant is always in a sum of money. Even in a *vindicatio*, where plaintiff asserts that he is owner of a piece of property in somebody else's hands, if he proves his case, his opponent will be condemned not in *ipsam rerem*, but for its value. I am not as foolhardy as to enter into the numerous controversies about this principle: does it come down from primitive procedure or evolve in the period of *legis actio*?, what needs does it serve?, how is an aside about its history in Gaius's *Institutes* to be understood?[47] All I have to say is that it is hardly accidental for the institution to be part of a system created by perhaps the most law-oriented lawyers ever. Their instinct counsels them that, once legal enforcement is sought, the thing to do is to dismiss any vestige of sentiment and look for the right figure.

The exceptions definitely support my approach. Freedom, the jurists declare, is *inaestimabilis*, "inassesable in money," and so is a head of family's power over his offspring. (The former statement comes from a discussion of matters not to be heard by municipal officers but to be sent on to Rome,[48] the latter from one of the unenforceability of a fideicommissary directive to emancipate children.)[49] The divisory actions between co-heirs, co-owners and neighbors, whose boundary is in dispute are particularly significant. Here the judge is empowered directly to allot property—say, give one heir the horses, the other the villa, or, between neighbors, make this stretch part of A's land, that one part of B's. In these relations, the fellowship component is very persistent. (True, already in the Republic, if an allotment is inevitably unfair—the inheritance consists of a Rembrandt and a Grandma Moses—an equalizing payment can be imposed.) The putting on the same level of neighbors not technically tied to one another with co-heirs and co-owners holding property in common underlines the importance in early times of personal closeness wherever occurring. I would

47. Gaius 4.48.
48. Digest 50.17.106, Paul II *ad edictum*; see O. Lenel, *Das Edictum Perpetuum*, 3rd ed. (1927), 55 f.
49. Digest 30.114.8, Marcian VIII *institutionum*.

remark that the gist of these reflections will require little modification if we follow Buckland's view (I am actually in sympathy with it) that boundary disputes are exclusively settled by surveyors till the age of Caesar, when the ordinary courts gradually take over.[50]

Psychoanalysts compare money to faeces, both the result of specifics dissolving into formless mass.[51] (I do not know whether the analogy has been carried further. Faeces, as fertilizer, in turn contribute to the growth of specifics; and similarly, any money I have in no time comes to life again in the shape of a dinner with Helen at Señor Pico's. In a way, Bacon saw it: "Money is like muck, not good except it be spread.")[52] Justice, too, could be said to be faecal, in a high degree denying the uniqueness of things. It is concerned with partnership as opposed to fellowship[53] and finds expression in abstract rules, to be administered indifferently, Book of Common Prayer, even-handedly, Shakespeare, ending where mystery begins, Burke. (One hopes that, deadly as it is in one way, it also enriches the soil from which individuality springs.) The tendency of money to link up with it may reflect this fundamental affinity.

It plainly goes on still. When I was young, a tip for a waiter was a tip, a Christmas gratification for an employee a gratification. By now, in many countries, 12% for service and an extra half-month's wages in December are compulsory. Yet this evolution has not so far spread to non-monetary items: the tie for the male secretary, the chocolates for the female one.

Take gracious living. Professor and Mrs. X, having dined with Professor and Mrs. Y, are expected to ask them back to a similar session. While the language might be quite legalistic—they owe them a meal, are in their debt, are under an obligation to them, should repay their invitation—they need fear no summons, only peer group censure. It is gift trade, not unlike archaic *mutuum*. And it is in the process of breaking down. If Y is Chairman of the Faculty or Director of the Laboratory, very likely he has an expense account for entertainment. If he has written a primer which

50. See W. W. Buckland, *Revue Historique de Droit Français et Étranger* (1936), 741 ff.

51. See O. Fenichel, *The Psychoanalytic Theory of Neuroses* (1945), 281 f., 487 f.

52. F. Bacon, *Essays*, 26, *Of seeming wise*.

53. See H. Coing, *Grundzüge der Rechtsphilosophie* (1950), 72 f.

he hopes X, editor of a series, will publish, the outlay for the evening will perhaps appear on his tax return among the deductions from the book's profits. Much hospitality in the city is shabby by King David's standard:[54] "Neither will I offer burnt offerings which cost me nothing." The point here of relevance is that all these cases involve a monetary mechanism, the gift to be dodged becomes a figure.

Lastly, a reminiscence from Camford. Certain perquisites of a College Fellow—free rooms and dinners, occasional excursions—once were on a level with what a parental home provides. It was when it became customary to compensate Fellows living outside—say, the College was occupied—that internal revenue got moving, and that university teachers with no College Fellowship demanded their salaries to be made up. *In Geldsachen hört die Gemütlichkeit auf,* "When it comes to money matters, that is the end of grooviness."

54. See above.

Fashions and Idiosyncrasies in the Exposition of the Roman Law of Property

I.

There is no scholarly effort independent of fashion—by which I understand a cultural trend—and idiosyncrasy—by which I understand a personal bent. In focusing on this aspect, I am myself providing an illustration. Distrust in the objectivity of academia is definitely the mode—in fact, it extends to what used to be the exact sciences and to mathematics—and my resentment against the authoritarianism under which I was brought up furnishes a private incentive. Of course, fashion and idiosyncrasy overlap: the former may owe much to the energy of an individual, the latter is usually coloured by prevalent conditions. I hasten to add that to be directed by these forces does not mean to go wrong. It may mean that, as may any route. But, say, a survivor of Auschwitz writing on existentialist ethics could come up with valuable ideas. Anyhow, the risk of error is presumably lessened by awareness of it.

II.

Let me begin with idiosyncrasy. A Roman usufructuary had the right to use and take the fruits of another's property. By way of exception, however, the offspring of a slave woman belonged, not to him, but to the owner. Quite a

[*Theories of Property*, eds. A. Parel and T. Flanagan, (Waterloo, Ontario: 1979), 35–50]

89

few explanations of this rule have been proposed, and I would here mention three.

1. When, in the late Republic, the institution of usufruct grew up, experts at husbandry confined the term "fruit" to produce regularly recurrent, capable of planned cultivation. "There is a sixfold division of seasons [says Varro][1] connected in some way with sun and moon, since virtually every fruit comes to its final perfection in five stages—preparation, sowing, nourishing, harvesting, storing—to be brought into use at the sixth—marketing." The jurists followed this definition they found in a prominent science. Nor, in so doing, were they forgetful of the practical consequences: the constant yield of a thing might well be deemed to be a usufructuary's main concern. A distant echo of this consideration may be contained in the Digest: "slave women are not hastily procured for the purpose of breeding."[2]

This, then, is solution number one of the puzzle, sober, academic. Something like it is advanced in many textbooks.[3] I taught it in my more earnest moods at Oxford.

2. Solution number two relies on another passage from the Digest which, not surprisingly, also appears in Justinian's Institutes:[4] all fruits are furnished by nature for mankind's sake, hence a member of mankind cannot possibly be "fruit." Few modern Romanists believe that such moral or philosophical esteem of humanity really caused or even contributed to the rule in question; they consider it—rightly, I think—a piece of late, cheap cosmetics. Girard calls it puerile,[5] Buckland remarks that "it must have seemed somewhat ironical to a slave"[6]—incapable of owning anything, indeed, a chattel. What difference does it make to a slave-baby whether its neck can be wrung by the mother's usufructuary or by her owner? Actually, if we look closely at the practical implications of the rule, the high-minded reason for it turns out quite inappropriate. There is enormous cruelty to the

1. Varro, *Res rusticae* 1.37.4. Translation based on W. D. Hooper, Cato, *On Agriculture*, Varro, *On Agriculture*, Loeb Classical Library (1936), 261 ff.
2. Digest 5.3.27 pr., Ulpian XV *ad edictum*.
3. See e.g. P. F. Girard, *Manuel Élémentaire de Droit Romain*, 4th ed. (1906), 247.
4. Digest 22.1.28.1, Gaius II *rerum cottidianarum*; Institutes 2.1.37.
5. Op. cit., 247.
6. See W. W. Buckland, *The Roman Law of Slavery* (1908), 21.

mother: as the child belongs to her owner, it will be physically separated from her who is being held in usufruct.[7]

Yet despite all this, Alan Watson accepts this number two as the true, historical background.[8] He speaks of a "noble" concept, though admitting that it might be imperfectly translated into practice. I would set this down to his upbringing in a deeply committed, non-conformist Scottish milieu: he wants to find a spark of idealism in the celebrated jurists.

3. The third attempt takes note of the fact that usufruct grew up as marriage without *manus* became prevalent. The wife, while retaining her prospects in her original family, would not, as in marriage with *manus*, acquire a daughter's rights to her husband's estate. Hence the latter would provide for her by will, appointing his children to be his heirs but leaving her a usufruct. In course of time usufruct was extended to other situations, yet a number of rules which had been laid down at the initial stage, in connection with widowhood, continued to live on—the one here discussed among them.

A man dies. His son inherits, the widow has a usufruct. A slave woman who is part of the estate gives birth to a child. More often than not, it will be the son's child. That is why, though apples and the young of animals and the earnings from leases go to the usufructuary, the offspring of a slave woman belongs to the owner—the son.

In the usufruct of the classical era, no longer specially associated with its original area of operation, the rule is an oddity.

The author of this explanation is John Kelly,[9] both a professor and

7. How M. Kaser can say that "it remains with the mother" and invoke humanitarian motives (*ZRG, RA* 75 [1958], 199), I do not understand.

8. *Tulane Law Review* 42 (1968), 291 ff., *The Law of Property in the Roman Republic* (1968), 216.

9. I have it from him: it has not appeared in print. —A slight contretemps. I sent him a xerox of my draft asking whether I reported him correctly, and I interpreted a prolonged silence as approval. But he was abroad, and now, at the proof stage, I hear from him as follows: "Your paraphrase of my suggestion is accurate, though what I really meant to emphasize was that the exception which the *partus ancillae* rule forms in usufruct would have been intolerable had there been a blood link between the usufructuary and the child; but as the *original* usufructuary was a woman, such a link was biologically impossible and so the curious rule avoided giving, so to speak, human offence. It is not necessarily part of

a politician. His works on Roman procedure stand out by looking beyond the dry law into what actually went on. He has also, under a pseudonym, published some lively fiction. Clearly, he knows where it's at.

Nowadays my heart prompts me to go along with him. And my head comes up with a helpful thought. If he is right, in the original setup—son-heir and widow-usufructuary living under the same roof (ordinarily)—mother and child stay together. This is distinctly consonant with sound economics and convenience.

Scholars will try to assess the relative plausibility of the three accounts. Some will make a choice, some will prefer a combination, some will reject all of them. If the debate leaves us in the dark about the subject-matter, at least it will shed light on the character of the participants.

III.

Turning to fashions, though generally my selection will be rather arbitrary, I feel I must open by a glance at the exposition of that central notion: ownership. In the popular mind, ownership as an individual's absolute legal power over an object is among the two or three most striking characteristics of Roman law. For several decades, however, Romanists have done their best to demonstrate first, that things were very different at the archaic stage, i.e. they resembled what we find in other ancient Indo-European cultures; secondly, that even the mature Roman ownership must be interpreted against a background of all sorts of extra-legal restraints such as tradition, ethics, state interest.

One of the factors accounting for the movement is the adoption by most civil law countries of modern codes which completely replace the original sources. As a result, the latter can be subjected to historical inquiry unfettered by any fear of how what emerges might affect actual decisions of the courts. Another cause far from negligible is this century's

---

this reflection that the *dominus nudae proprietatis* would typically be the child's father—if he lived on the premises, of course this would very regularly be the case—but it might equally be the offspring of a male slave living in *contubernium* with the mother." So his phantasy is more restrained than I represented it as being. But where does this leave me?

reaction against the last one's apotheosis of private capitalism.

Up to very recently, it was agreed that classical law allowed an owner of land unlimited freedom to build: if his neighbour's light was totally cut off, it was just too bad. Alan Rodger now has made a strong case against this view. Indeed, he argues persuasively that, from the middle of the first century B.C., even a valuable pleasant view must not be blocked.[10]

At times, the current re-evaluation is perhaps overdone. One could imagine flickers of absolute ownership existing even in the epoch of *legis actio*, when litigation looks like having concentrated on the relatively better right of one of two pretenders. From what moment would a child begin to feel that certain objects are his, or somebody else's, versus any third party's interference?[11]

Too much can be made of the absence from early Latin—or Greek or Hebrew—of a term for "ownership."[12] A social phenomenon no less than one in nature may considerably antedate its final labelling by a noun. Table manners and extradition went on long before so named. This is not to deny that such naming is a significant step; it is merely to warn against too far-reaching conclusions.

We must not forget that, in a way, it is easier to become aware of minor rights over an object than of the all-embracing title. In the latter case, the thing itself stands in the light: in the absence of painstaking reflection, the owner is apt to think of having it rather than of having a legal relationship to it. There is no such block with regard to servitudes and usufruct, hence they will more readily appear as rights over the thing encroaching on the owner's position. (At least after that remote period when a rustic servitude made the owner of the dominant estate a sort of co-owner with his neighbour.)

The tangle here in question is equally common outside the law: a material datum engrossing the attention slows up recognition of the abstract, general one back of it. The Old Testament has no inclusive designation for

10. See A. Rodger, *Owners and Neighbours in Roman Law* (1972).

11. Cp. A. M. Honoré, in *Oxford Essays in Jurisprudence*, ed. A. G. Guest (1961), 114.

12. See E. Rabel, *ZRG, RA* 36 (1915), 341 f., M. Kaser, *Eigentum und Besitz im Älteren Römischen Recht* (1943), 3 ff.

"to commit suicide;" it sticks to the concrete "to fall upon one's sword," "to strangle oneself." One of the earliest passages in Jewish literature with the comprehensive notion has regard to a prospective action: the Fourth Gospel represents people as wondering whether Jesus proposes "to kill himself."[13] No actual, solid incident obstructs the view. A comparable case is furnished by the Greek word for time, *chronos*, first used with reference to the interval between events—battles, raids and the like; while they go on, time is unnoticed. Just so, in the *Winter's Tale*, Shakespeare brings Time on the stage to represent, summarize, the fifteen quiet years separating the remarkable happenings of the first part and those of the second. Even today, when I say that this morning I have no time since lecturing but I shall have time in the evening, I am speaking of time not covered over by some going-on. An illustration from the XII Tables is *iniuria*, unlawfulness, denoting an assault that leaves no permanent, visible damage: a slap in the face, for example. The same section deals with *membrum ruptum*, a limb torn off, and *os fractum*, a bone broken: here people concentrate on the visible horror and not on the unlawfulness behind it. Gradually, of course, it is realized that these cases no less than a slap involve unlawfulness.

How long-lasting the effects of this type of development can be is shown by the fact that, even in Justinian, while servitudes and usufruct are classed as incorporeal things, more specifically, things existing in or by the law, ownership is still not so classed, being evidently mixed up with the object, the corporeal thing; and it is significant that by *iura praediorum*, rights of estates, is still meant only the servitudes attaching to the dominant property; the term never includes the owner's right.[14]

IV.

If, not acting at your behest, I made a new thing—a chair, a vessel—with your raw material—your wood, your gold—according to the Sabinians,

13. John 8:22. See D. Daube, *Philosophy and Public Affairs* I (1972), 395 f., rpt. *Suicide and Life-Threatening Behaviour* 7 (1977), 140 f. [*Ethics*, 73].

14. Institutes 2.2. See D. Daube, in *Studi Solanni* (1948), 49 ff. of reprint.

the thing was yours, according to the Proculians, mine. Many authorities regard the Proculian standpoint as a refinement, in one or both of the following respects: (1) it put the spiritual, the form, above crude matter, (2) it opted for social progress, the right of labor, a sort of proto-socialism.[15]

Whether correct or false, these characterizations obviously imply not only heavy value judgments but also the conviction that mankind, or at least ancient Roman jurisprudence, moves from lower values to higher ones. It is also clear that the two postulates—the Proculians recognize form, the Proculians recognize labour—must have been first elaborated in different eras and milieus.

How unlikely they are to have paid homage to the right of labour may be seen from the fact that, even for them, if I worked at your behest—say, you commissioned a statue and supplied the gold—the product belonged to you. I might be the greatest artist in the world, it made no difference. The technical justification would be that at no moment in the process were you divested of possession. I never had more than "detention."

A view rapidly gaining currency is much more plausible: it was the Sabinians who innovated.[16] The original setting of the problem was surely, not academic reflection, but litigation. Suppose I, not acting under your orders, made a chair with your wood and you brought a *vindicatio*. In primitive times, you could not declare: "this chair is mine." All you could show was that you had owned the wood—which was gone. This must lead to the Proculian result: you lost, I was owner of the new object. The Sabinians got away from the rigid interpretation of "this chair." They allowed your material to live on in the artefact. Having owned the wood, you were also entitled to say: "this chair is mine." The new object was yours.

The jurists seem to have enjoyed expanding on the respective merits of the two solutions. Actually, yet a further one was added; and the matter was not finally settled till Justinian plumped for the third one. A major reason indecision could be tolerated so long is that the consequences in actual life were minimal. (The same goes for not a few of the drawn-out

15. See R. von Jhering, *Geist des Römischen Rechts*, III.1, 6th and 7th ed. (1924), 323: *Recht der Arbeit*.
16. See F. de Zulueta, *The Institutes of Gaius*, II (1953), 79.

disputes between the schools.) As already remarked, if I used your material by agreement with you, no question arose: it was never doubted by anyone that you owned the omelette I made as your cook with your eggs, or the shoes I made as your employee with your leather. If I stole your material, I was liable for a multiple of its value as thief; whether what I worked it into belonged to you or me would not be terribly important. This leaves mainly the case where I used your material in good faith—having *bona fide possessio*. It could not have occurred too frequently, and even when it did occur would mostly be disposed of amicably. No doubt one may think up some other relevant situations; but, on the whole, there was plainly no undue pressure to cut short pleasurable controversy for action.

The practical unimportance explains also why Justinian could pronounce in favour of the third solution, the most awkward of the lot. If I made cider from your apples, mistakenly believing them to be mine, it belonged to me (since irreducible to the raw material); if Cellini made candlesticks from your ingot, mistakenly believing it to be his, they belonged to you (since reducible). Stupid, but harmless.

The restriction of the problem to independent work, not under the owner's orders, has not been lost on medieval and modern thinkers trying to find here help in shoring up private property. Pius XI's encyclical *Quadragesimo Anno* affirms: "The only form of labor, however, which gives the working man a title to its fruits is that which a man exercises as his own master." The German translation adds the adverb *natürlich*: "naturally" this is the only form entitling him.[17] A hint, I suppose, that the ultimate source of the doctrine is natural law.

V.

In paragraph III I stressed linguistic aspects, and increased attention to this province is definitely one modern trend. I have participated in various ways—for example, by commenting on the action noun derived from a verb,

---

17. See D. Daube, *ZRG, RA* 90 (1973), 5 (in German), *Juridical Review* 85 (1973), 128 f. (in English) [above, 56].

expulsion from expel, termination from terminate.[18] For an action noun to be introduced, there must have been a good deal of reflection on the activity concerned. People sell and donate for a long time before sale and donation come in as a result of abstraction, systematization, classification. The doings have become institutions.

To seize an object is *occupare*, to abandon one *derelinquere*. The institutions *occupatio* and *derelictio* never occur in the Roman sources. To transfer something to the heir is *transmittere ad heredem*; *transmissio* is first met in a law by Justinian.[19] How slow this kind of abstraction was in making its way is shown by the absence from the classical texts of so basic a concept as *acquisitio*; they speak only of *acquirere*; the noun emerges at a snail's pace in post-classical ones.[20]

Much can be learned by taking note of the earlier or later birth of one action noun compared with another. In contradistinction to *acquisitio*, *alienatio* is classical. General rules about making over property—one may think of groups with restricted powers, women, prodigals—were formulated by the jurists long before general rules about receiving property. *Auctio* is frequent already in Plautus:[21] that special case of *augere*, a public bidding competition, very early became an established thing.

As for the agent noun[22]—baker, seer, from bake, see—it is often narrower than the verb, singling out him who performs the action in a striking fashion. A baker bakes for a living, a seer sees what is invisible to others. An illustration from Roman obligations is *sponsor*, describing not everyone who *spondet*, promises, but only him who, peculiarly, promises in support of another person, the surety. The use of *auctor* in the law of property is not so dissimilar. This term designates not everyone who *auget*, augments, but only him who, remarkably, augments, warrants, somebody else's title.

18. See D. Daube, *Roman Law* (1969), 11 ff.
19. Code 6.30.19.1, A.D. 529.
20. E.g. *Ulpiani Regulae* 19, rubric.
21. E.g. *Menaechmi* 5.9.93 ff., 1153 ff.
22. See D. Daube op. cit., 2 ff.

VI.

For the past fifty years or so, the contact of Roman law with rhetoric has excited much interest;[23] and for the past twenty-five, quite a few writers in this field have speculated on the role of the rhetorical doctrine of the *topica*, arguments which, though rational, yet lack absolute cogency.[24] We possess Aristotle's and Cicero's versions of this doctrine. For Viehweg,[25] it forms the backbone of the casuistic method of the leading classics who proceeded, not from a system into which the problem in hand would be fitted, but from the particular problem to be solved by bringing together and weighing up any relevant considerations. His first illustration is a discussion of usucapion by Julian.[26]

A significant contribution may be found in Dieter Nörr's monograph on *praescriptio longi temporis*, the protection of one who has been in possession of an object for a long time. This institution, unlike many, did not grow up in the obscurity of the early Republic: it dates from the late classical period, around A.D. 200. Yet it presents an extraordinary number of doubtful features. According to Nörr, this is due neither to the scarcity of texts about it nor to deficient modern analysis but to its "topical" nature. Its creators, that is, pragmatically gave prominence now to substantive law, now to procedural; now to possession, now to presumption of title; now to security, now to the analogy of usucapion; now to one figure for "long time," now to another.[27]

One of the stimuli behind this involvement in rhetoric is the desire to place Roman law in a living context. It—or much of it—was meant, after all, to serve or obstruct a party to a dispute. Of considerable importance, too, is the—by now pretty universal—recognition that the quasi-mathe-

---

23. Sparked by J. Stroux, *Summum ius summa iniuria* (1926).
24. This line was initiated by T. Viehweg, *Topik und Jurisprudenz* (1954).
25. Op. cit., 5th ed. (1974), 46 ff.
26. Digest 41.3.33, Julian XLIV *digestorum*.
27. D. Nörr, *Die Entstehung der longi temporis praescriptio* (1969), 6 f., 42 ff., 62, 112 f. The main results of the book are already offered in *The Irish Jurist* N.S. 3 (1968): 352 ff., but with no explicit reference to the *topica*. In a letter written to me after I showed him a xerox of my draft, he informs me that in the meantime he has revised his views about the topical in law.

matical logic that used to be attributed to Roman law was an illusion. Even the logic of the sciences has been taken down a peg or two: we have become very self-critical, there are no more gods among us. The latter development indeed plays a somewhat paradoxical part in the debate about the influence of the *topica* on the jurists. At first blush, it would seem to support the side believing in this influence. In reality, it has been held to speak against it. The way the jurists set about their task is so general, it has been maintained, that there is no need to bring in the *topica*.[28] Clearly, one of those controversies which may never be settled to the satisfaction of all or even a majority.

VII.

In a sense, the question of Roman law and rhetoric is a segment of the general one of foreign input. Here, fashions and idiosyncrasies play an extraordinary part. It is not only that a discovery like that of the Code of Hammurabi or a cache of papyri may produce a wave of interest. Quite apart from this, scholarly attitudes vary to an astonishing degree in different periods, countries, persons. Apparently deep emotions favouring a positive or negative approach are involved.

Nor should we overlook mundane factors. For instance, the alien material is often in a difficult language, which must make it tempting a priori to deny its relevance. (The treatment of modern writings in an unaccustomed tongue provides analogies. Some while ago, I received a Bulgarian treatise on Roman law. I can plough my way through Russian, but Bulgarian is beyond me. So I console myself with the thought that the book probably contains little that is new.) While it would be wrong to assume that no gifted linguist will defend the autarky of the classics, as a rule no one but a gifted linguist will be keen on discovering foreign influence. One of the conclusions Alan Watson reaches in his work *Legal Transplants* is: "most changes in most systems are the result of borrowing."[29] Such a statement is

28. See F. Horak, *Rationes Decidendi* I (1969), 45 ff.
29. See Alan Watson, *Legal Transplants* (1974), 95.

not likely to come from one who is unilingual.

Pignus, pledge, was a mode of real security which left the debt-or owner of the object pawned: the creditor obtained only possession. In course of time, it became possible to pawn a thing without even handing it over. The creditor, that is, would have a possessory remedy or an action in rem only when the debt was due. In most texts, this relaxed variant goes under the old designation *pignus*. A fair number of them, however, call it *hypotheca*—a Greek word. Some authorities conclude that the idea originated in Greece; others that the texts concerned are spurious; yet others that, while the institution is native, already middle and late classical lawyers made occasional use of a distinction met in Greek terminology. The third view—advocated, for example, by Wolfgang Kunkel[30]—appears the most attractive to me.

VIII.

This brings us to interpolations, alterations of classical statements by later editors and Justinian. In the first third of the century, there was intense preoccupation with them. Especially in Germany, the enactment of the *Bürgerliche Gesetzbuch*, by turning the *Corpus Juris* into a purely historical monument, no longer to be treated by anyone as a consistent, unitary legislation, opened the way to uninhibited critical probing. As a result of such enthusiasm, many a passage was held spurious on inadequate grounds. By now the climate is different, perhaps owing not only to the normal swing of the pendulum but also to a longing for security. In fact, there may be a little too much zeal to pronounce in favour of genuineness.

A fragment from Ulpian runs:[31] "Ownership has nothing in common with possession; and therefore one who has begun a real action for the thing is not refused the interdict *uti possidetis*; for by bringing the real action he is not considered to have renounced possession."

---

30. See W. Kunkel, *Römisches Recht*, on the basis of P. Jörs, 3rd ed. (1949), 156.
31. Digest 41.2.12.1, Ulpian LXX *ad edictum*. Translation by F. de Zulueta, *Digest 41, 1 & 2, Translation and Commentary* (1922), 57.

Beseler, in an article published in 1925, maintains that the initial clause, "Ownership has nothing in common with possession," is without substantive content and lends no support to the opinion. The classical utterance starts "One who has begun a real action," and the reason for the verdict comes at the end, "for by bringing the real action" etc.[32]

Probably no colleague of mine nowadays accepts any of this. The text is constantly quoted, never with any question-mark.[33] In Buckland and McNair's *Roman Law and Common Law*, it figures as epitomizing the Roman distinction between ownership and possession.[34]

Yet I wonder whether a grain of truth may not be salvaged. Beseler in this piece is out to prove that the classics do not employ *et ideo*, "and therefore." No doubt he goes too far. But the phrase is indeed a rather easy connective and frequently resorted to by the compilers when they abbreviate or re-arrange the original.

That one who has sued—scil. unsuccessfully—by means of the interdict may go on to sue by means of the real action is mentioned by Paul.[35] The ban on suing twice for the same thing does not operate since, as he remarks, the interdict has regard to possession, the real action to ownership. This solution can never have been questioned. A foremost function of the interdict is precisely to prepare the real action, i.e. by determining possessor and non-possessor to allot the superior role of defendant and the inferior one of plaintiff in the action about title. Paul here gives the theoretical justification for the practice: the statement comes from his chapter on the bar to a second process about the same matter.[36]

Ulpian's problem is not simply the reverse: may one who has lost the real action go on to institute the interdict? What he asks is whether the latter may be instituted by one who has begun the former, scil. while it is on. One can think of situations where this might plausibly be wanted; for instance, it is only after commencing the real action that plaintiff comes upon

32. See G. v. Beseler, *ZRG, RA* 45 (1925), 479.
33. See e.g. M. Kaser, *Das Römische Privatrecht* I (1955), 325.
34. See W. W. Buckland and A. D. McNair, *Roman Law and Common Law*, 2nd ed. by F. H. Lawson (1952), 62.
35. Digest 44.2.14.3, Paul LXX *ad edictum*.
36. See O. Lenel, *Palingenesia Iuris Civilis* I (1889), 1085.

evidence showing defendant to have been allowed onto the land by plaintiff's deceased father's *precario*, under a revocable licence—so his possession is no good against plaintiff.[37] It should be noted that Ulpian must be dealing with a dispute about land: the interdict he names is *uti possidetis*. And the fragment, as we know from Lenel,[38] goes back to a part of his work mainly devoted to defective possession, i.e. possession obtained by force, clandestinely or by licence. (But Lenel did not see how the fragment fitted into this part.[39] He would have been pleased with my suggestion.)

How is he likely to have answered? Presumably he made a preliminary reference to the inapplicability of *non bis in idem*: to assert possession is not the same as to assert ownership. But his observation would be far more subdued than the present opening. For the chief difficulty of the case lies elsewhere. It stems from the principle that the real action is brought by the non-possessor against the possessor. Plaintiff in a real action, therefore, may be said to be acknowledging defendant's possession. Has he not, then, debarred himself from turning around midway through the litigation and demanding that the roles be reversed?

To go by the report before us, Ulpian declared that he is not estopped. Perhaps he did take this straightforward, liberal stand. Quite possibly, however, it is substituted by the compilers for something a little less absolute; say, the interdict is feasible till *litiscontestatio* moves the real action from the magistrate to the judge. In Justinian's procedure, this division no longer exists; so the limitation would be crossed out.

Three conclusions emerge as pretty certain. First, the jurist's exposé contained more detail than is preserved. At least, there must have been a brief indication of the circumstances (such as *precarium* granted by the *de cuius*) in which the problem could arise. Secondly, the opening sentence reveals a type of rewriting Justinian is given to: a sober classical explanation of a decision is changed into a maxim.[40] Indeed, as often, the latter is

---

37. Digest 43.26.8.1, Ulpian LXXI *ad edictum*; 43.26.12.1, Celsus XXV *digestorum*.

38. See Lenel, *Palingenesia*, II.822.

39. See O. Lenel, *Das Edictum Perpetuum*, 3rd ed. (1927), 469 n. 13 where, despairingly, he labels it as an excursus or appendix to either defective possession or *interdicta utilia*.

40. See D. Daube, *ZRG, RA* 76 (1959), 176 ff., P. Stein, *Regulae Iuris* (1966), 117 ff.

too sweeping. That "ownership has nothing in common with possession" is an exaggeration. Actually, *nihil commune* stands in front, which makes the denial of any tie even more emphatic—"Nothing in common has ownership with possession." (Already Buckland apparently found it a bit much: he calls it "a strong statement").[41] Thirdly, "and therefore" papers over one of the cracks resulting as the codifiers revised the discussion.

IX.

This may be the place for a reminiscence.

In the late 1920s and early 30s I often visited Lenel, then in retirement at Freiburg. My parents' house was Goethestrasse 35, about seven minutes on foot from his Holbeinstrasse 5. In his whole long career he had in fact only two personal pupils (at least that is how he saw it): Josef Partsch, who died at age 43 in 1925 and whose obituary in the *Savigny Zeitschrift*—a moving tribute—was written by Lenel,[42] and me. Which lends Kantorowicz's reconstruction of Lenel's academic genealogy[43]— showing an unbroken chain of transmission right from Irnerius around 1100—particular meaning for me and my personal pupils.

One morning when I called on him, he showed me a postcard just received from Beseler:

41. See Buckland and McNair loc. cit. Cp. also Kunkel, *Römisches Recht*, 113 n. 11: *nicht immer werden indessen Eigentum und Besitz einander so scharf gegenübergetreten sein.*

42. See O. Lenel, *ZRG, RA* 45 (1925): V ff. This issue of the *Zeitschrift* was curiously focal in my early days as a Romanist. Besides the obituary of Partsch and the article on *et ideo* quoted above, it contains Lenel's *Interpolationenjagd*, to be mentioned presently, as also W. Kunkel's debut, a brilliant if slightly overbold attack on the classicality of *diligentia* and *neglegentia* (266 ff.). Four years later, he left Freiburg for Göttingen and I followed him as his student. When Hitler came to power, I found refuge at Cambridge; Lenel had given me a letter to H. F. Jolowicz, who sent me to W. W. Buckland. Buckland thought Kunkel's thesis far too extreme: in *Studi P. Bonfante* II (1929), 85 ff., *Law Quarterly Review* XLVIII (1932), 217 ff. Kunkel's rejoinder may be found in *Römisches Recht*, 177 n. 23 and 178 n. 31.

43. See H. Kantorowicz, *ZRG, RA* 50 (1930): 475 ff.

+

considerare

R. I. P.

Which meant that yet another word was to be consigned to the post-classical rubbish heap. To appreciate the communication, one must remember that in 1925 Lenel had sounded the alarm against hypercriticism, singling out A. Albertario and G. v. Beseler.[44] The title of the paper, *Interpolationenjagd,* "Interpolation hunt," became a slogan. From then, he repeatedly opposed Beseler's radical methods.[45] The latter, besides replying in print,[46] took a naughty boy's pleasure in needling authority—hence this frivolous announcement designed to shock the old master. He definitely succeeded. Lenel sadly shook his head and looked at me as if imploring help.

Beseler, besides absolute command of the material and a natural affinity with classical legal thinking, had a genius's flair for the subtleties of Latin usage. He also had many a genius's knack of putting people's backs up. At the time of this incident, though he far surpassed most others in his field, he was still *Honorarprofessor* at Kiel, where he had begun as *Privatdozent* some twenty-five years before. No university ever offered to make him *Ordentlicher Professor.* Lenel was the greatest Roman lawyer, *stricto sensu,* since Julian whose Edict he reconstructed.

X.

What fashions may we expect in the next decades? I hope for two, above all.

1. The position of women in regard to property needs re-examination. Not enough attention has so far been paid to subtler modes of discrimination—for example, *privilegea odiosa,* fake privileges which, while ostensi-

---

44. See Lenel, *ZRG, RA* 45 (1925), 17 ff.
45. See e.g. Lenel, *ZRG, RA* 49 (1929), 7 ff.
46. See e.g. G. v. Beseler, in *Studi P. Bonfante* II (1929), 62.

bly helpful, in reality degrade.[47] Taxation may be one of the areas in need of re-evaluation.

2. Anthropological and psychological—even psychoanalytical—insights should be put to greater use. The earliest meaning of *contrectare* seems to have been "to touch obscenely." When the jurists employed it as a criterion of theft, were they "personalizing," even "sexualizing," property? We are not surprised to hear a sailboat referred to as "she;" and to many a youngster his motorcycle or car offers a relationship passing the love of women. The Romans may have gone further.[48]

47. See D. Daube, in the *Memorial Volume for Walter Fischel*. Appeared as "Johanan ben Beroqa and Women's Rights," *ZRG, RA* 99 (1982), 22–31 [*TL*, 143–152].

48. More comments on this in a forthcoming paper by me on Lucrece.

The Marriage of Justinian and Theodora: Legal and Theological Reflections

Perhaps no Pope has been acclaimed as a father *urbi et orbi* so universally as John XXIII. If I may use a Jewish expression, he was among the *ṣaddige 'ummoth ha 'olam*, among the righteous of the peoples of the world. It is fitting that a lecture in his honour sponsored by a renowned centre of jurisprudence should furnish an illustration from the history of law of the fraternization of Eros and Agape. I shall present a piece of legislation from ancient Byzantium which, brought about by the loves and hates of the mighty, and serving their personal interests, yet aimed at widening the scope of charity and extending a helping hand to many in lowlier positions. With its roots in worldly errors, entanglements and aspirations, it reached out towards the divine—and it did achieve lasting good.

Around A.D. 523, the Emperor Justin I lost his wife and was left without children. He was about seventy years of age. He had been born of poor parents near Skoplie, in present-day Yugoslavia, had risen in the army and had finally gained the throne in that great state which, with its centre on the eastern shores of the Mediterranean, carried on the name and heritage of Rome. He was illiterate; indeed it is his description by the contemporary historian Procopius which has bequeathed the term "analphabet" to modern Western languages.[1] (About Procopius I shall have a

[*Catholic University of America Law Review* 16 (1967): 380–399. Delivered as the third annual Pope John XXIII Lecture, Catholic University of America.]

1. *Anecdota* 2.17. Considering that this term appears on and off in Greek writings from about 400 B.C., I am a bit puzzled why Procopius introduces it as somewhat special: he tells us that Justin had not learnt the letters, adding "and he was, to use a familiar phrase (*to legomenon*), analphabet." Apparently, the word was still not quite ordinary. (As we meet it in the third century A.D.—Athenaeus, *Deipnosophists* 176E—it cannot be a

little to say further on.)[2] But he had summoned his brilliant nephew Petrus Sabbatius, whose original home was in the same region as his own, to join him at the capital, Constantinople, had adopted him—on which occasion the two names Petrus Sabbatius were replaced by the one name Justinian, to indicate the relationship—and had given him an excellent education. Justinian was about forty years old at the time.[3]

For several years the nephew had wanted to marry one Theodora, then in her early twenties. But Justin's wife, Justinian's aunt, firmly opposed the match; and though Justin had long left virtually all government in the younger man's hands, in this matter he deferred to his wife who had the law—time-hallowed law—on her side.[4] Theodora had been an actress—of a rather inferior type—and possibly worse. Justinian, of course, was now a member of the aristocracy, the senatorial class. Under the then prevailing marriage regulations which, basically, dated from the founder of the monarchy, Augustus, a member of the aristocracy could not marry an actress. Nor did her giving up her profession make any difference: once an actress, always an actress.[5]

---

question of its having become obsolete by Procopius's time and his reviving it.) That it is this chapter of Procopius from which modern languages get the term is demonstrable. It is not only that other passages containing it are too recondite; we can actually trace the route, namely, via the tenth-century lexicon *Suidas*, where the term is listed with just this reference, *Suidae Lexicon*, ed. Adler (1928), I.175. In Du Cange, incidentally, *Glossarium Mediae et Infimae Latinitatis*, ed. Favre (1883), 238, it is said that *Suidas* applies the epithet to Justinian. *Suidas*, however, correctly names Justin. The slip in Du Cange is due to the Benedictines who added the entry *analphabetus*, not given in the first edition by Du Cange himself. It is a slip easily committed, Justinian being so much more in the historian's mind than Justin. In the authoritative eleventh-to-twelfth-century MS of Justinian's Code, Casinas 49, the legislation which forms the main subject of this lecture, Code 5.4.23, Justin A.D. 520–23, is mistakenly attributed to Justinian; see *Corpus Juris Civilis*, 11th stereot. ed., 2 [*Codex Justinianus*, ed. Krueger [1954)], 196. Similarly, the MS of John of Ephesus' *Lives of the Eastern Saints*, ch. 13 at the beginning, substitutes Justinian for Justin; Brooks, in Migne, *Patrologia Orientalis* 17 (1923), 187.

2. See below.
3. See Vasiliev, *Justin The First* (1950), 92 ff.
4. Procopius, *Anecdota* 9.47 ff.
5. Digest 23.2.44, Paul I *ad legem Juliam et Papiam*; *Codex Theodosianus* 4.6.3 (Code 5.27.1), Constantine, A.D. 336; *Novellae Marciani* 4.3.2 (Code 5.5.7.2), Valentinian and Marcian, A.D. 454. Paul quotes the statute as referring to *quae ipsa cuiusve pater*

This is a socio-legal point of some interest. The law then, as today, knew conditions which stuck to a person, involving permanent degradation, and conditions which did not stick. For example, if you were found guilty of certain offences—theft, assault—you suffered various disabilities in civic life, and these went on forever.[6] In the case of disreputable trades, there was more discrimination. Lasting infamy was incurred by a man who sold himself, hired himself out, as a gladiator.[7] (It is against this background that we must read the Talmudic stories about Resh Laqish, an eminent Rabbi of the middle of the third century A.D., who in his youth had fought in the arena and then switched over to sacred studies—not the normal career for a Rabbi. Though immensely respected, to the end of his life he was liable to be taunted by his colleagues with his earlier occupation and remained sensitive to such taunts.)[8] Similarly, prostitution,[9] pimping[10] and,

---

materve artem ludicram facit fecerit, "one who herself or whose father or mother practises or has practised stagecraft." *Codex Theodosianus* 4.6.3 (Code 5.27.1) attacks even concubinage, a recognized union of a lower grade, between a senator and an actress or her daughter. It would appear, incidentally, that even an ordinary freeborn citizen was forbidden to marry an actress, though not her child: *Ulpiani Regulae* 13.2, 16.2. There is some uncertainty and I shall not go into the matter.

6. See Lenel, *Das Edictum Perpetuum,* 3d ed. (1927), 77, *Tabula Heracleensis* 110 f.

7. Lenel, *Edictum Perpetuum,* at 79, *Tabula Heracleensis* 112 f.

8. *Babylonian Gittin* 47a, *Baba Metzia* 84a; see Bacher, *Die Agada der Palästinensischen Amoräer* (1892), I.342 ff. Lenel points out that a gladiator's infamy resulted, not from fighting, but from selling himself to fight. Significantly, the Talmud does speak of Resh Laqish having sold himself. It should be borne in mind, however, that the Talmudic stories refer to social snubs, not (or not directly) to legal disabilities.

9. See Lenel, *Edictum Perpetuum,* at 76, *Tabula Heracleensis* 122 f. Both the Edict and the *Tabula* contemplate males only: women are excluded from advocacy and City Councillorships by virtue of their sex, so no special bar in the event of misconduct is needed (cp. Lenel, *Edictum Perpetuum,* at 90). The Edict, incidentally, penalizes pathics in general, not prostitutes only—though pathics often are prostitutes.

10. Lenel, *Edictum Perpetuum,* at 77, *Tabula Heracleensis* 123, both contemplating male pimps only (see the preceding note). It is true that the *Tabula* says *lenocinium faciet,* "practises pimping," instead of, as in comparable cases of permanent infamy, *fecit fecerit,* "has practised or shall have practised." But this is mere carelessness. That a pimp becomes infamous for good is clear not only from general considerations but also from the *Edict,* which has *fecerit,* "has practised," in this as in all cases of lasting disability. It has long been seen that in the *Tabula* the clause about pimping does not come where, logically,

indeed, the theatre[11] rendered a man infamous for good: no use turning respectable. By contrast, a public crier or auctioneer was reduced in status only while holding that job.[12] The distinction was not just a game of the jurists; the ordinary citizen was fully alive to it. In Cicero's correspondence we meet a craftsman of a superior kind anxiously enquiring whether a municipal constitution just put into force denies membership of the Council even to a former auctioneer, and Cicero is able to reassure him.[13]

It was far from the only distinction in this field: there were countless shades of degradation in law. A certain measure attached to anyone engaged in a mercenary occupation;[14] an auctioneer, even while at the job, suffered less of it than an actor;[15] an actor suffered less than a prostitute.[16] Even the antithesis of permanent reduction and transitory reduction covers a multitude of degrees. One way in which a legal system can manipulate

---

it ought to. It ought to come a little earlier on, together with prostitution. Omitted in its proper place, it is appended after the instructor of gladiators and the actor. Such addenda are frequently slipshod. There is much literature; see above all Gradenwitz, *Sitzunberichte der Heildelberger Akademie der Wissenschaften*, Phil. Hist. Klasse 7 (1916), no. 14, 18, and v. Premerstein, *ZRG, RA* 43 (1922), 120 f. (where Mommsen's implausible explanation of the crux is adduced). I am expressing no view on the nature of the *Tabula Heracleensis*. Cp. below, note 20.

11. Lenel, *Edictum Perpetuum*, at 77, *Tabula Heracleensis* 123, both contemplating male actors only (see the preceding two notes). The Edict reads *qui artis ludicrae pronuntiandive causa in scaenam prodierit*, "he who has appeared on the stage in order to act or recite"; the *Tabula queive lanisturam artemve ludicram fecit fecerit*, "or he who has practised or shall have practised the instruction of gladiators or stagecraft." Both definitely embrace the past as well as the present.

12. So expressly *Tabula Heracleensis* 104 f., *dum faciet*, "while he practises."

13. *Ad familiares* 6.18.1. The questioner's anxiety becomes all the more understandable if, as is likely, earlier, similar constitutions were less liberal: see v. Premerstein (note 10), at 49.

14. See Greenidge, *Infamia* (1894), 12, 34, 194.

15. Unlike the actor, the auctioneer does not figure in the Edict: see Lenel, *Edictum Perpetuum*, at 77. His right of advocacy was not restricted.

16. While an actor's right of advocacy was severely restricted, a pathic lost it completely: Lenel, *Edictum Perpetuum*, at 76 f. It is largely failure to take seriously enough the legal differentiation between an actress and a harlot which has led scholars to overlook major points in Code 5.4.23—the enactment I propose to analyze—and to misinterpret subsequent reforms by Justinian such as Novels 117, A.D. 542; see below, notes 53 and 64 ff.

the matter is by the extent to which it will recognize truth as a defence in an action brought on the ground of injury to reputation. Obviously, where truth is an absolute defence, a tainted past mercilessly remains a tainted present. The Roman discussions of the action show remarkably little concern with this question; possibly because, as damages were assessed according to what was equitable in each individual case, it presented no particular difficulty—truth was a defence where it seemed equitable that it should be (a full defence or a partial one, according to the circumstances) and no defence where it seemed wrong.[17] Professor T. B. Smith, for Scots Law, favors the retention of the doctrine—prevalent in several states of the U.S.A.—that wanton publication of an old scandal is actionable irrespective of truth.[18] To outline the precise implications of permanency of infamy at Rome would mean to present almost every group affected individually and follow it up through the centuries.

There were strange quirks. When Caligula imposed a tax on harlots, he saw to the insertion of a proviso extending it to retired harlots. The very fact that he needed a special clause shows that, but for it, they would not have been thought of as included—even though they did share with practising harlots a number of disabilities, for instance, the incapacity to act as witnesses in certain cases.[19] The disabilities which stuck to them were such as had their *raison d'être* in inferiority of character: the character of a prostitute does not ordinarily change when she retires. A tax on trade, unless vindictive, is designed to take a slice from the earnings: a retired prostitute does not earn, and to apply the principle of permanency to this area was unfair. Suetonius, the Roman historian from whom we learn of

17 Digest 47.10.18 pr., Paul LV *ad edictum*, represents truth as an absolute defence. But Justinian's compilers may well have simplified the classical decision. There need not be much interference with the wording: the mere suppression of the original context might produce the present unconditional ruling. Even as it stands, it makes equitableness the basic consideration.

18. See *Scotland, The Development of its Laws and Constitution*, ed. Keeton (1962) 2.732 f.

19. Digest 22.5.3.5, Callistratus IV *de cognitionibus*. He quotes the *lex Julia de vi* as referring to her who *palam quaestum faciet feceritve*, "practises or has practised prostitution."

Caligula's procedure, does condemn it.[20]

A striking feature of the Augustan and subsequent marriage regulations was that a parent's condition might be transmitted to the offspring. Augustus kept even the children of an actor or actress from marriage into the senatorial class.[21] This harsh—if understandable—course was taken by lawgivers more persistently in regard to daughters than in regard to sons. In the ordinances of Constantine and his successors we hear only of the daughter of an actress or, say, the daughter of a female tavernkeeper or a pimp, not of the son.[22] A young man was more likely than a young woman to strike out on his own, away from his background; and once he had attained a position to attract a lady from the upper orders, it no longer made much sense to enquire into his antecedents. A young woman might find a noble suitor interested in her looks even if she was still very much part of her original setting. There seems to be no evidence, incidentally, that the daughter of a harlot was as such placed under any marriage restriction.

When we add to the nuances sanctioned by the legal order those which would enter into a person's social relations, the matter becomes infinitely complicated. Then, as today, legal evaluation might be in conflict with social. Mere poverty did not in law exclude a woman from an aristocratic union; in social reality it might be as serious a handicap as a legal bar,[23] but, manifestly, it was curable from one moment to the next. In modern life, a person sentenced for fraud may be re-established within a short time as far as the law is concerned, yet remain unclubbable for ever; while a political offence may entail civic disabilities of long duration, yet have only the briefest effect on social status. Language may afford clues. The expression "to live down" a reproach exists exclusively in English, though German, for instance, would have no difficulty in producing a corresponding formation, *niederleben* (or French *souvivre* or *dévivre*). Originally it was

20. *Caligula* 40. Retired pimps were also taxed.

21. Digest 23.2.44, above note 5.

22. *Codex Theodosianus* 4.6.3 (Code 5.27.1), *Novellae Marciani* 4.3.2 (Code 5.5.7.2), quoted above note 5.

23. Actually, in some circles it was evidently thought that it did constitute a legal bar, and the Emperors had to declare this opinion unfounded: *Novellae Marciani* 4.1 (Code 5.5.7 pr., 1).

used of the rebuttal by years of blameless behaviour of an unjust imputation. Among the elements that went into this usage were a simple division of good and evil, an optimistic belief in the power of the former and a dose of self-righteousness. The earliest recorded evidence dates from 1842, when non-conformism is declared (by a non-conformist) to have lived down the prejudice against it.[24] The idea, though not the expression, can be paralleled in antiquity: it was by his exemplary life that Socrates—so his disciple Xenophon affirms[25]—prepared his defence before the court that was to try him, and Augustus, according to Suetonius, "refuted the defamatory charge of unnatural vice by the chastity of his present and subsequent mode of life."[26] It was only at a later stage that "to live down" acquired the sense in which it is now common: to cause a discreditable past to be forgotten by prolonged, consistent good behaviour.[27] To this there are no really close approximations in antiquity.[28]

Theodora had renounced the stage and become a serious Christian before she met Justinian. None the less his aunt was adamant. She had not prevented her Emperor-husband from conferring the high rank of a Patrician on the lady their nephew courted, but of marriage she would not hear. Who was this puritan Empress?

She had been born a slave, and originally was called Lupicina. Justin had bought and manumitted, freed, her; and she assumed the more decorous name of Euphemia when she ascended the throne with him. But how could a freedwoman, a woman of servile provenance and only released from slavery in the course of her life, be married to the Emperor? The very same Augustan statutes which forbade a member of a senatorial family to marry an actress or her daughter also forbade him to marry a freedwoman, and

24. *Oxford English Dictionary*, ed. Bradley (1903), 6, pt. 1, 357, quoting Edward Miall, *Non-Conformist* 2.1.

25. *Apology*, towards the beginning.

26. *Augustus* 71: *infamiam impudicitiae refutavit et praesentis et posterae vitae castitate*.

27. The earliest occurrence quoted by the *Oxford English Dictionary* is in Archibald Clavering Gunter, *Miss Dividends* (1892), 158: "How long do you think it will take in New York society for a girl with sixty thousand dollars a year to live anything down?"

28. It would be easier to find approximations to the related, yet different, slang phrase "to make good."

later enactments extended the prohibition even to a freedwoman's daughter.[29] There is indeed some evidence that, to begin with at any rate, she was merely Justin's concubine, a kind of recognized mistress.[30] But from Constantine onwards, even concubinage between a senator and a freedwoman or her daughter was outlawed,[31] and in any case Euphemia almost certainly finished up with the full status of wife.[32]

The answer is twofold. For one thing, her union with Justin probably antedated his rise to senatorial rank;[33] and already the late classical jurists, around A.D. 200, had wondered whether an existing, valid marriage between an ordinary citizen and a freedwoman should be dissolved by the former's elevation to the aristocracy.[34] However, this can hardly be the complete solution, if only because the prevalent opinion seems to have been that the marriage was indeed ended; it was Justinian himself who, later on when he had succeeded his uncle as Emperor, reversed this harsh trend.[35] Anyhow, we may be sure that, if there was a non-controversial method of keeping or rendering his union lawful, Justin must have chosen it. There was such a method, and this brings me to the second point of the answer.

From some date in the second half of the second century A.D., a slave

29. Digest 23.2.44, *Codex Theodosianus* 4.6.3 (Code 5.27.1), *Novellae Marciani* 4.3.2 (Code 5.5.7.2), quoted above.

30. Procopius, *Anecdota* 6.17: *pallake*. My slight doubt stems from the consideration that Procopius, whenever making a damaging statement about the imperial house, is not absolutely trustworthy; see below. For other sources see Vasiliev, *Justin the First*, at 61.

31. *Codex Theodosianus* 4.6.3 (Code 5.27.1), quoted above. That went against the widespread feeling that, however highly placed a man was, at least concubinage with a slave woman he had himself manumitted was all right: Digest 23.2.41.1, Marcellus XXVI *digestorum*; 25.7.1 pr., Ulpian II *ad legem Juliam et Papiam*; 48.5.14 pr., Ulpian II *de adulteriis*.

32. A letter of A.D. 519 written by the Patriarch of Constantinople to the Pope speaks of Justin's "most pious spouse, our daughter, Euphemia," *piissimam eius coniugem, nostram autem filiam, Euphemiam, Patrologia Latina* 63 (1860), 450. Procopius himself writes loc. cit.: "He lived in wedlock with her as wife," *gynaiki xynoikei*.

33. Under Anastasius I, 491–518; see Vasiliev, *Justin the First*, at 63.

34. Code 5.4.28 pr., Justinian, A.D. 531 or 532: *apud Ulpianum quaerebatur*, "the question was raised in Ulpian."

35. Code 5.4.28, just quoted; cp. below note 78.

could not only be freed but also be made freeborn.[36] This sounds, and is, queer, but it is a historical fact; I shall come back to it.[37] It was indeed a very special thing, and whereas freedom could be conferred by a slave's master, freebornhood could be conferred only by the Emperor. The institution belongs to those interferences with the past held possible in certain settings in antiquity, and maybe even in our day. Remember the "new creation" of the New Testament,[38] drawing on the then current Jewish teaching about proselytism: a convert to Judaism was newborn in so real a sense that he was no longer related to, say, his sister and (provided she too converted) could marry her.[39] A freedman made freeborn by the Emperor had never been a slave. As Mommsen noticed,[40] if, for example, such a man, prior to the grant of freebornhood, held one of those offices which were normally entrusted to freedmen, his tomb inscription, in recording his career, would suppress it. It would do so even though the office might have been extremely important and honorable: as by the time of his death he was freeborn, he could never have held it. If you study successive editions over the past fifty years of the leading German or Russian encyclopedias, you will find not dissimilar modern attempts to refashion the past in this direct manner. I have with my own eyes seen a group painting of a party conference where one of the heads originally there had been erased: that man now never was at the conference. George Orwell in *Nineteen Eighty-Four* depicts in detail this control of yesterday. Doubtless Lupicina-Euphemia was made freeborn, so the Augustan marriage restrictions were not applicable to her, her union with Justin was unobjectionable.

Otherwise quite passive in politics, she put her foot down against Justinian's marriage plans. She was simple, worthy, narrowly old-fashioned, and an ex-actress was just not tolerable. But about A.D. 523, as remarked, she died.

---

36. For details, see part IV (Interference With the Past) of my lecture "Greek and Roman Reflections on Impossible Laws," delivered at Notre Dame University in October 1964: *Natural Law Forum* 12 (1967): 188–201.

37. Below, notes 44 f.

38. 2 Cor 6:17.

39. *Babylonian Yebamoth* 22a, 97bf., *Palestinian Yebamoth* 12a.

40. *Römisches Staatsrecht* 3.I.518 f.

Now Justinian got his uncle to legislate. This law, laying down that a penitent actress can be rehabilitated, is preserved in Justinian's Code and commented on by Procopius, whom I have mentioned already, in his *Anecdota* or *Secret History*.[41] As he flourished under Justin and Justinian, and therefore was a witness of those events, his account is invaluable—yet it must be taken with a grain of salt. He was Justinian's court historian and obtained many tangible expressions of the Emperor's gratitude for eulogistic descriptions of his wars, his buildings and so forth. But all the while the same author was engaged on a venomous attack on the reign—the *Anecdota*—taking good care to see that it was not published till after his death. His hatred for Justinian and Theodora was clearly extreme, so in using his work some allowance must be made for distortion. Let us now inspect the law.

An introductory paragraph says that the Emperor has the welfare of his subjects at heart; that women who have slipped into a dubious way of life should be offered suitable aid; and that they should not be deprived of hope of rehabilitation which might work as a stimulus to renounce their objectionable doings. In this way (the paragraph concludes) the Emperor can imitate the clemency of God, always willing to accept a penitent sinner and reinstate him in a better condition. If the Emperor fails to do so to his subjects, he himself will not be worthy of divine forgiveness.

There is much here that is reminiscent of New Testament thought: the role of hope, the inducement to be held out to the erring, the emulation of the example of God—*imitatio Dei*—the latter's mercy to penitent sinners, the postulate that you must forgive if you want to be forgiven.[42] Nevertheless we must not forget that remarkably similar sentiments are entertained by pagan Stoic ethics. This ethics had long been a major influence on Roman imperial ideology and categories derived from it were deeply entrenched in the legislative tradition inherited by Justin and Justinian. They must have been a far from negligible factor contributing to the result before us. It will

41. Code 5.4.23, Justin, A.D. 520–3, Procopius, *Anecdota* 9.30. As for the mistaken attribution of the enactment to Justinian in the inscription of Casinas 49, see above.
42. E.g., Matt 6:2, 14 f., 7:1 f., 18:23 ff.; Mark 11:25 f. Cp. also Ecclus 28:1 ff., *Tosephta Baba Kamma* 9:29 f., *Babylonian Shabbath* 151b, and (for gentle chastisement with a view to reform) *Zadokite Fragments* 13:9 f.

suffice to quote Seneca:[43] "Since I have made mention of gods, I shall do well to establish this as the standard after which the prince should model himself—that he should be so to his citizens as he would wish the gods to be to himself. Would he, then, desire to have deities that cannot be moved to show mercy to our sins and errors?" And again: "You will more easily reform offenders by a lighter punishment. For he will live more carefully who has some unspoilt good left. No one looks after honour that is lost."

The next paragraph starts with a strange reference to the grant of freebornhood, that curious institution on which I have already touched. May I recall: slaves could always be released, and from the early Empire they could be given the rights of freeborn citizens. But from, roughly, the reign of Commodus, around A.D. 180, a more radical transformation was recognized: they could be made freeborn (not only given the rights) by imperial grant. Sometimes this was interpreted as a new creation, sometimes as an elevation of the person to the ideal status which prevailed in the golden age before the breaking up of mankind. Here, then, in the paragraph under discussion, Justin—the uncle who is legislating, but we must always remember that the guiding hand is Justinian's—asserts that it would be unjust that slaves can be fully helped up in this manner whereas penitent actresses should have no chance.

The argument is quite unconvincing, based as it is on a highly defective parallel. Slaves are what they are without fault, actresses by their own choice. Why does he put up such a bad analogy? We might indeed ask: why does he need an analogy at all?

Very possibly there is here an allusion to, almost a refutation of, the dead Empress who had blocked the plans of Justinian and Theodora though herself secure in her marriage only by virtue of a grant of freebornhood, which had lifted her out of her subordinate class. A far more important point, however, is revealed by the provisions enunciated in the following, substantive, portion of the enactment. Henceforth, it is ordained, a penitent actress may apply for an imperial grant of full marriage privileges, upon which the highest aristocrat may marry her: all blemish, all *macula*, attaching to her from the stage is utterly wiped out and—now I quote—"she

43. *De clementia* 1.7.1, 1.22.1.

is so to speak handed back to her pristine, native condition."[44] Here lies
the main reason for the introduction of the parallel. By the imperial grant
of freebornhood a man born a slave "was handed back to his native condition"—this was a technical term[45]—in the sense that he was born afresh
in freedom or (an alternative interpretation) was placed under the ideal
dispensation of the golden age with no gulf in society. This institution was
the nearest available model in the law for a grant with a direct effect on a
person's past, not just remedying what had happened but altering it head-
on. Theodora must be flawless. It was not enough to rule that, from now,
she was acceptable. The blemish must never have been, must be totally
eradicated even from the past. She was to be restored to her sinless state
at birth or the ideal state of the world before sin entered. For such a step, a
model—the only one in law, as distinct from religion or philosophy—was
provided by the grant which made a man who was born a slave a freeborn
man. This feature of directly getting at the past was so desirable for blot-
ting out her taint as an actress that the weakness of the analogy—the slave
being innocent, an actress guilty—was brushed aside.

Of course, these attempts to interfere with the past are never more
than partially successful. The law enjoins that, once the grant is obtained,
she is no longer to be called an actress, "no longer to be so dishonorably
designated."[46] Would it be permissible to say that she had been one? I suppose so, even though all taint is gone and she is as pure as on the first day.
Remember the tomb inscriptions of freedmen made freeborn, suppressing
all indication of an unfree origin. I suppose she was an actress in a different life just as a convert, newborn, a new creation, would still have a former
life in the dark.

The law continues with a paragraph to the effect that the children of
an actress who marries after rehabilitation are legitimate; and yet a further
paragraph lays down that a daughter from such a marriage does not count

44. *Quasi suis natalibus huiusmodi mulieribus redditis.*
45. Digest 39.2.3.1, Ulpian XII *ad edictum.* Often "to restore (*restituere*) to native
condition": Digest 40.11.2, Marcian I *institutionum*; 40.11.5.1, Modestinus VII *regula-
rum*; Code 6.55.6, Diocletian and Maximian, A.D. 294.
46. *Neque vocabulum inhonestum eis inharere de cetero.*

as the daughter of an actress. As for the latter provision, I observed above[47] that Augustus had ruled unfit for marriage into the aristocracy the children of actors, whether sons or daughters; but that in course of time the ban was confined to daughters. That is why this paragraph makes no mention of the former: they were no longer in need of relief.

Strictly, indeed, both paragraphs—that the children from such a marriage are legitimate, and that a daughter does not count as the daughter of an actress—might be judged superfluous: once the mother is rehabilitated and her marriage with a senator recognized without reservation, what these two paragraphs state follows automatically. If it was thought prudent not to rely on inference in this matter, and to create one-hundred-percent clarity, it was because, potentially, the future of the dynasty was involved: there must not be the shadow of a doubt as to the legitimacy of any offspring that might result from the proposed union, and as to the unsullied status of any daughter. We know that Justinian and Theodora badly wanted children, from the tragic scene in A.D. 530, when they had been married some seven years and Abbot Sabas had an audience with Theodora.[48] She fell at the holy man's feet and asked him to entreat God to grant her a child. The abbot, however, was orthodox while she was a Monophysite. So in answer to her request he prayed: "God the Lord of all may guard your Empire." She asked him again, and this time he prayed: "The God of glory may preserve your Empire pious and victorious." Tearfully she got up and he left her. When questioned by his entourage why he had been so hard, he replied: "Believe me, Fathers, that no fruit will come from her womb, lest it should suck of the tenets of Severus and trouble the Church worse than Anastasius."[49] They never in fact did have a child. But at the time the law enabling them to marry was promulgated, obviously the position of offspring would be very much in their minds.

The case of an actress's daughter born before her mother's reinstatement is not overlooked: she will be entitled, the law ordains, to an imperial

---

47. See notes 21 f.

48. *Kyrillos Von Skythopolis*, ed. Schwartz (1939), 173 f. (*St. Sabas* 71); see Nagl, "Theodora," *Paulys Real-Encyclopädie* 2d ser., 5 (1934), 1782.

49. Severus of Antioch, the Monophysite leader, and Anastasius I, the Monophysite Emperor.

conferment of unrestricted marriage capacity. It is worth noting that Theodora had a daughter from an earlier union who, if she so desired, might
benefit from this provision. Bury claims[50] that this daughter was the fruit of
her mother's pre-marital friendship with Justinian himself. This is incredible. It is not hinted at by a single source; and the argument from silence is
strong in this case, since the writers hostile to the couple would have been
happy to mention the point had it been remotely plausible.

Bury is definitely wrong on a fundamental issue. So far I have accepted what Procopius reports in his *Secret History*—that this legislation
was passed for the purpose of Justinian's marriage with Theodora. Some
forty years ago Bury argued[51] that the law was not needed at all because,
some while before, Justin, the uncle, had promoted Theodora to the Patriciate, a high dignity (bestowal of which Euphemia had not prevented);[52] and
a woman-Patrician was at liberty to marry anyone, however noble, even if
she was an ex-actress. This thesis of Bury's is taken over by several scholars.[53] It is, however, based on an enormous fallacy. The regulation that a
woman-Patrician, even if previously an actress, may marry anyone was
introduced in a paragraph of the very law we are considering, the very law
enacted by Justin for his nephew's sake. So Procopius is perfectly right:
but for this law, Justinian could not have married Theodora though she was

50. *History of the Later Roman Empire* (1939), 2.27.
51. Ibid., at 29.
52. See above.
53. E.g., by Vasiliev, *Justin the First*, at 100 f. Not, e.g., by Nagl, "Theodora," at
1778; Holmes, *The Age of Justinian and Theodora*, 2d ed. (1912), 347; Schubart, *Justinian and Theodora* (1943), 34; Stein, *Histoire du Bas-Empire* (1949), 2.236; Ure, *Justinian
and His Age* (1951), 200; Rubin, *Das Zeitalter Justinians* (1960), 107. There are, however,
a number of other recurrent errors: Vasiliev (at 97, 395), Nagl, Holmes, Schubart, and Ure
throw together actresses and prostitutes and believe that Justin's enactment encouraged
both equally to return. Ure in the decisive sentence actually forgets about the former: the
enactment repealed, he says, "the law which prohibited senators from marrying courtesans, and Theodora became Justinian's lawful wife." Cp. above note 16, and below, notes
64 ff. Rubin falls into a different blunder: he thinks the enactment authorized a senatorial
marriage only with such ex-actresses as were Patricians. Nagl's position is quite self-
contradictory: she does not accept Bury's conclusion, yet she does share his mistaken
premise that from the moment Theodora was a Patrician, there was no longer any obstacle.
The confusion is truly remarkable.

indeed a Patrician.

It is true that the paragraph giving women who have received a dignity full marriage privileges does constitute a problem. But the proper question to ask is: why does the law do two things when, apparently, one—either of the two—would suffice? In its principal part, which I have reviewed at some length, the law says that a penitent actress may apply for an imperial grant which will abolish her stain. Then a special paragraph adds that a woman promoted to high rank—such as the Patriciate—is likewise rid of blemish. Either of the two provisions, it looks at first sight, would have done, would have achieved what Justinian wanted. Why, then, do we get both? Pursuing this line of inquiry we shall see just how wrong Bury and his followers are: every detail of the law is tailored to the particular dilemma of Justinian and Theodora—which does not exclude the effectiveness of wider, charitable considerations.

Let us begin by imagining that the law had confined its remedy to a woman raised to the Patriciate or an equivalent honour. The result would have been most unsatisfactory, for such a law would have been a crudely individual favour for the couple in question, and the general formulation— the reference to any woman-Patrician—would have deceived no one; it would only have played into the hands of the critics who would have seen how specious it was. In that age, it just was not on the cards that there would be a series of further cases of circus girls being ennobled. The law might just as well have acknowledged, in a short sentence, without much ado, the particular marriage between Justinian and Theodora. If this was not good enough, then a wider regulation, a regulation going beyond Patricians, became inevitable.

There is a further aspect we should do wrong in neglecting. We must give some credence to the benevolent and pious feelings expressed in the law. The three, Justin, his nephew and the bride-to-be, were really inspired by religious-moral fervor. They did want to extend to others, to ordinary mortals, the remedy which made marriage possible in this instance. This is not speculation: Justinian's subsequent legislative reforming activity as sole Emperor after his uncle's death proves it.[54] The immediate purpose

54. See Biondi, below note 73. Cp. also above note 35, and below note 78.

of the law was *ad hoc*, but this does not mean that it was not at the same time intended to give encouragement to fellow-beings in similar plight. We may conclude, then, that though it would have been open to the lawgiver merely to annul the lapse of a Patrician, that course was rejected for two reasons: it would have been impolitic, too crassly personal, and it would not have satisfied the genuine charitable aspiration to come to the assistance of penitent actresses in general, high or low.

This leaves us with the question why the law contains more than the principal part authorizing penitent actresses to seek rehabilitation: why, in addition, does it contain the special little paragraph saying that an ex-actress admitted to the Patriciate is equally fit to marry anyone? Here again the main reasons are two. For one thing, this was a gallant gesture to Theodora, who was thereby relieved of applying to the Emperor as a penitent actress. It was he who did all that was necessary; her promotion automatically put her on a level with an actress who had received a grant. This object, of sparing her the awkwardness of the procedure and of representing her rehabilitation as freely offered her by the old Emperor's goodwill, comes out in the wording of the paragraph. We are told that the privileges acquired by penitent actresses who have sought a grant shall be enjoyed also by women "who, without supplicating to the most Serene Emperor, have prior to their marriage been honoured with high rank by his spontaneous gift."[55]

However, there is more—far more—to this extra paragraph which confers free marriage ability on a Patrician. It has never been noticed that the ruling differs in a significant substantive detail from that about an ordinary penitent actress. The latter obtains an imperial grant, whereupon the blemish of the stage is wiped out. In the case of a Patrician, her rank, the law declares, wipes out not only the blemish of the stage but "also any other blemish whatsoever" which might impede a high union.[56]

Theodora was widely reputed to have been a prostitute, and thus, quite apart from her theatrical past, to belong to a category not to be taken in

55. *Quae dignitatem aliquam, etsi non serenissimo principi supplicaverunt, ultronea tamen donatione ante matrimonium meruerint.*

56. *Aliam etiam omnem maculam per quam certis hominibus legitime coniungi mulieres prohibentur.*

marriage by any freeborn man, let alone a senator.[57] Neither she nor Justinian nor Justin would admit this for one moment; on the contrary, they were greatly concerned to mark off her venial offence, the theatre, from prostitution which, in this world, remained in principle unredeemable. Even Justinian's later humanitarian reforms, we shall see,[58] never ameliorated the status of a penitent harlot. Accordingly, the bulk of the enactment is devoted to penitent actresses, of whom Theodora was avowedly one. Yet something had to be done about the graver charge, warranted or unwarranted, if only for dynastic reasons. I have already adverted to the couple's hope for progeny. Suppose there would be children, and after Justinian's death their claim to the succession would be contested because the father's marriage with an ex-prostitute had been invalid. If the law cleared Theodora only from her career as an actress, then, rightly or wrongly, somebody would attack the marriage on that other ground: on a monarch's death, all sorts of things happen. Justinian had to provide against the day when he could no longer cow those who held this view of his wife into silence or clandestine rumour. Which means that it was essential to render the marriage lawful even should it be assumed that she had in fact been guilty of prostitution. Here we have a further weighty reason—in addition to consideration for her feelings, sparing her the application—of the special paragraph regarding a Patrician: by it, a woman promoted to high dignity was enabled to contract an aristocratic marriage however low she had once fallen.[59]

It will be noticed that this paragraph was not likely to benefit any group of persons. I previously observed that in that age it was not to be expected that the Patriciate would be conferred on other actresses; still less would it be conferred on worse offenders. There was indeed no intent to generalize the relief, no intent to do anything for ex-prostitutes at large.

57. Digest 23.2.43 pr. ff., Ulpian I *ad legem Juliam et Papiam*; 23.2.44.8, Paul I *ad legem Juliam et Papiam*; *Ulpiani Regulae* 13.2. In Digest 23.2.43.4 Ulpian states that "not only she who practises prostitution but also she who has practised it, though she has now ceased to do so, is marked by this statute: for her vileness is not abolished by discontinuance," *non solum autem ea quae facit (palam corpore quaestum) verum ea quoque quae fecit, etsi facere desiit, lege notatur: neque enim aboletur turpitudo quae postea intermissa est.*

58. Below notes 64 f.

59. Whether the paragraph would have made a difference if put to the test is another question. It would be rash to deny that in certain circumstances it might have done so.

The paragraph was designed as a strictly personal protection of the couple and their issue should Theodora at some future time be deemed—unjustly, from the lawgiver's point of view—to have been in that despicable trade. We have before us an admirable specimen of legislative craft. The task before the lawgiver was, while not conceding the reproach, to see to it that it would do no harm even if accepted as true; and again, while seeing that it would do no harm in this particular case, not to blunt its consequences in other cases (since ex-prostitutes remained damned); and again, to achieve all this without openly singling out the people concerned. The task is solved by this paragraph.

Actually, the draftsman has performed an even subtler feat. The provision is formulated in so subdued a fashion and tucked away in so subordinate a place that it is barely noticed. The lawgiver did not wish it to be noticed, certainly did not wish its major point to be understood at that time. He was forced to put it in just in case, after Justinian's death, the more serious aspersion against Theodora might be voiced and, but for the paragraph, create obstacles for their offspring; but for the moment it was to be as inconspicuous as ever possible. Significantly the particular charge in view of which the provision was needed is not even specified: that would indeed have attracted attention—but all we get is a bland, innocent-looking phrase, "any other blemish." How successfully it has been done may be gathered from the fact I have just noted, that until now nobody has spotted the thrust of this little section—remarked that the law goes much further in rehabilitating a Patrician than a mere penitent actress, and connected it up with the gossip about Theodora.

There is one exception: Procopius (and I regard this as confirmation of my analysis). If love makes blind, hate makes seeing. Procopius in his *Anecdota* alleges that the enactment legalized marriages between senators and courtesans; to this monstrous concession, he claims, Justinian's infatuation had led. This is, of course, a perversion of the truth, but not without the proverbial grain. The grain lies in the singling out by the law of ex-actresses elevated to high dignity—meaning, in effect, Theodora alone, but speaking in general terms—whose entry into a senatorial family was not to be impeded by anything at all that could be said against their character.

In the history of legislation, this case of a camouflaged provision is far from unique; many illustrations could be given from present-day law. It would indeed be interesting to examine systematically the technique of authorities throughout the ages in employing the device. At first sight one might perhaps assume that in modern democracies, with free and open debate of proposed legislation, this kind of thing could not happen. But it does: what is required is an understanding between those charged with the debate or (quite enough) between the knowing ones among them. Where to look for examples? Constitutions are worth probing—say, the section dealing with the emergency powers of the head of State. Immigration acts—the way it is made possible, if the worse comes to the worst, to keep a group or race out. Currency exchange laws. Income tax laws. Lower down the scale, a university's (or a professional body's or a country club's) admission or disciplinary code. If we go still lower down, into the arena of contract, it is well known—though rarely looked at from this angle—that, say, standardized insurance terms, money-lending arrangements, hire-purchase agreements, tenancy forms, are all apt to contain stipulations overlooked by the unwary and meant to be overlooked, but no less operative if need be.[60]

The ill-founded dismissal of Procopius's information that the law was promulgated with a view to the marriage between Justinian and Theodora has produced much basic misrepresentation. Vasiliev infers that the law "was merely one step in the process of the emancipation of women which goes back to the fourth and fifth centuries and was in accordance with Christian sentiment."[61] This is an exaggeration. No doubt the law marks a stage in a gradual advance of the kind he envisages. But that such advance was not its central purpose comes out in many ways. Why were only penitent actresses considered and no other female sinners? Why no other female sufferers with better claims and more comparable to slaves or freedmen not responsible for their unfortunate condition?[62] It was not till some twenty years later that Justinian allowed senators to marry, say, the daughters of female tavernkeepers or pimps.[63] Harlots who repented

---

60. I refrain from illustrations: far be it from me to give away an artist.

61. Vasiliev, *Justin the First*, at 395. Holmes more judiciously takes the law to be *ad feminam* at the same time as chiming with the development of Christian sentiment.

62. See above.

63. Novels 117.6, A.D. 542, abolishing the restrictions of *Codex Theodosianus*

were never relieved of their disabilities even by Justinian—contrary to the prevalent view which credits his great reform Novel with a range it does not have.[64] Procopius both in his official and in his secret writings describes their seclusion on inaccessible islands off-shore, expanding on their ensuing happiness and saintliness in the official account, on their misery and unwillingness to be saintly in the secret one.[65]

Here a word may be said about Theodora's actual standing. Beyond question she had led a dissolute life (being brought up to it from earliest childhood, as the only means of mitigating total destitution). Procopius's biography, however biased, is too circumstantial to be dismissed as a pack of lies, and, above all, its main thesis is corroborated by John of Ephesus, equally contemporary, a Monophysite who would not unnecessarily testify against the admired benefactress of his creed.[66] No use trying to explain it away.[67] In fact, for John of Ephesus there was something wonderful in this conversion and exaltation which proved such a blessing for the true faith. (It would be of some interest to work out to which types of modern historians and theologians the thought is abhorrent.) In law, it would be very material whether she fell under the definition of a prostitute or only came near being one: I think she was in the latter case. She was free with her favours and not averse to earning money, yet, refusing to become a mere tool, she was not technically a prostitute.[68] But she did come close and many considered her guilty. As I have already pointed out, the long, principal portion

---

4.6.3 (Code 5.27.1), Constantine, A.D. 336, and *Novellae Marciani* 4.3.2 (Code 5.5.7.2), Valentinian and Marcian, A.D. 454.

64. See Buckland, *Text-Book of Roman Law,* 3d ed. by Stein (1963), 115; Kaser, *Das Römische Privatrecht* (1959), 2.113. Above notes 16, 53, 58.

65. *De aedificiis* 1.9.1 ff., *Anecdota* 17.5 f.

66. "The good God... directed the virtuous Stephen to Theodora who came from the brothel, who was at that time a Patrician, but eventually became Queen also with King Justinian." Brooks (note 1), at 189.

67. Vasiliev, *Justin the First,* at 97, rightly rejects such attempts. As mentioned above, note 53, where he goes wrong, here as elsewhere (e.g., at 395), is in missing the vital legal distinction between actress and prostitute. He says: "The two terms were almost synonymous." That may be so in many social, moral, and theological contexts. In law, there was a huge difference.

68. Digest 23.2.43.1, Ulpian I *ad legem Juliam et Papiam: palam autem sic accipimus, passim, hoc est sine delectu.*

of the law under discussion is carefully designed to convey that she could be accused of nothing worse than acting, and the relative lightness of this lapse is insinuated by means of ingeniously picked moderate terms—such as "ill-considered choice."[69] (We are also given to understand that women go in for the stage from "feminine weakness,"[70] presumably misled by ruthless men.[71] Ruthless men, however, are responsible for prostitution too.)[72] The continued harshness displayed by Justinian and Theodora against ex-prostitutes, out of keeping with the general trend of their government, may have been partly motivated by the urge to demonstrate that she had nothing in common with this category. It was malice which prompted Procopius to fasten on the subsidiary paragraph which provided against the possibility of her being misjudged; and, disregarding the religious-moral aims of the law, to suggest that it paved the way for unions with former prostitutes. That was definitely not true.

Biondi is the author of a book on Justinian as a Catholic ruler and an admirable three-volume work on the Christian law of Rome.[73] He quotes the law some ten times, but never once mentions its purpose of authorizing the marriage between Justinian and Theodora. For him, whatever Procopius may say, it is a "veritable hymn to the redemption of women and the benevolence of God whom the lawgiver seeks to imitate,"[74] nothing but an example of Christian pity for the sinner and facilitation of repentance. He cites the stretch: "We hold that their lapses should be remedied by a suitable means and we ought not to deprive them of the hope for a better condition in order that, looking forward to this, they may more readily give up their ill-considered and shameful choice." And he adds: "Who does not see in these phrases the distant echo of the gospel episode of the adulterous woman in John?"[75] The echo, however, is highly dubious. In John,

69. *Improvida electio.*
70. *Imbecillitate sexus*; cp. Digest 16.1.2.2, Ulpian XXIX *ad edictum.*
71. Cp. Code 1.4.33, Justinian, A.D. 534.
72. Procopius, *De aedificiis* 1.9.2 f.
73. *Giustiniano Primo Principe e Legislatore Cattolico* (1936), *Il Diritto Romano Cristiano*, 1 and 2, (1952), 3, (1954). As this article is going to press, I learn of this great and high-minded scholar's death.
74. *Giustiniano*, 62 f .
75. *Il Diritto* 2.166; John 8:3 ff.

it is not a question of making it easier for adulteresses to give up their way of life, but—an entirely different matter—Jesus reprieves an adulteress caught in the act. Nor is there any significant verbal affinity between the episode in John (in its Latin versions) and Justin's legislation. Biondi continues: "Towards those women the lawgiver feels not contempt but humane understanding calculated to bring about penitence and redemption." "These women" is very ambiguous; from the context it seems to include both actresses and adulteresses. But the latter are not contemplated by Justin's law; in fact their treatment at the time was far from lenient.[76] Biondi also quotes the passage where the law speaks of actresses who "spurning their evil condition have turned to a better intent and have fled their dishonorable profession, have embraced a worthier life and have turned to decency." He asks: "Who does not hear in these provisions the echo of the gospel warnings in Matthew concerning prostitutes who convert?"[77] Here the echo is not dubious but plainly imaginary. What Matthew complains about is that, while publicans and prostitutes, both of them outcasts, believed the Baptist, the Pharisees, the elite, though offered more evidence, showed no repentance. This is not a portion of the gospel to which the law is specifically indebted.

The law is permeated by the spirit of Christianity and rich in thought and sentiment deriving from the New Testament, directly or indirectly, and merging with Stoic culture. But over-idealization ultimately enhances neither the stature of the *dramatis personae* nor the value of their legislation as *exemplum*, as stimulus and guide—not to mention the violence done in the process to the gospel texts invoked. What is moving about the law is precisely the interplay of self-interest and generosity. The primary impulse comes from Justinian's passionate resolve to marry Theodora. Nothing wrong with it, but it is a personal cause. The two have, however, thought profoundly about their situation and terrible difficulties, and about why it is right to seek an escape not only for themselves but for any couple similarly placed. The law, while assisting them, extends relief to many and,

76. See Mommsen, *Römisches Strafrecht* (1899), 698 f.; Biondi, *Il Diritto* III.473 ff.

77. *Il Diritto* II.168; Matt 21:32.

indeed, propagates considerations which would inevitably be an incentive to further progress.[78] No point in de-humanizing the measure. Some fifteen years later, at the age of fifty-five (about my age), in another reforming law, Justinian, by now the greatest Byzantine Emperor ever, avowed: "For we know, though we are lovers of chastity, that nothing is more vehement than the fury of love."[79] This is Justinian speaking, not any member of his Legislative Council, not Tribonian, his Minister of Justice. No official, however high, would have thought of putting in a confessional aside of this nature. It is the same mind that we meet in the law signed by Justin I.

Theodora died in A.D. 548, so they had about twenty-five years of married life, during which she exercised an enormous and—if we make allowance for their historical setting—beneficial influence. The mosaics in the choir of S. Vitale at Ravenna, showing the two, date from A.D. 547, one year before her death. Justinian died in A.D. 565, aged eighty-three. From the moment of Theodora's departure, however, his government had declined: he lost his grip, or rather, he lost her grip. He was succeeded by his nephew Justin II, as he had succeeded his uncle; only, unlike his uncle, he never made his nephew his co-regent, he remained sole ruler to the last. On the morrow of his death, Justin II issued a proclamation in which he declared: "We found the treasury crushed by debts and reduced to the last degree of poverty"—it almost sounds like Harold Wilson taking over from Sir Alec Douglas-Home, or Governor Reagan from Brown.

In conclusion, a philological remark. It would be worth going into the vocabulary of the law (and other laws by Justinian as well as his predecessors) and investigating its relation to the Latin versions of the Bible, Itala and Vulgate—especially, of course, where Scripture is cited or alluded to. Complicated problems are involved.[80] For example, the law uses *venia* for

---

78. We may compare, or contrast, Code 5.4.28, A.D. 531 or 532, referred to above, note 35. Justinian here laid down that a marriage between an ordinary citizen and a freed-woman was to remain intact even should the husband become a senator. The memory of his uncle's problem may well have played a part; yet by this time the object of the law was entirely altruistic, it was only others who could benefit.

79. Novels 74.4, A.D. 538.

80. Far more complicated than in the case of the *Collatio legum Romanarum et Mosaicarum*. For literature concerning the Biblical quotations in the *Collatio* see Wenger, *Die Quellen des Römischen Rechts* (1953), 547.

"forgiveness,"[81] *ignoscere* for "to forgive,"[82] *sublevare* for "to remedy."[83] All three words are found in the Old Testament, none in the New, where different ones are preferred.[84] The first question, therefore, is what significance, if any, to assign to this distribution: the answer might throw light on the role of these words generally in the area of theology. Another question is whether the distribution has been a factor in the phrasing of the law; in other words, is there some specific Old Testament influence at work? With respect to *venia* at any rate, the answer is in the negative. Surely, this word comes down from the Roman imperial tradition: the exercise of *venia* was

81. In the introductory paragraph discussed above: if the Emperor does not emulate God's mercifulness, "we ourselves shall not be worthy of forgiveness."

82. In the same paragraph: it is incumbent on the Emperor to imitate the benevolence of God "who always deigns to forgive."

83. "We hold that their lapses should be remedied by a suitable means."

84. *Venia* denotes "forgiveness" in Gen 4:13 (Cain: "My iniquity is greater than that I can merit forgiveness"), Num 15:18 (the priest obtains forgiveness for a man who has sinned in error), Wisdom 12:11 (God refused forgiveness to the Canaanites). It can mean "indulgence," "patience": Ecclus Prol. (where the translator asks his readers' indulgence should he be guilty of an occasional slip), 3:15 (enjoining patience with a senile father), or "permission," "freedom": 25:34 (a warning against giving a wicked woman freedom to go about). Both in the Old Testament and in the New we find *dimittere* and *remittere* for "to forgive," though, in the Old, *remittere* is confined to Psalms. *Remissio* in the sense of "forgiveness" and *donare* in that of "to forgive" occur only in the New Testament (in the Old, *remissio* signifies "release of debt" in the Jubilee and the like). *Sublevare* is an Old Testament word (except for John 6:5. and 17:1, *sublevare oculos*, "to lift up the eyes"); and in several passages the meaning is comparable to that in Justin's law—Deut 15:10 (a slave gaining his statutory freedom has a right to some provision, nor must his master be grudging about "his necessities to be remedied"), Prov 29:25 (he who trusts in God "shall be relieved"), Jonah 2:7 ("thou will lift up my life from corruption"). Other terms, of course, are of interest. *Lapsus*, which is used by Justin ("We hold that their lapses should be remedied"), is met only in the Old Testament, and even here in a different sense: the "stumbling" of a foot. *Macula* is frequent in the Old Testament, rarer in the New (Eph 5:27, 1 Tim 6:14, 2 Pet 2:13, Jude 12, Rev 14:5). *Poenitentia* is frequent in both Testaments. *Benevolentia* and *clementia* are divine attributes Justin wishes to imitate, and the law itself is styled a *clementissima sanctio*, "a most clement disposition." *Benevolentia* occurs once only in the entire Latin Bible, in Ecclus. Prol. just quoted: the reader is asked to approach the translation with "benevolence." On *clementia*, see below note 87.

always a prerogative and ornament of the Emperor.[85] How powerful that tradition was is brought out by the fact that, in the *Codex Theodosianus*, about one hundred-and-twenty years after the Edict of Milan, there is next to no direct quotation of Scripture.[86] An enquiry on the lines indicated would certainly illumine the blend and relative weight in these laws of Christian and pagan notions; also the greater or lesser dependence on different Church Fathers and doctrines; and, conceivably, here and there, we might even gain a little more information about textual readings current at the time. I wonder whether the Benedictines, who have already done so much in this field, would add this formidable enterprise to their program.

As I was looking into terms like *clementia*, *benevolentia* and their synonyms, I came upon what must be the most optimistic passage in world literature—in the Epistle to Titus, where God is praised for his *humanitas*,

---

85. The word occurs in Pliny's famous letter to Trajan about Christians and in Trajan's reply, 10.96 f. Suetonius, among his illustrations of the promising start of Domitian's reign, mentions the *venia* with which he presented certain minor offenders: *Domitian* 9.3. Professor Stein of Aberdeen University, who kindly read this lecture in typescript, draws my attention to Waldstein, *Untersuchungen zum Römischen begnadigungsrecht* (1964). This is a broadly based, meticulous analysis of the various uses of *venia*, *indulgentia* and allied terms in the province of law from the late Republic down to Justinian. The latter, Waldstein points out (at 198), employs *venia* only in one constitution, Code 5.74.3 pr., 2, A.D. 529. In a sense, however, we may add Justin's enactment about ex-actresses, Justinian being its intellectual author.

86. I have heard it affirmed that there is none. A few passages, however, do come rather near being quotations. *Codex Theodosianus* 9.40.2 (Code 9.47.17), Constantine, A.D. 315, prohibits the branding of a criminal's face, "in order that the face, which is shaped in the likeness of the celestial beauty, be not stained," *quo facies, quae ad similitudinem pulchritudinis est caelestis figurata, minime maculetur.* This is a reference to the creation; though, to be sure, there must be an intermediate theological authority—or more than one—between Gen 1:26 f. and the enactment. For one thing, in Gen 1:26 f. it is man who is created similar to God (*faciamus hominem ad imaginem et similitudinem nostram, et creavit Deus hominem ad imaginem suam*), in the enactment it is his face alone: hands or legs may be branded. Again, Gen 1:26 f. speaks of creation in the likeness of God, the enactment more distantly of creation in the likeness of the heavenly beauty. (*Pulchritudo* and *pulcher*, incidentally, are both peculiar to the Old Testament.) Lastly, Gen 1:26 f. employs *facere*, "to make," and *creare*, "to create" (and Gen 2:7 *formare*, "to form"), the enactment *figurare*, "to shape." (Has this to do with the emphasis on the face? In French, *figure* ultimately acquired the sense of "face.")

"humanity": "But after that the kindness and humanity of God our Saviour appeared."[87] The life and work of Pope John seem like a justification of this charming usage. *Zikhrono libherakha*, may his memory be for a blessing.

87. Tit 3:4, *cum autem benignitas et humanitas apparuit salvatoris nostri Dei*. The Greek is *philanthropia*. In Code 5.16.27.1, Justinian, A.D. 530, *humanitas* is the Emperor's means of imitation of God. It should be observed that to ascribe *humanitas* to God is still not quite the same as to describe him as *humanus*: one would hardly expect the latter in a careful writer. This example shows that, in tracing the history of such concepts, it is advisable to be mindful of possible divergences between noun, adjective, adverb and so forth. The excellent article on *Clementia* by Winkler, in *Reallexikon für Antike und Christentum*, ed. Klauser, 3 (1957), 206 ff., suffers from too little attention to this aspect. The adverb *clementer* is met twice only in the Latin Bible, both times in Gen (43:27, 45:4), both times in the sense of "courteously," "graciously"—approximated by *pro tua clementia* in Acts 24:4.

Dividing a Child in Antiquity

I make a claim upon a person, expecting something from him. I lay claim to an object, in competition with others. This distinction, however, is not absolute. On the one hand, I may make a claim upon an object—my dog, for example, or even my racing car, personified. On the other, I may lay claim to a person, as an object or objectified. In earlier times, there might be disagreement as to the ownership of a slave or villain; a number of creditors might dispute the services or body of an insolvent debtor; the ladies of a harem might enter into a contest over the husband—Leah "hired" Jacob from Rachel for a night.[1] To list some familiar instances: the partners in a firm may fall out as to which is going to have the typist that day; two society hostesses as to which may invite the visiting royalty; one state may request from another the extradition of a criminal or permission for a minority to emigrate to the state preferring the request; men may fight about a woman; angels and demons about a soul, alive or dead.[2] Within the family, father, mother and governess may compete for a child; several children for a parent; father and son for the mother; mother and daughter for the father.

Often, though by no means always, where I lay claim to a person, I make a claim upon him at the same time. Leah expected Jacob to honor her pact with Rachel: "Thou must come in unto me." A partner quarrelling with the others about a typist may try to win by a direct appeal. So may a state asserting a right to a minority in another state, though hardly one

[*California Law Review* 54 (1966), 1630–7]
1. Gen 30:16. See D. Daube, *Studies in Biblical Law* (1947), 16–24, and "Concerning Methods of Bible-Criticism," *Archiv Orientální* 17 (1949), 96–99 [*BLL* 47–50, 86–89].
2. See, e.g., Rivière, "Rôle du Démon au Jugement Particulier chez les Pères," *Revue des Sciences Religieuses* 4 (1924), 43–58. His denial of pagan influence (Iranian, Egyptian) is not, however, acceptable.

requesting an extradition. So may a man fighting about a woman: the fifty
sons of Aegyptus wrested from Danaus his fifty daughters, but one only of
the bridegrooms survived the wedding-night—Lynceus, who won Hyperm-
nestra's love. During a man's life, angels and demons, besides warring for
him against one another, do their best to enlist his cooperation, though
death puts an end to the latter possibility. So long as a child is in the cradle,
his competing elders will each lay claim to him; as he grows up, claims
upon him will be added. *The Father* by Strindberg strikes a neat balance.

While marriage lasts, the law is reluctant to take up the conflicts over
a child. In most systems, modern or ancient, control resides either with the
father or with the mother. In a Roman marriage, in principle it is with the
father, though at the latest, from Antoninus Pius (middle of the second century A.D.), sometimes it is with the mother.[3] Save in extreme cases, it is left
to spouses to make, or not to make, the necessary adjustments, without the
help of the courts. On divorce or separation, in modern law, things become
different. Though even at this stage control is as a rule adjudged to one of
the parents, at least with regard to physical presence a child is practically
divided. Not, fortunately, as Solomon proposed to divide a baby between
two harlots each alleging to be his mother,[4] or as the Twelve Tables allowed
a defaulting debtor to be cut up by his creditors.[5] A child, humanely, counts
as indivisible with respect to his body; hence the division is in time, father
and mother take turns. (Indivisible things have none the less been split
up. Plutarch tells us of two brothers, joint heirs, so insensate as to halve a
silver cup and a cloak).[6] In English law, this starts with the equity courts
expressing sympathy for, and now and then giving some actual support to, a
mother's desire for access to her child.[7] Nowadays elaborate arrangements

---

3. Digest 43.30.1.3, 3.5, Ulpian LXXI *ad edictum*.
4. I Kgs 3:24, 25.
5. III 6.
6. Plutarch, *De fraterno amore* 483E.
7. In *Ball* v. *Ball*, 2 Simon 35 (1827), the spouses of a subsisting marriage lived
apart, the husband keeping the child and entertaining an adulterous union. The Vice-
Chancellor regretted his inability to help the mother. He said he was "nearly certain"—so
not absolutely certain, which is remarkable—that Lord Eldon in a similar case (except
that the estrangement was due to the husband's Catholicism) had refused the petition for
access.

may be imposed to attain a fair result—with what success, who can say?[8]

In antiquity, the party who is out is out; no legal guarantee of access, shared holidays or the like. Where there are several children, the problem may be mitigated if the law distributes them between the parents. Some laws do—a distribution according to sex is suggested to, and rejected by, the Roman Emperors Diocletian and Maximian (end of the third century A.D.); evidently, the custom was known in some corner of the Empire.[9] But many laws do not admit distribution, and in any case there may be only one child. Again, in some laws, a child below a certain age belongs to the mother, above that age to the father. In medieval Jewish law[10] a child belongs to the mother. But in the case of a son, once he is seven, the father may stop paying for his maintenance and thus, if she is poor, force her to hand him over. This is not, however, the kind of rotation which prevails in modern law. It simply means that at one point control may pass, for good, from one party to the other.

Why do we not find division in time—access or taking turns—in ancient systems? There are three reasons, interrelated, reinforcing one another. (One might think of a fourth, that children were less valued, but this would be fallacious.) First, in the absence of a developed apparatus of state, with means of investigation, communications and organs of enforcement, it would be too difficult to formulate or compel observance of such regulations. Secondly, ancient law is even more unwilling than modern to interfere in personal affairs; modern law looks away from struggles over a child during marriage, ancient law goes on looking away when the marriage has broken up. Thirdly, even during marriage in antiquity, that parent who is not in legal control no doubt receives less consideration than his modern counterpart. The enormous power of the head of family at Rome is proverbial—and he need not even be the father; if the father's father or grandfather is still alive, it is he who has control. As for Greece, Agamemnon sacrificed Iphigenia while he was married to her mother; nor, for that mat-

---

8. "'You're so stupid about children, Richard. They don't like being split,' said Molly." Lessing, *The Golden Notebook* (1962), 1.

9. Code 5.24 (A.D. 294); see Yaron, "Reichsrecht, Volksrecht and Talmud," *Revue internationale des droits de l'antiquité* 11 (1964), 296–98.

10. Maimonides, *Mishneh Torah*, Personal Status 21.17.

ter, did Abraham ask Sarah's permission when he set out to offer up Isaac. True, this is not the kind of thing that happened every day—in historical times, it would no longer be permitted—and writers like Aeschylus and Pindar represent Clytemnestra as deeply resentful.[11] Still, even in Plato's age, a father could expose, cast out, a new-born child, regardless of the mother's wishes.[12] Measured, then, by what people have to expect *constante matrimonio,* the situation *soluto matrimonio* is not so radically changed.

This third point goes far towards providing the answer to a further question that might be asked: granted it is not feasible for ancient law to assist the party who is out, why do we not come across more complaints or laments in general literature? As far as plays are concerned, the explanation is simple: divorced women do not appear on the Greek or Roman stage. This is no accident, but the subject cannot here be pursued. However, there would be ample room for exhibiting the plight of the forsaken parent in epic, history, moral essays, letters and so forth. That nothing of the sort occurs is accounted for by the harsh conditions during marriage, preparing the ground, so to speak, for those prevailing on divorce.

There is a tremendous exception: Medea. She is divorced, or about to be divorced, yet far from remaining confined to tales and poems, she is chosen as heroine by the greatest dramatists. Moreover, in Seneca, where she alone is exiled by King Creon, she pleads for time to bid her children a last farewell;[13] indeed, at one point she asks Jason, the father, to let her take them with her.[14] In Euripides, interestingly, Creon banishes her together with her children, so this ground of grievance does not arise (except for a moment, when the children are to be reprieved).

The case of Medea is hardly less extraordinary than that of Iphigenia.

11. See B. Daube, *Zu den Rechtsproblemen in Aischylos' Agamemnon* (1938), 159–66.

12. Plato, *Theaetetus* 151C.

13. E.g., Seneca, *Medea* 288–93 (ed. Miller, *Tragedies* [1918]).

14. Lines 541–43. The words *genetricem abstrahit natis,* 144–45, however, may express sorrow, not at her loss of the children, but at the latter's loss of their mother. Miller, taking *natis* as an ablative, equivalent to *a natis,* translates: "He (Creon) tears mothers from their children" (239). But *natis* may be a dative, *dativus incommodi.* The meaning may be: "He robs the children of their mother." Concern about the fate in store for the motherless children recurs, e.g., lines 282–83.

Even so, it definitely shows that the feelings were there. Only, most of the time, people put up with them, as they did with much other pain, without making a fuss. For the distress to come fully into the open, it needed outrageous circumstances like those depicted in this tragedy, with faithlessness, cruelty and hatred carried to extremes. Another conclusion is strongly suggested by this case. Authorities on ancient family law emphasize the financial obstacles in the way of divorce; say, a husband would have to return a substantial dowry. This is perfectly correct. But too little attention has perhaps been paid to the question of children. Surely, where the divorcing spouse would lose them—without the share he would normally be allotted by present-day law—that must act as a brake. As remarked above, medieval Jewish law assigns a child to the mother. Whatever may be the origin and intention of the rule, in a system which accords the husband an unfettered right to divorce his wife, and no corresponding right the other way round, the result must be to restore the balance somewhat.[15]

The idea of rotation as such is quite familiar to antiquity. Oedipus uttered a curse on his two sons, that they should divide their inheritance with the sword. In order to escape this doom, they agreed to take turns—year by year one would leave the country while the other ruled as king. Alas, it did not work.[16] From the beginning, the highest offices of the Roman Republic are each occupied by two colleagues—two consuls, two praetors—who take turns; at home, for instance, the two consuls of the year change every month, in the field every day.[17] Nor is the method restricted to the sharing of functions; it extends to objects and persons. Under Roman law, the owner of land on which water rises can give the right to it to two neighbors, for different times;[18] or again, if joint holders of a usufruct wish to divide it—and it might be a usufruct over a slave—it can be done by mutual guarantees

15. How such pressures work may be gathered from as early a Biblical code as the Mishpatim. Here it is considered as not unlikely that a slave, if on release he would have to leave his wife and children with his master, will prefer to remain a slave together with them (Exod 21:3–6), see D. Daube, *The Exodus Pattern in the Bible* (1963), 48 f. [BLL, 127–28].

16. E.g., Euripides, *Phoenissae.*

17. See Jolowicz, *Historical Introduction to Roman Law*, 2nd ed. (1952), 45.

18. Digest 10.3.19.4, Paul VI *ad Sabinum*; 43.20.5 pr., Julian IV *ex Minicio*.

for alternate turns.[19] The briefest mention may do for the strange *ménage à trois* carried on by Amphitryon, Jupiter and Alkmena. Two myths, however, involving the division of a child, deserve a closer look, though in neither is the child divided between the parents.

There is, first, the rape of Persephone by Hades. Her mother, Demeter, disconsolate, prevails on Zeus to order her restoration. However, anyone who has tasted food in the nether world must return there again. Accordingly, for some months of the year she dwells with her mother and for some with her husband: in the Homeric Hymns[20] she spends two thirds with the former, one third with the latter; according to Ovid[21] half the year with each. (Obviously, a version written at Berkeley would have sent her down for a fortnight in December at most.) It is conceivable that, at one of the many stages of this myth, the accent lay less on the collision between the right of the mother and the magic of the food than on that between the right of the mother and the right of him who, without complying with the requisite forms, has yet in fact made the daughter his wife. Ovid tends a little this way: "If you are bent on a separation," says Jupiter (Zeus) to Ceres (Demeter), and "if you are set on breaking the bonds of bed once contracted."[22] The ancient world knows the queerest gradations of *patria potestas* and wedlock. We need not even go outside Rome. To this day there is controversy as to the status, under the Twelve Tables,[23] of a woman lawfully united to a man without *confarreatio* or *coemptio* and—an interesting feature this, in the present context—leaving his home once every year for three nights (or, maybe, the three All Souls' Nights).[24] It would not be surprising if some of those who worked on the story of Persephone had been stimulated to a measure of legal or semi-legal speculation. In Ovid, it may be observed, Jupiter does act as "mediator," "arbitrator," *medius*.[25]

19. Digest 10.3.7.10, Ulpian XI *ad edictum*.

20. 2 (Hymn to Demeter) 400, 445–47, 463–65.

21. *Metamorphoses* 5.564–67; *Fasti* 4.613–14.

22. *Metamorphoses* 5.529–30 (*tanta cupido si tibi discidii est*); 4.602 (*statque semel iuncti rumpere vincla tori*).

23. VI 4.

24. See Jolowicz, *Historical Introduction*, 112–16, 549–50, Koschaker, in *ZRG, RA* 63 (1943), 447.

25. *Metamorphoses* 5.564.

So here a child is divided in time between mother and husband or abductor. Curiously, the child, Persephone, figures also in the second myth to be considered, this time as a claimant, a foster-mother unwilling to return her charge. Aphrodite, angry with Smyrna, causes her to fall in love with her father and become guilty of incest. The girl is turned into the myrrh-tree—*smyrna* in Greek and Latin. Adonis is born of it, and Aphrodite hides the beautiful boy from the gods in a chest and entrusts him to Persephone, in the underworld. Persephone takes to the boy herself and refuses to hand him back. (Considering his broken home background, it is astonishing he did as well in the end as he did.) The case is brought before Zeus who, according to Apollodorus, decrees that for one third of the year Adonis should stay by himself, for another third with Persephone and for another third with Aphrodite. Adonis at once, understandably, makes over his own share to the latter.[26] According to another version, probably of later origin, Zeus passes the case for decision to a lesser figure—the muse Calliope in Hyginus,[27] her son Orpheus in a papyrus.[28] In this account, half a year's possession is awarded to each of the two litigants; and Aphrodite, enraged at not obtaining sole enjoyment, takes vengeance by instilling into the Thracian women or the Maenads such frenzied love for Orpheus that they tear him to pieces. It will be noticed that as in the rape of Persephone, there is a shift from a year two-thirds happy and one-third unhappy to a year equally divided. How far this has to do with the calendars of different cults or regions, how far with varying climatic and agricultural experiences, may be left open.

This myth has distinct legal overtones. The dispute itself is less fantastic for early times than it looks today. Aphrodite saves a foundling, who may thereby turn into her slave, her foster-son or her adoptive son. The daughter of Pharoah did, it seems, adopt Moses: "And he became unto her a son."[29] But we know of many cases where this does not happen, and

26. Apollodorus, *Biblioteca* 3.14.4.
27. Hyginus, *Astronomica* 2.7. Of course Zeus here is Jupiter and Aphrodite is Venus.
28. Pap. Berlin 13426, brilliantly edited by Schubart, "Papyruskunde," *Einleitung in die Altertumswissenschaft* 1.9, 42–43, ed. Gercke and Norden (1924).
29. Exod 2:10.

besides, even adoption proper in antiquity can create a more or less tight relationship. Anyhow, Aphrodite immediately hands the child on to Persephone, who doubtless becomes a foster-mother. A foster-mother who does her duty may acquire strong rights to the child.[30] The case, then, is rather subtle: the foster-mother who has actually brought up the child defending her title against the woman—owner, first foster-mother or adoptive mother—from whom she received him.

Especially in the later version, the manner in which the dispute is handled is reminiscent of the Greek action of co-owners for partition, an action initiated before an officer of state and then decided by "distributors," *datetai*. Needless to say, the litigation over Adonis is so unusual that it would be ill-advised to use it for settling the various controversies regarding the action for partition: did the official appoint the "distributors" or did he request a court to do so?; was the action available to any co-owners or only to joint heirs?; was it available even where one of the parties denied the very existence of co-ownership, maintaining that he was the sole owner?[31] To solve these problems, we must still rely on the legal sources proper.

Perhaps the verdict in the myth establishes something like a joint usufruct, to be exercised in rotation. Or maybe it makes the competing women into a kind of co-owners, defining the precise extent of each one's share. In systems less rigidly analytical than the classical Roman, co-ownership with the parties alternately owning for a time would be quite feasible.[32] Nor would the grant of a third of the year to Adonis himself—this we find in the earlier version—necessarily conflict with this construction. He, too, is a co-owner; for that third he belongs to himself: in ancient law, to belong

30. For a first orientation, see Koschaker, "Adoption," in *Reallexikon der Vorgeschichte*, ed. Ebert (1924), 1.24–27.

31. See J. W. Jones, *The Law and Legal Theory of the Greeks* (1956), 210–12; Lipsius, *Das Attische Recht und Rechtsverfahren* (1912) 2.2, 576–77; Pappulias in *ZRG, RA* 26 (1905), 550–52.

32. On the institution of co-ownership in functional shares, see Koschaker, in *ZRG, RA* 58 (1938), 254–66; Koschaker, "Über einige griechische Rechtsurkunden aus den östlichen Randgebieten des Hellenismus," in *Abhandlungen der Sächsischen Akademie, Phil.-Hist. Klasse* 42 (1931–4), 46–48.

to oneself and to be free are often the same thing.[33] We may indeed detect here an allusion to *paramone*, "staying with the master." This is the designation of a widespread ancient Greek practice: a slave is freed and therefore belongs to himself, at the same time remaining bound to continued service and therefore belonging to his master. (A debtor or apprentice could be in a similar state of *paramone*).[34] Apollodorus employs the verb *menein para*, "to stay with," for the three parts of the year Adonis is "to stay with himself, with Persephone and with Aphrodite." Admittedly, *paramenein* would be even closer to *paramone*. Of course, the transfer of his share to Aphrodite spells the end of any pretensions on his part to independence.

The vengeance of the goddess in the later account is a beautiful example of punishment fitting the crime. She loves Adonis so much that to be given turns is a deep hurt. Orpheus now, through her doing, is loved by a horde of women so passionately that they will not contemplate a peaceful arrangement; they dismember him. The physical division instead of division in time, threatened by Solomon by way of bluff (and successfully avoided so far by the Beatles), is here translated into reality. If it is Orpheus' mother Calliope who rendered the offensive decision, the retribution is even more precise: she is being taught what it means to have to "share" a beloved child.

Both in the story of Persephone and that of Adonis, the parties laying claim to the child are thought of as making claims upon her or him at the same time. Already in the Homeric Hymns Hades exerts himself to win over Persephone,[35] and in some elaborations of the myth she actually prefers his company to her mother's.[36] Lucan goes very far: Persephone hates

---

33. For Greek law, see Koschaker, "Über einige griechische Rechtsurkunden," 47, 55, 74. According to *Mishnah Gittin* 9:3 the writ of emancipation of a slave-woman runs: "Lo, thou art a free woman, thou art unto thyself." In the bill of divorcement supplied by Maimonides, *Mishneh Torah*, Divorce 4.12, the following passage occurs: "That thou mayest be authorized and empowered over thyself, to go and be married to any man."

34. See Jones, *Law and Legal Theory*, 212–15; Berneker, "Paramone," in *Real Encyclopädie der Classischen Altertumswissenschaft*, 18.2 (1949), 1212–14; Koschaker, supra note 32, at 16–32.

35. 2 (Hymn to Demeter) 361–69.

36. Virgil, *Georgics* 1.39; Columella *De re rustica* 10.272–74.

her mother and loves her abductor with an unholy love;[37] and indeed, her mother, because of some terrible thing the daughter has undergone, does not want her back."[38] The latter feature is unique, and we are in ignorance of what is behind it. Lucan's own relation to his mother seems to have been miserable; this remains probable even if the horrid detail in his life recounted by Suetonius should be exaggerated or untrue.[39] As for Adonis, the earlier account of the myth represents Aphrodite as eminently successful in her dealings with him: he himself assigns his own third to her.

These two myths, it may be said, show the modern method of dividing a child hovering on the verge of materialization, like hope under the rim of Pandora's jar. Relatively little, one feels, would be needed to make it part of legal life. As it is, centuries had to pass before the courts were in a position to make practical use of the idea.

The writer would be happy if Professor Albert Ehrenzweig, *levem non aversatus honorem,* found these reflections of some interest.

37. *Pharsalia* 6.698, 740–41.

38. 6.741–42.

39. Orthodox opinion (see Anderson, "Lucan," in *Oxford Classical Dictionary* [1949], 514) rejects it as a fabrication, accepting the conclusions of Plessis who wrote at the beginning of the century in *La Poésie Latine* (1909), 547–49. But Plessis is highly speculative. For him, this detail is an invention of Nero: Lucan had pretended to be the Emperor's equal as a poet; let him live on in history, the Emperor decided, his equal as a monster of a son.

Did Macedo Murder His Father?

It is to be feared that he did.

I.

A *senatusconsultum* under Vespasian,[1] called *senatusconsultum Macedonianum*, provided that a man lending money to a *filiusfamilias* should have no action even after the father's death. During the latter's lifetime, enforcement of a claim against his son had always been barred by the general rules. This decree, in the case of money loans, refused an action even when the son had since become *sui iuris*.

The following texts comment on the reasons for, and aims of, the law.

1. Ulpian, in Digest 14.6.1 pr., records the words of the *senatusconsultum*.

> Cum inter ceteras sceleris causas Macedo,[2] quas illi natura administrabat, etiam aes alienum adhibuisset, et saepe materiam peccandi malis moribus praestaret qui pecuniam, ne quid amplius diceretur, incertis nominibus crederet; placere, ne cui qui filio familias mutuam pecuniam dedisset, etiam post mortem parentis eius cuius in potestate fuisset, actio petitioque daretur, ut scirent qui pessimo exemplo faenerarent nullius posse filii familias bonum nomen expectata patris morte fieri.

[*Zeitschrift der Savigny-Stiftung für Rechtsgeschichte, Romanistische Abteilung* 65 (1947), 261–311]

1. See, however, below, section VII, for an alternative date, slightly earlier.

2. On the curious position of this name in the Latin text (there is a hyperbaton, "Whereas to the other causes for his crime Macedo, which his nature furnished him, added also debts"), see below, section V.

Whereas Macedo, to the other causes for his crime, which his nature furnished him,[3] added also debts, and whereas he who, dispensing with detailed transactions, lends money under no specific business headings—or perhaps: and whereas he who, in order that no details should appear, lends money without entering the headings in his cash-book—is likely to drive such as indulge in vice to illicit courses; it has been decided that no one lending money to a *filiusfamilias* may be given any action even after the death of the parent in whose *potestas* he was, in order that the usurers who lead people astray shall know that no son's debt can be made good by waiting for his father's death.

One minor question may be discussed at the outset. Two possible translations are here given of *qui pecuniam, ne quid amplius diceretur, incertis nominibus crederet*, neither of them orthodox. The main thesis of this article is indeed unaffected if we keep to the traditional rendering, "he who, to say no more, lends money on dubious obligations),[4] where *incerta nomina* is taken as referring to obligations which offer the creditor little security, and *ne quid amplius diceretur* as implying that the senate, if it wanted, could be more outspoken about the practices of moneylenders. A point speaking in favour of this rendering is the use of *bonum nomen* towards the end of the fragment, in the sense of "a good claim": at first sight, this looks like being contrasted with *incerta nomina*.

None the less, the orthodox rendering is unsatisfactory. For one thing, *ne quid amplius diceretur* can hardly mean "to say no more," "to use no stronger terms." If that meaning were intended, one would expect *ne quid amplius dicatur*. The imperfect subjunctive suggests that the clause expresses, not an action or omission of the senate issuing the decree, but one of the usurer *qui crederet*, "who lends money." Nor does it seem possible to find any convincing alternative interpretation of *ne quid amplius diceretur* so long as we translate *qui incertis nominibus crederet* by "he who lends money on dubious obligations," "he who lends where there is little security." For another thing, the phrase *certis nominibus debere*, which occurs in Cicero *Pro Quinctio* 38, does not signify "to owe on good security"; and

---

3. On this notion of causes furnished by nature, see below, section V.
4. See Buckland, in Monro, *The Digest of Justinian* 2, ed. Buckland (1909), 407.

it is tempting to suppose that *incertis nominibus* in the *senatusconsultum Macedonianum*, ought to denote the opposite of *certis nominibus* in Cicero.

In *Pro Quinctio* 38, Cicero observes that his client's opponent waited for a year and a half before claiming a sum which, he now alleges, was owing *certis nominibus*. The phrase, when considered in its context, may mean either of two things. It may mean that the debt, in the other party's contention, was owing "as a result of clear, specific transactions"—so that his not suing at once cannot be due to the necessity of complicated investigations. Or it may mean that the debt, in the other party's contention, was owing "as entered in the creditor's ledger"[5]—and as such entries, if valid, impose an absolute obligation on the debtor, the hesitation to institute proceedings cannot be due to the necessity of elucidating the legal position.

If we proceed from this basis, *incertis nominibus* in the *senatusconsultum Macedonianum* must mean either "as a result of no specific transaction" or "without entries in the creditor's cash-book." In other words, the *senatusconsultum*, in the sentence under notice, may be expressing disapproval of the usurer who grants pure money loans, as opposed to an ordinary business man giving credit to, say, a buyer or hirer: "whereas he who, dispensing with detailed transactions, lends money under no specific business headings drives to illicit courses.[6]" Or it may be expressing disap-

---

5. The claim in dispute must have arisen either out of a partnership between the deceased brother of Cicero's client and the other party, or out of contracts concluded between the two independently of their partnership, or out of both; see *Pro Quinctio* 37 (and cp. 15), where Cicero denies any debt either *ex societatis ratione*, "on account of the partnership," or *privatim*, "on a private basis." It should be noted that, even if the ultimate origin of the debt lay in the partnership, a consensual contract giving a *bonae fidei iudicium*, there would be nothing surprising in its being claimed "as entered in the creditor's ledger." That debts incurred in the course of a partnership were not infrequently turned into "literal debts," debts resting on entry in the ledger, is attested by Gaius 3.129: *A re in personam transscriptio fit, veluti si id quod to ex emptionis causa aut conductionis aut societatis mihi debeas, id expensum tibi tulero*, "A literal obligation is made *a re in personam* where, for instance, I enter to your debit what you owe me on account of a purchase, hire or partnership."

6. If *ne quid amplius diceretur* were translatable by "to use no stronger term," we should get: "whereas he who lends money under—to use no stronger term—no specific headings." The sentence would then contain the additional implication that such general loans are used for immoral purposes. The stronger term that the senate could have put

proval of a usurer who, in order to keep his dealings with the *filiusfamilias* secret, does not put them down in his ledger: "whereas he who, in order that no details should appear, lends money without entering the headings in his cash-book drives to illicit courses."

Either of these two interpretations treats *ne quid amplius diceretur* as having regard to an action of the usurer, not of the senate. The former interpretation receives support from a point to which we shall return: the *senatusconsultum Macedonianum* was in fact directed solely against pure money loans to *filiifamilias*, not other transactions on credit. For the latter, one might adduce a passage like *Pro Quinto Roscio Comoedo* 9, from which it appears that people did omit from their cash-books such headings as they wished to remain private. *Nolebas sciri debere tini Roscium*, "You did not want it to be known that Roscius was indebted to you?"—Cicero ironically asks the party who demands payment of a debt from his client without being able to shew a proper entry in his ledger. One or the other of these renderings is probably correct. But it may be repeated that the thesis to be submitted is not dependent on them; it remains valid even if the orthodox translation should be preferred.

2. The essential tendency of the enactment is noted by Suetonius, in his *Life of Vespasian* 11.

> Libido atque luxuria coercente nullo invaluerat. auctor senatui fuit decernendi, ut quae se alieno servo iunxisset ancilla haberetur; neve filiorum familiarum faeneratoribus exigendi crediti ius umquam esset, hoc est, ne post patrum quidem mortem.

> Wantonness and revelry, as no one had taken measures against them, had assumed larger dimensions. Vespasian proposed the *senatusconsulta* that a freewoman cohabiting with another person's slave should herself be considered a slave; and that those who lent money to *filiifamilias* should never become entitled to exact the debt, that is to say, not even after the fathers' death.

---

might be something like *turpibus nominibus* instead of *incertis nominibus*, "he who lends money for disgraceful ends." However, as remarked above, it is highly doubtful whether *ne quid amplius diceretur*, with the imperfect subjunctive, may be taken in this way.

3. In Digest 14.6.3.3, Ulpian comes back to the idea underlying the *senatusconsultum*. He explains that debts incurred by a *filiusfamilias* in the course of ordinary dealings, i.e. dealings not pure money loans, do not fall under the ban—because that is not the sort of thing to be feared.

> Is autem solus senatus consultum offendit qui mutuam pecuniam filio familias dedit, non qui alias contraxit, puta vendidit locavit vel alio modo contraxit: nam pecuniae datio perniciosa parentibus eorum visa est.

> But he alone transgresses the *senatusconsultum* who lends money to a *filiusfamilias*, not he who transacts any other business with him, e.g. he who sells or lets to him or otherwise enters into business with him: for it is the lending of money that has been held dangerous to their fathers.

4. From Marcian also we hear about the point of the law. He says, in Digest 12.6.40 pr., that if a *filiusfamilias* borrows money and, in ignorance of the defence granted by the *senatusconsultum* (or more precisely, of those circumstances on account of which the case comes under the *senatusconsultum*),[7] repays if after having become *sui iuris*, he cannot claim it back. This is a most remarkable provision. We know indeed that deliberate ratification of the old debt by one who had become a *paterfamilias*—ratification, that is, in full knowledge of the facts—was permissible. (Code 4.28.2, e.g., of A.D. 198, says: *Zenodorus cum... suae potestatis constitutus... agnovit debitum, non esse locum decreto amplissimi ordinis rationis est*, "If Zenodorus acknowledged the debt after becoming *sui iuris*, the logical decision is that the *senatusconsultum* should not apply.") But the rule discussed goes much further: there is to be no *condictio*, no recovery, even if the old debt has been settled in ignorance of the defence. The rea-

---

7. If his error is entirely one of law, a *condictio* is probably excluded by more general principles; see Buckland, *A Text-Book of Roman Law*, 2nd ed. (1932), 542. The question is not relevant to the argument of this article. What is alone relevant is the fact that, according to Marcian (and others to be quoted presently), there were cases of payment in error—no matter what was their exact nature—where, normally, a *condictio* would lie, but none lay if it was payment by one who had borrowed while a *filiusfamilias* and now was *sui iuris*.

son, Marcian says, is that the law is intended to deny the moneylender an action for the debt, but not to help the borrower.

Qui exceptionem perpetuam habet, solutum per errorem repetere potest: sed hoc non est perpetuum. nam si quidem eius causa exceptio datur cum quo agitur, solutum repetere potest, ut accidit in senatus consulto de intercessionibus: ubi vero in odium eius cui debetur exceptio datur, perperam solutum non repetitur, veluti si filius familias contra Macedonianum mutuam pecuniam acceperit et pater familias factus solverit, non repetit.

He to whom a perpetual *exceptio* is available may reclaim what he has paid in error. But this is not always true.[8] For if indeed an *exceptio* is granted in the interest of the defendant, he may reclaim what he has paid in error, as is the case under the *senatusconsultum Velleianum* (forbidding women to make themselves liable for others, by way of surety, for example). But where an *exceptio* is granted to thwart[9] the creditor, what has been paid in error cannot be reclaimed; for instance, if a *filiusfamilias*, contrary to the *senatusconsultum Macedonianum*, has borrowed money and, after becoming a *paterfamilias*, has repaid it, he cannot claim it back."

5. Pomponius doubtless has the same case in mind in Digest 12.6.19 pr.

Si poenae causa eius cui debetur debitor liberatus est, naturalis obligatio manet et ideo solutum repeti non potest.

If it is in order to penalise the creditor that the law releases the debtor, a natural obligation remains and, therefore, what has been paid in

---

8.   The clause *sed hoc non est perpetuum* is declared spurious by several writers who think it must mean "but this *exceptio* is not perpetual"; see, e.g., Siber, *Naturalis Obligatio* in *Gedenkschrift für Ludwig Mitteis verfaßt von Mitgliedern der Leipziger Juristen-Fakultät* (1926), 55. Even if this were correct, it would not affect the gist of the fragment. In point of fact, however, the words simply mean "but this is not always true," "but not in every case"; they are used in exactly the same sense in Gauis 1.200.

9.   On this use of *in odium*, a few words will be said below, section V. Monro, in *The Digest of Justinian* 2, ed. Buckland (1909), 320, has "to punish," which is equally possible, though perhaps a little too strong and straightforward to serve as an accurate equivalent of the Latin phrase.

error cannot be reclaimed.[10]

6. A brief remark about the motives of the senate in enacting the *senatusconsultum Macedonianum* is made by Justinian in Institutes 4.7.7.

Quae ideo senatus prospexit quia saepe onerati sere alieno creditarum pecuniarum, quas in luxuriam consumebant, vitae parentium insidiabantur.

The senate laid this down for the reason that frequently those who were burdened with debts contracted by borrowing money, which they wasted in revelry, tried to take their parents' lives.

7. It is, however, in Theophilus's paraphrase on this text that we find an exact description of the immediate occasion of the *senatusconsultum*.

Μακέδων τις οὕτω λεγόμενος γέγονεν ἐν τῇ ῾Ρώμῃ. ὑπεξούσιος ὢν τῷ οἰκείῳ πατρὶ ἐδανείσατο παρά τινος, ἐλπίζων ὅτι τελευτήσαντος αὐτοῦ τοῦ πατρὸς δυνήσεται τὸ χρέος ἀποδιδόναι. πολλοῦ χρόνου διαδραμόντος, ὁ δανειστὴς ἐπέκειτο τὸ χρέος ἀπαιτῶν. ὁ Μακέδον οὐκ ἔχων πόθεν ἀποδῷ (πῶς γὰρ ὑπεξούσιος ὤν;) ἀνῖλε τὸν ἑαυτοῦ πατέρα. ἐγνώθη τοῦτο τῇ συγκλήτῳ κἀκεῖνος μὲν δίνας δέδωκε πατροκτονίας δόγμα δὲ λεγόμενον Μακεδωνιανιον γέγονε.

There lived at Rome one called Macedo. When still in *patria potestas*, he borrowed money from somebody, hoping that after his father's death he would be able to repay the debt. As time dragged on, the creditor pressed him hard, demanding his debt. Macedo had nothing wherewith to pay—how could he, being in *potestas*? So he killed his father. The matter was brought before the senate: Macedo suffered the penalties of *parricidium*, and the *senatusconsultum* called *Macedonianum* was made.

When these statements are put together, the following picture emerg-

10. There is a third text setting forth this aspect of the *senatusconsultum Macedonianum*, namely, Digest 14.6.9.4, from Ulpian. But the fragment is not free from serious corruption, and has given rise to much controversy; see Siber, op. cit., 55 f. It is not necessary for the present purpose to go into this text.

es: For a considerable time before the *senatusconsultum Macedonianum*, the situation had been unsatisfactory. A moneylender knew, of course, that he could not effectively sue a *filiusfamilias* while his father was alive. If he lent money to a *filiusfamilias* nevertheless, he did not do so from charity. It is safe to assume that he not only charged an exorbitant rate of interest, but also saw to it that, somehow or other, he did obtain certain guarantees of repayment within a reasonable period. A son who had no property of his own could still get hold of, and make away with, his father's jewels. This is the kind of illicit course to which the *senatusconsultum* alludes, and which, indeed, we know from the Roman comedy. Moreover, it was inevitable that the parties to such a loan should often look forward to the father's death as a welcome event: it was the father who stood between the *filiusfamilias* and his inheritance and freedom, and between the moneylender and an unhampered prosecution of his claim.

Things were brought to a head by the deed of a *filiusfamilias* of the name of Macedo, who, when his father proved long-lived and his creditor became troublesome, murdered the former. The senate now decreed that loans to *filiifamilias* should never be actionable, not even when a *filiusfamilias* became independent on his father's death. This was a radical but effective stroke. In the first place, it was bound to make loans to *filiifamilias* highly unpopular with usurers: a usurer would think twice before parting with money which, it must be quite clear to him, the law would never assist him to recover. In the second place, a usurer who still took the risk at least would no longer harass the *filiusfamilias* so mercilessly that parricide was the only way out. For, from now, the father's death did not improve the creditor's position; it did not, as it had done before, give him a sanction to his claim. Rather it weakened it, inasmuch as his debtor acquired greater freedom generally.

So far, then, Macedo does not seem to have a chance. The sources declare him guilty of a heinous crime.

II.

Yet his defence has been conducted with such skill that, by this time, some authorities regard him as entirely innocent, while others at least deny that he committed parricide: if murder there was, they say, it was not of his father. Let us survey the arguments.

Beseler is the great advocate of Macedo's acquittal. According to him, the account given by Theophilus is "a silly Byzantine legend,"[11] and that part of Digest 14.6.3.3 which appears to support this account (to wit, *nam pecuniae datio perniciosa parentibus eorum visa est,* "for it is the lending of money that has been held dangerous to their fathers") is spurious. If—thus Beseler reasons—Macedo had been pressed by his creditor, as Theophilus would have us believe, it would have caused him, not to kill his father, but, on the contrary, to wish his father a very long life, since it was precisely during his father's lifetime that he was safe from an enforcement of the claim. A *filiusfamilias* could be effectively sued only after his father's death: why should Macedo have brought about just that position, the most unfavorable to him?

There is, however, in Beseler's view, a second, even stronger consideration against adopting the version of Theophilus. Supposing, he says, it were true that Macedo murdered his father in order to come into property of his own, the *senatusconsultum Macedonianum* would have been the least intelligent method of preventing a repetition of such a crime. In fact, Beseler urges, it would have rendered this crime more instead of less frequent. Before the *senatusconsultum,* a *filiusfamilias* who wanted money could go to the moneylenders and, so long as he had not absolutely exhausted their goodwill, there was no need for him to kill his father. After the *senatusconsultum,* hardly any credit would be given to a *filiusfamilias,* and a *filiusfamilias* who wanted money must now kill his father at once. Evidently, Beseler concludes, the protection of the latter's life cannot have been among the objects of this enactment. This aspect was not considered at all. There had been no such thing as a parricide, for had there been, the senate would have made loans to *filiifamilias* easier, not more difficult.

What, then, was Macedo's true role? That a person of this name did exist, and that some act of his did play a part in the deliberations of the

---

11. See *Beiträge zur Kritik der römischen Rechtsquellen* 4 (1920), 130 f.: "eine alberne byzantinische Legende."

senate, is not denied by anyone. The *senatusconsultum* itself, preserved
in Digest 14.6.1 pr., mentions his offence as having led to the new regulation and the designation *Macedonianum* is indisputably classical (Digest
14.6.1 pr., for instance, begins: *Verba senatus consulti Macedoniani haec
sunt*, "These are the words of the *senatusconsultum Macedonianum*").
Connected with this question is the other: What was the real purpose of the
senatusconsultum, if it was not, as the sources tell us, to remove the basis
for those underhand dealings and crimes—chief among them elimination
of an inconvenient father—so often resulting from loans to *filiifamilias?*

Beseler's solution is that Macedo was simply a *filiusfamilias* borrowing and spending a great deal of money. But he perpetrated no real crime
whatever. True, the *senatusconsultum* says that he did. This statement,
however, Beseler argues, ought not to be taken too seriously. His "crime"
consisted in nothing worse than his unfilial attitude of mind: a loving son,
the senate gave the public to understand, would not contract a debt which
he and the creditor were both aware would become fully operative only on
his father's death.. This calculating contemplation of his good father's future death, in Beseler's opinion, was Macedo's whole "crime." Nor, Beseler
goes on to say, was the senate at all worried by this side of the matter. It was
a very different idea which governed the *senatusconsultum Macedonianum*:
its true object, Beseler holds, was to protect a *filiusfamilias* against his own
improvidence. A *filiusfamilias*, in his own interest, should no longer be in
a position to waste his inheritance even before he had it, and any who provided him with the means of doing so should suffer for it.

There is no dearth of other theories about the real Macedo. Mitteis,
in his revision of Sohm's *Institutionen*,[12] remarks, that he cannot have been
quite so blameless as Beseler thinks. If he had merely shewn himself lacking in good feeling, the senate would not have spoken of *scelus*, "a crime,"
and, indeed, the decree would not have been called after him. On the other
hand, Mitteis inclines to agree with Beseler that Theophilus's· story must
be apocryphal: the *senatusconsultum* can hardly have been intended to
stop sons from scheming against the lives of their fathers, and, consequently, Macedo's offence, in view of which the enactment was made, can

12. See 17th ed. by Wenger (1923), 393 n. 1.

hardly have consisted in murdering his father. Mitteis, therefore, suggests that Macedo may have been a *filiusfamilias* who, when he had borrowed more money than he could repay, killed—not his father—but either some wealthy person who had nothing to do with his loans at all or, perhaps, his creditor, the usurer, himself. To prevent this from happening again, the rules against loans were enacted.

A still further conjecture seems to enjoy some popularity. Once we give up the account of Theophilus as impossible, it has been argued, there is no reason why we should stick to any of its details. Above all, there is no reason why we should continue ascribing to Macedo the status of a *filius-familias*, or more particularly, that of a *filiusfamilias* in debt. Quite likely, this argument goes on, the Macedo who is stigmatized as a criminal in the *senatusconsultum* was the very opposite of such a *filiusfamilias*: he was, in fact, a moneylender who committed some wrong be it murder, intimidation, a monetary delict or any other wickedness.[13] On the basis of this view, that is, Beseler is right in rejecting the "silly Byzantine legend." Only he is too conservative as to the position of Macedo. Macedo, in spite of what the sources report, was not a *filiusfamilias* at all, he was a usurer whose misconduct precipitated the intervention of the senate.

Regarding the intention of the decree, the followers of this theory share Beseler's opinion that it was not to put an end to unlawful dealings or even murder. It may have been, as Beseler assumes, to guard sons from their own carelessness. But, possibly, the original object of the *senatusconsultum* was yet narrower, more technical: namely, to exclude the *actio de peculio* against the father. Before this enactment, though a son could not be effectively sued while in *patria potestas*, the father himself, where he had entrusted his son with a separate fund, a *peculium*, was liable on his son's contracts to the extent of that fund. The jurists—as we know from several texts (e.g. Code 4.28.6 pr.; of A.D. 245: *Si filius tuus in potestate tua agens contra senatus consultum Macedonianum mutuam sumpsit pecuniam, actio de peculio adversus te eo nomine efficaciter dirigi nequaquam potest*, "If your son, in your *potestas*, raised a loan contrary to the *senatusconsultum Macedonianum*, an *actio de peculio* can by no means be effectively

---

13. *Deus sum, commutavero* might be the proud motto of this proposition.

brought against you on that account")—decided that, under the regime of the *senatusconsultum*, a man who lent money to a *filiusfamilias* with a *peculium* should not be entitled to bring the *actio de peculio*. It is this refusal of the *actio de peculio* against the father which some of those who say that Macedo was a usurer assert to have been the true object of the *senatusconsultum Macedonianum*.

It may be noted that Professor Buckland, both in his *Manual*[14] and in his *Text-Book*,[15] looks upon Macedo as a usurer. Indeed, he does not even mention—a most unusual omission with him—that there might be grave doubts, and that the texts offer an entirely different version. In his *Manual*, he says that the *senatusconsultum* was "enacted as the result of the proceedings of a certain usurer, Macedo"; and in his *Text-Book*, that it was "named, it seems, after the person whose malpractices led to its enactment"—obviously again meaning the moneylender, not the *filiusfamilias* who had borrowed from him. As for the meaning of the law, he favors different theories in the *Manual* and *Text-Book*. In the former, he describes the law as "aimed at thriftless young men 'with expectations' and those who took advantage of them"; while according to the latter, it is the exclusion of the *actio de peculio* which "was probably its primary purpose."

By now, it looks as if for some fourteen hundred years Roman lawyers had been too hard on Macedo. He was no parricide. And the only question still open is whether he was a thoroughly law-abiding, though somewhat selfish, young man; or a young man who, encumbered with debts, killed a rich person or, maybe, his creditor; or a moneylender of a disagreeable sort.

III.

The vindication of Theophilus's description of the affair may be conveniently divided into two parts. In the present section, it is proposed to shew that the alternatives substituted for his account are untenable; and in the next three sections, that his account is so probable that "s'il n'existait pas,

14. See 2nd ed. (1939), 273 f.
15. See 2nd ed. (1932), 465.

il faudrait l'inventer."

The alternatives offered, it is submitted, are untenable. To begin with, with one exception, they do not fit the text of the *senatusconsultum*, the exception being the theory sponsored by Mitteis, to which, as will be shewn below, there are fatal objections on other grounds. Surely, that an explanation of the occasion and tendency of the decree should not conflict with its very words is the minimum requirement which ought to be satisfied.

Beseler holds that Macedo did no serious harm. But the *senatusconsultum* uses *scelus*, a strong expression. As remarked above, Mitteis boggles at this, even though disposed to accept Beseler's main thesis. Beseler further contends that Macedo's only "crime" was to borrow money on the—unfilial—understanding that it should be repayable after his father's death. But the *senatusconsultum* says that *inter ceteras sceleris causas... etiam aes alienum adhibuisset*, "to other causes for his crime he added also debts." This means that his debts were among the causes, the motives, for his crime; and it follows that they were not the crime itself. Whatever that crime may have been, it must have been something resulting from his borrowing, it cannot have been the mere borrowing as such. Again, Beseler asserts that Macedo's behavior, and similar occurrences, did not worry the senate at all: it was a different consideration—the protection of youth against thoughtless expenditure—that led to the enactment. But the *senatusconsultum* says, *Cum... Macedo aes alienum adhibuisset, et saepe materiam peccandi praestaret qui pecuniam... crederet, placere*, "Since Macedo added his debts, and he that lends money is likely to drive to illicit courses, it has been decided." There is here an unambiguous causal *cum*. The affair of Macedo and frequent experiences of the same kind—though presumably less dreadful—are represented as the direct cause of the senate's action. Obviously, Beseler's theory would make the *senatusconsultum* utterly untranslatable.

Professor Buckland, both in his *Manual* and *Text-Book*, adopts the standpoint of those who believe Macedo to have been a wicked moneylender. But the *senatusconsultum* says that *aes alienum adhibuisset*, "he added debts," sc. to the other causes for his crime. The point to be noted about this is that *aes alienum*, literally, "another man's money," means "debt" only in the sense of "a debt which I owe" (since only in this case have I taken "another man's money"), never in the sense of "a debt which is owing to me." The debts which were among the causes for Macedo's crime must, therefore, have been debts which he had incurred, not debts which he wished to exact. In other words, he was the debtor in that affair, not the creditor, not the moneylender. To take him as the latter is to turn the phrase used by the text into its opposite.[16]

Nor does the text warrant the theory, quoted with approval in the *Text-Book*, that the primary object of the *senatusconsultum* was to bar the *actio de peculio* which, otherwise, would have lain against a father where he had given his son a separate fund to manage. The words of the decree are *ne cui qui filio familias mutuam pecuniam dedisset, etiam post mortem parentis..., actio petitioque daretur*, "that no one lending money to a *filiusfamilias* may be given any action even after the death of his parent"; and again, *ut scirent... nullius posse filii familias bonum nomen expectata patris morte fieri*, "in order that they shall know that no son's debt can become good by waiting for his father's death." It could not be expressed more clearly that the chief effect of the decree was meant to be the refusal of an action even when the son became independent. A father's death, it was laid down, should not render the debt enforceable; a man lending money to a *filiusfamilias* should never have a good claim. This is what we learn direct from the text of the enactment. If we substitute exclusion of the *actio de peculio* as the gist of the measure—which would make it very much tamer not only in its actual effect but also as regards its range of application, since, after all, only a certain number of *familias* had *peculia*—we must also invent another text.

Even apart from the actual words of the *senatusconsultum*, however, the whole tenor of its regulation and the whole trend of what we hear about it from the Roman writers are incompatible with the doctrines put forward by the critics of Theophilus. As we have seen, Beseler and Professor Buckland in his *Manual* maintain that the *senatusconsultum* contemplated the welfare of lighthearted youngsters: they were to be kept from squandering

16. Curiously, in his translation of Digest 14.6.1 pr. (in Monro, *Digest of Justinian* 2 [1909], 407), made twelve years before the first edition of his *Text-Book*, Professor Buckland interprets *aes alienum* perfectly accurately: "whereas Macedo, to the other causes..., added also indebtedness." Here Macedo is clearly the debtor.

beforehand their future possessions. It was, as Professor Buckland puts it, "aimed at thriftless young men."

But in a fragment already quoted, Digest 12.6.40 pr., from Marcian (and Digest 12.6.19 pr., from Pomponius, confirms his point), we are told in so many words that the lawgiver had not intervened in the interest of the borrowers. More than that, the fact is stated as the reason for the rule that a *filiusfamilias* who by mistake repays a loan after reaching independence will not be able to recover the money.

> Si quidem eius causa exceptio datur cum quo agitur, solutum repetere potest... ubi vero in odium eius cui debetur exceptio datur, perperam solutum non repetitur, veluti si filius familias contra Macedonianum mutuam pecuniam acceperit et pater familias factus solverit, non repetit.

> If indeed an *exceptio* is granted in the interest of the defendant, he may reclaim what he has paid in error. But where an *exceptio* is granted to thwart the creditor, what has been paid in error cannot be reclaimed; for instance, if a *filiusfamilias*, contrary to the *senatusconsultum Macedonianum*, has borrowed money and, after becoming a *paterfamilias*, has repaid it, he cannot claim it back.

Had the senate meant to safeguard the "expectations" of a *filiusfamilias*, this rule would be absurd. Why, once we assume that intention, should the law refuse its help to one who, having become a *paterfamilias*, repays an old loan in ignorance of his defence (or rather, of circumstances entitling him to this *exceptio*?)[17] Is there anything making this case less worthy of protection than others? That a deliberate acknowledgment of his old debt by one who has attained independence should be valid and irrevocable is one thing: that might be reconcilable with the interpretation of the decree as in the interest of the careless young. But the rule here in question does not contemplate a deliberate acknowledgment. It contemplates the case of a man who repays the old loan unaware of the fact that he need not do so. Why may he not demand restoration when he discovers his mistake? The only possible solution is to accept as correct Marcian's (and

---

17. Where repayment takes place as a result of a mistake of law, *condictio* is probably excluded on more general grounds: see above, n. 7.

Pomponius's) express information that the welfare of the borrower was not the object of this law.[18]

The chief error underlying the opposite view is a confusion—a not uncommon one in several fields—of *filiifamilias* and young men, two very different classes of the population. A *filiusfamilias*—and he alone fell under the decree—might well be sixty years of age and a consul. Had the senate approached the question from the angle suggested, had it intended to defend youth against its own thoughtlessness, the way would have been to legislate, not about *filiifamilias*, but about persons, *filiifamilias* or *sui iuris*, below a specified age. But this was not what the senate did. It singled out *filiifamilias*, of whatever age.

Nor did the lawyers hesitate to draw the consequences. According to Ulpian, in Digest 14.6.3.4, if a *filiusfamilias* promised repayment of a loan before actually receiving the money, and by the time that he actually received it had become *sui iuris*, the *senatusconsultum* did not apply: the final, decisive lending was to a *paterfamilias*. Again, Scaevola, in Digest 14.6.6, tells us that if a person *sui iuris* promised to repay a loan before actually receiving the money, and by the time he actually received it had become a *filiusfamilias* through *adrogatio*, adoption, the *senatusconsultum* did apply: the final lending was to a *filiusfamilias*.

> Si a filio familias stipulatus sim et patri familias facto crediderim..., debet dici cessare senatus consultum.

> If I received a promise of repayment from a *filiusfamilias* but lent him the money when he had become a *paterfamilias*, it is right to hold that the *senatusconsultum* does not apply.

> Contra etiam recte dicitur, si a patre familias stipulatus sis, credas postea filio familias facto, senatus potestatem exercendam.

> Conversely, it is rightly held that if you received a promise of repayment from a *paterfamilias* but lend him the money when he has become a *filiusfamilias*, the senate's authority is to be exercised.

In the first case, all arrangements for the loan were made while the bor-

---

18. For details concerning the true place of the rule under notice, see below, section V.

rower was still a *filiusfamilias*. Why should they become less thoughtless by his subsequent change of status? But the second case is even more striking. All arrangements were made while the borrower was a *paterfamilias*—and consequently, on the basis of the view here combated, of a cautious disposition. Why, then, should they come under the ban merely because of *adrogatio* before receipt of the money? He is older, not younger, now than when he made the original arrangements. The truth is that we cannot understand the *senatusconsultum Macedonianum* if we take it as enacted for the good of the young. Young and *filiusfamilias* are not the same.

As a matter of fact, there are indications that people did feel that the decree was a little hard on a *filiusfamilias* grey-haired and a prominent statesman. Apparently they asked the jurists whether no concessions were here possible. But the answer was in the negative: even in such a case, the jurists replied, a man lending money to a *filiusfamilias* would never be entitled to an action—in other words, even in such a case, loans must be prevented. Ulpian says in Digest 14.6.1.3:

> In filio familias nihil dignitas facit quominus senatus consultum Macedonianum locum habeat: nam etiamsi consul sit vel cuiusvis dignitatis, senatus consulto locus est.

> So long as a man is a *filiusfamilias*, rank by no means excludes the application of the *senatusconsultum Macedonianum*. For even if he be consul or of any conceivable rank, the *senatusconsultum* will apply.

Clearly, this decree was concerned with *filiifamilias* as *filiifamilias*, not with the young and careless.

There is a further point telling strongly against the assumption that the *senatusconsultum* was designed to preserve intact a son's prospective wealth. It is that only pure money loans came under the ban, no other dealings. A *filiusfamilias* could still, for example, buy whatever he liked on credit, that is to say, the seller's claim would be enforceable against him after his father's death. The *senatusconsultum* did not interfere with such a transaction, provided, of course, that it was not a mere mask, a dodge to evade the ban. Indeed, a *filiusfamilias* might even become a surety for a loan given to another person. Here, too, on his father's death, he would be fully liable (except, again, in the case of fraud on the *senatusconsultum*):

it was a matter, not of a pure money loan, but of standing surety. Digest 14.6.3.3 has already been quoted. The relevant section is:

> Is autem solus senatus consultum offendit qui mutuam pecuniam filio familias dedit, non qui alias contraxit, puta vendidit, locavit.

> But he alone transgresses the *senatusconsultum* who lends money to a *filiusfamilias*, not he who transacts any other business with him, e.g. he who sells or lets to him.

To this may be added Code 4.28.3, of A.D. 198:

> Si filius familias aliquid mercatus pretium stipulanti venditori cum usurarum accessions spondeat, non esse locum senatus consulto, quo faenerare filiis familias prohibitum est, nemini dubium est: origo enim potius obligationis quam titulus actionis considerandum est.

> If a *filiusfamilias*, buying something (on credit), promises the vendor the price and, in addition, interest as well, nobody doubts that the *senatusconsultum* by which loans to *filiifamilias* are forbidden does not apply: for the origin of the obligation (in this case, a purchase on credit—which is permitted) is decisive rather than the form of action (in this case, the same that would fit a pure money loan).

There is further Digest 14.6.7 pr., again from Ulpian:

> Item si filius familias fideiusserit, Neratius...cessare senatus consultum ait.

> Again, if a *filiusfamilias* becomes surety by *fideiussio*, Neratius says that the *senatusconsultum* does not apply.

In fact, the limitation of the ban to pure money loans is contained in the very text of the decree, which withdraws the aid of the law from him *qui filio familias mutuam pecuniam dedisset*, "who has lent money to a *filiusfamilias*." There is no reference to other transactions on credit: *mutua pecunia*, "money advanced," alone is mentioned. We saw that, quite conceivably, it is with this limitation that we have to connect also one of the reasons set forth by the lawgiver for the decree, namely, the evil influence of a man *qui pecuniam, ne quid amplius diceretur, incertis nominibus crederet.* This may well be a condemnation of one "who, dispensing with detailed transactions, lends money under no specific business headings"— though, indeed, as pointed out at the beginning of this study, there is another possible interpretation of the sentence.

The *senatusconsultum*, then, was not directed against, say, the keeping by a *filiusfamilias* of any number of horses or gladiators bought on credit, or his breakfasting every morning on nightingales equally unpaid for. Similarly, it was not directed against a *filiusfamilias* making himself responsible, as surety, for a prodigal friend's debts, however enormous those debts might be. Would this be so if the decree had been laid down in the interest of improvident young men?

In his *Text-Book*, Professor Buckland subscribes to the doctrine that the primary object of the *senatusconsultum* was refusal of the *actio de peculio* against the father. That this cannot be reconciled with the text of the decree was pointed out above. Here three considerations may be added.

First, the text of the decree, in just this respect, is borne out by evidence from lay literature. Suetonius, in the passage already cited, regards as the gist of the law, not the exclusion of the *actio de peculio* (which he does not mention at all), but the exclusion of an action against the son after he has reached independence. The senate, he tells us, ordained *neve filiorum familiarum faeneratoribus exigendi crediti ius umquam esset, hoc est, ne post patrum quidem mortem*, "that those lending money to *filiifamilias* should never be entitled to reclaim it, that is to say, not even after the father's death." There is also the testimony of Tacitus, *Annals* 11.13.2, concerning a similar, earlier step taken by Claudius:[19]

> Et lege lata saevitiam creditorum coercuit, ne in mortem parentum pecunias filiis familiarum darent.

> And by means of a law he checked the ruthlessness of creditors, restraining them from making loans to a *filiusfamilias* recoverable at the father's death.

It is always the action against the son on his becoming *sui iuris*, never

---

19. Maybe it was not a similar earlier step, but the *senatusconsultum Macedonianum* itself. On this possibility, see below, section VII.

the *actio de peculio* against the father, to bar which appears as the principal aim of the legislator.

Secondly, passing to the treatment of the *senatusconsultum* by the jurists, we do not find a single text that attaches superior importance to the exclusion of the *actio de peculio*. There is not the faintest sign that, in the original conception of the senate, the decree was limited to the case where a father had confided to his son a separate fund, a *peculium*; not the faintest sign that, in the original conception, a moneylender might hope to acquire a sanction to his claim through the father's death. The contrary is true. The absence of a sanction even where the son had become *sui iuris* is the prominent feature of this regulation throughout.

Thirdly, one of the objections to be raised against the view that the decree was designed to benefit lighthearted youth is valid also against the view that it was chiefly intended to bar the *actio de peculio*. Why, if the senate's main object was to give the father a defence against this action, was the ban restricted to pure money loans? Why did it not apply to purchase on credit of horses and gladiators? It is difficult to think of a convincing answer.

The attitude of Mitteis is very curious. It was said above that he alone of those who disbelieve Theophilus has taken care to bring his version of what happened into harmony with the text of the *senatusconsultum*. But he pays a high price for it. For his version is open to the very attacks that have been levelled against that of Theophilus—and to one or two more. In fact, his procedure is illustrative of the not infrequent phenomenon of a critical theory perpetuating itself even when its *raison d'être* has been lost sight of.

Mitteis thinks there is something to be said for Beseler's thesis that Macedo—whom they both admit to have been a *filiusfamilias* in financial distress—cannot have murdered his father: why should he have done so, seeing that he was safe from his creditors precisely while his father lived?, and if he had done so in order to get money of his own, would the senate have reacted by putting new obstacles in the way of loans to *filiifamilias*, which must increase the likelihood of desperate deeds? On the other hand, says Mitteis, contrary to what Beseler maintains, it is evident that Macedo did commit a grave offence, otherwise the *senatusconsultum* would not have called it a *scelus*, "a crime." It follows, in Mitteis's view, that Macedo probably killed a rich person not his father, maybe the usurer himself. But, clearly, we may now ask the same questions which render Theophilus's account so impossible in the eyes of his critics: Why should Macedo have killed anybody, even if it was not his father, since he did not have to trouble about his creditors? And had he killed a third party in order to get free money, money not under his father's control, would the senate have reacted by imposing fresh restrictions on loans to *filiifamilias*, thus increasing the likelihood of such desperate acts? As Mitteis is unable to follow Beseler all the way because of the term *scelus*, and as his compromise involves exactly the same difficulties as the story given in the sources, one would have thought he might have found it simplest to put up with the latter.

As a matter of fact, Mitteis's conjecture suffers from a flaw which is certainly not present in the story as offered in the texts: his conjecture does not explain at all why the lawgiver interfered solely with loans to *filiifamilias*, but not with loans to persons *sui iuris*. Mitteis suggests that Macedo, loaded with debts, may have killed a wealthy man other than his father, possibly the importunate creditor himself. This, however, would have been a crime which anyone unscrupulous enough might commit, not only a *filiusfamilias*; and even when we suppose that such a deed, in a particular instance, happened to be committed by a *filiusfamilias*, that would hardly have justified legislation exclusively affecting this section of the population. So long as we go by Theophilus's description, at least there was a crime having its roots in the peculiar position of a *filiusfamilias*: there was parricide, murder of a father for the sake of independence and the inheritance. On this basis, it is easily intelligible how the senate· came to concern itself with loans to *filiifamilias*—*filiifamilias* and no one else. If we accept Mitteis's correction, Macedo's crime was essentially unconnected with his status as *filiusfamilias*, and the senate's coming down upon *filiifamilias* makes little sense.

One cannot help feeling that, if any of the theories set up to replace the information supplied by Theophilus were to be met with in the *Digest*, modern students of Roman Law would deliver a unanimous verdict of interpolated—and rightly.

I V .

Theophilus's account is absolutely convincing. Loans to *filiifamilias* had been too often accompanied by dishonest machinations or worse, and Macedo's parricide furnished terrible evidence of the dangers threatening fathers if the situation was allowed to continue. The *senatusconsultum Macedonianum*, by ordaining that the creditor's claim should remain unenforceable even after the father's death, not only made those loans unattractive for usurers, but also stopped such as still took the risk from driving a *filiusfamilias* to the worst of crimes.

But what of the two arguments against the trustworthiness of this story? The first is that Macedo, had he been worried by his creditor, would have done everything to prolong his father's life rather than murdered him: it was precisely while his father was alive that the creditor was powerless to exact the debt.

This, however, is not a very serious consideration. It is a highly academic idea to think that a usurer, as he could not enforce his claim through the law-courts while his debtor's parent lived, had no means of becoming troublesome—outside the law-courts. In many cases, a *filiusfamilias*, by the time the moneylender pressed for repayment, would have committed a number of minor or major illegalities which he did not wish to have divulged. Actually, the mere threat to inform an unsuspecting father of his son's debts—a threat the execution of which might lead, for example, to disinheritance—would frequently be enough to make the son resort to extreme remedies. A *filiusfamilias*, the detractors of Theophilus quite forget, as a result of his dependence and limitations, was particularly susceptible to blackmail; and the son who fears, not a lawsuit, but exposure is a stock character of the Roman comedy, though, of course, in a comedy, the ugly possibilities inherent in this situation are never allowed to mature. A simple man like Phil Squod knew that "mischeevious consequences is always meant when money's asked for" by a usurer that is "a leech in his dispositions, a screw and a vice in his actions, a snake in his twistings and a lobster in his claws."

Fortunately, there exists positive evidence that the Romans did consider excessive debts a probable motive for parricide in a *filiusfamilias*.

The advocates of the view here combated, in their *a priori* reasonings, have failed to note that we possess a speech, *Pro Sexto Roscio Amerino*, delivered by Cicero in defence of a man accused of parricide; and that, making due allowance for the orator's bias, we may learn from it a good deal concerning what the Romans really thought in this matter.

It ought to be mentioned that the accused is represented as having had the status of a *filiusfamilias* up to his father's death. This is plain both from the general relationship between him and his father as depicted in the speech—for example, his career was entirely determined by his father—and from the consideration that anything like an *emancipatio*, a release from the family, would have been eagerly seized on by the prosecution, as proving their point that there had been an estrangement between father and son; but no hint at such an argument of the prosecution occurs in Cicero's speech. Moreover, in 48, Cicero explains that his client's father made him take up those pursuits which *a patribus familias maxime laudantur*, "which are most esteemed by *patresfamilias*."

In 39, Cicero points out that his client's character shews none of the features which you would expect were the charge well-founded. Was he— he exclaims—driven to such a deed by *aeris alien magnitudo*, "the magnitude of his debts"? And he answers: *nihil autem umquam debuit*, "he never had any debts."

We shall have to come back to the whole passage below. For the moment, it is sufficient to remark that the brief extracts quoted utterly demolish the first of the two arguments against Theophilus. Obviously, the Romans did not hold that a *filiusfamilias* entangled in debts had special reason to wish his father a long life. On the contrary, it was a commonplace that excessive debts might induce a *filiusfamilias* to kill his father—a commonplace allowing Cicero to infer his client's innocence from the absence of debts. Needless to say, this conclusion remains valid even if Cicero's facts should be wrong; though, in this particular, they seem to have been admitted by the prosecution, and it is indeed perfectly credible that a *filiusfamilias* employed by his father to look after somewhat remote farms— such was the position of Sextus Roscius—had no opportunity or desire to borrow money.

V.

The other argument—the principal one—on account of which Theophilus's story has been rejected says that if Macedo had killed his father
on purpose to obtain property of his own, the senate would have tried to
prevent the repetition of such a crime, not by a restriction on loans to *filiifamilias*, but rather by the opposite course. For, clearly, that restriction
made the position of a *filiusfamilias* worse than it had been before. Before,
a *filiusfamilias* had had money to spend at least for some while, namely,
money borrowed from usurers. But the *senatusconsultum* frightened usurers off these loans, and, normally, a *filiusfamilias* now had no money free
from his father's control at all. Consequently—thus the argument runs—
a *filiusfamilias*, if he absolutely wanted uncontrolled money, now had no
choice but to kill his father: parricide, that is, was likely to be committed,
not, as before, after a long period of riotous living, as a last resort, but in
order that the riotous living might commence. The combating of parricide,
it is inferred, cannot have been the object of the *senatusconsultum*, and
Theophilus's report of Macedo's murder is a piece of fiction.

There are two serious flaws in this criticism. In the first place, whether, taken as a whole, the senate's legislation was a sound mode of stemming
the crime of parricide or not (and we shall see that, in the circumstances,
it was), it undeniably eliminated one danger at least: the usurer urging a
filiusfamilias to do away with his father. Under the new system, a usurer
would only rarely consent to a loan to a *filiusfamilias*, knowing that he
would never be entitled to sue for repayment. But even if, in an exceptional
case, he did take the risk, he had no interest in the father's death. That
event might indeed bring the son a fortune, but it left the lender's claim
without a sanction. In some respects, it even weakened his position, since
his debtor, now quite independent, would henceforth be better capable of
standing up to general, extra-legal threats.

When we contrast this state of affairs with that prevalent before
the *senatusconsultum* was enacted, we shall be less inclined to distrust
Theophilus. Before the decree had been enacted, the death of a father not
only gave his son the inheritance, but also rendered the usurer's claim
against the son fully enforceable. Surely, there must have been more than

one moneylender who, having acquired some power over the *filiusfamilias* indebted to him, persuaded, or rather, compelled the latter to hasten his father's end. One great factor favoring parricide, then, the *senatusconsultum* did remove, whatever we may think of its general effect.

Read with impartiality, the texts imply that the senate attached the highest importance to this point. The *senatusconsultum* itself declares that wicked moneylenders frequently are the moral authors of crimes of the kind perpetrated by Macedo: it is the usurer who *saepe materiam peccandi malis moribus praestaret*, who "often drives such as indulge in vice to illicit courses." This fact, it should be noted, is given as one of the reasons for the legislation: *cum... praestaret*, "since a usurer often drives." It may also be recalled that, possibly, the description of the usurer as lending *incertis nominibus* constitutes a direct reference to the shady, disreputable nature of these loans to *filiifamilias*—namely, if we translate the phrase by "without entries of the headings in his ledger."

True, the clauses so far quoted have no specific application to parricide; they embrace any kind of offence a *filiusfamilias* will come to once he has fallen into the hands of moneylenders, theft, forgery, murder. But, going on with the text, we meet with a very specific statement: the *senatusconsultum* itself emphasizes the result that, in future, a moneylender will derive no profit from inciting a *filiusfamilias* to parricide. Indeed, the language is very strong: *ut scirent qui pessimo exemplo faenerarent nullius posse filii familias bonum nomen. expectata patris morte fieri*, "that the usurers who lead people astray shall know that no son's debt can be made good by waiting for his father's death."

There is a significant detail about this. The *senatusconsultum* consists of three parts: (a) the reasons for the decree, *Cum... Macedo... aes alienum adhibuisset, et saepe materiam. peccandi... praestaret qui pecuniam... crederet*, "Whereas Macedo added debts, and whereas he who lends money is likely to drive to illicit courses"; (b) the actual law, *Placere, ne... actio petitioque daretur*, "It has been decided that no one may be given any action"; and (c) the wider purpose of the regulation, the effect hoped for, *Ut scirent... nullius posse filii familias bonum nomen... fieri*, "In order that they shall know that no son's debt can become good." That this is a carefully chosen, artistic division is clear from the fact that exactly the same form recurs in the *senatusconsultum Trebellianum*, of Nero's reign, i.e. very close in date to the *senatusconsultum Macedonianum*, and preserved in Digest 36.1.1.2, from Ulpian:

> Cum esset aequissimum... iudicia... eos subire in quos ius fructusque transferretur potius quam cuique periculosum esse fidem suam; placet, ut actiones... dari... his et in eos quibus... fideicommissum restitutum fuisset, quomagis in reliquum confirmentur supremae defunctorum voluntates.

> Whereas it is only equitable that those to whom the right and benefit are transferred should also shoulder the liabilities rather than that anybody should incur risk by keeping faith, it is being decided that actions must be given in favour and against those to whom an inheritance left by way of *fideicommissum* has been made over, in order that, in future, the last wishes of the deceased shall be upheld.

Here also, there are three parts, (a) introduced by a causal *cum*, the reason for the decree, (b) introduced by *placet*, the actual law, and (c) introduced by *quomagis* (where the *senatusconsultum Macedonianum* has a final *ut*), the aim of, the effect intended by, the decree.[20]

Now, in the *senatusconsultum Macedonianum*, part (c) does not bring anything substantially new; the only new point in it is that grave insinuation concerning the role of moneylenders. The actual law, part (b), makes it quite clear that one who lends money to a *filiusfamilias* will never have an action, not even *post mortem parentis*, "after the death of the latter's parent." Part (c) repeats this—only in a most biting tone: the moneylenders shall know that there will never be an action. "Those vermin," we may paraphrase, "shall no longer be tempted to work for the death of decent citizens." This is the part setting forth the fundamental object of the enactment; it corresponds to the *quomagis... confirmentur supremae defunctorum voluntates*, in order that the last wishes of the deceased shall be upheld," of the *senatusconsultum Trebellianum*. Evidently, to get rid of

---

20. The two parts (a) and (b) were common in *senatusconsulta*, though (a) did not come in until the Principate; see Mommsen, *Römisches Staatsrecht* 3.2 (1888), 1008 f. (he enumerates these parts as nos. 7 and 8). But the tripartite form, with part (c), is extremely rare and not noticed by Mommsen.

the moral, indirect author of parricide was a major consideration of the lawgiver.

Very possibly, the idea of the elimination of the usurer as an instigator of parricide has determined also the formulation of *Annals* 11.13.2, quoted above and concerning a law of Claudius.[21] By it, we are told, *saevitiam creditorum coercuit, ne in mortem parentum pecunias filiis familiarum faenori darent*, "he curbed the ruthlessness of creditors, restraining them from lending money to a *filiusfamilias* recoverable at his father's death." *In mortem parentum*, here translated by "recoverable at his father's death," has an ominous sound: "secured on his father's death" or "in anticipation of his father's death" would perhaps be a better rendering, imitating the ambiguity of the original.

Above all, however, there is the rule, to which reference has repeatedly been made, that a *filiusfamilias* who borrows money and, in ignorance of the defence available to him by virtue of the *senatusconsultum* (or it may be more accurate to say, in ignorance of circumstances forming a ground for this defence), repays it after becoming *sui iuris* cannot claim it back. We find it in Digest 12.6.40 pr. and 12.6.19 pr., both times explicitly rested on the fact that the decree was enacted *in odium eius cui debetur*, "to thwart the creditor," or *poenae causa eius cui debetur*, "to penalise the creditor." That the provision is certainly incompatible with any interpretation of the *senatusconsultum* as saving youngsters from the consequences of their improvidence has been remarked above. But the question relevant at this point is: For exactly what misdeeds is the moneylender to be thwarted or penalized? It cannot be for the ordinary, minor offences of his trade, since, if they were meant, the rule under notice would be quite incongruous. More precisely, had it been on account of the minor offences of his trade—such as charging too high a rate of interest, accepting stolen goods as pledge and so on—that the *senatusconsultum* refused a moneylender an action even after his debtor reached independence, it would be unintelligible why he might keep what his debtor, on reaching independence, repaid him by mistake. Indeed, one would think that in such a case, where the debtor must be of a particularly ingenuous nature, the presumption of crooked behavior

21. Or, possibly, the *senatusconsultum Macedonianum* itself; see below, under VII.

on the part of the usurer would be stronger than in others.

The rule makes perfectly good sense, however, as soon as we realize—and only if we realize—that it is the moneylender in his role as instigator of parricide who is to be thwarted and penalized. It was the elimination of this danger to which the senate attached major importance, and to
bring about which loans to *filiifamilias* were declared for ever unenforceable: a moneylender must no longer have any interest in the murder of a
father. But, clearly, once a father has died and the debtor become *sui iuris*,
the danger described ceases to exist. If, now, the debtor repays the borrowed money, be it even in ignorance of his defence, the usurer need not
return it. A usurer must have no action through a father's death—else he
would plot to bring it about. But whatever he obtains, without an action,
after his debtor's father has died he may keep. The law is not designed to
help the borrower, who is presumably not much better than the lender: he
is indeed branded by the legislator as of *mali mores*, as "indulging in vice."
It is designed to fight parricide, and in particular, the usurer *qua* instigator
of parricide. In the special situation contemplated by the rule discussed,
this object of the *senatusconsultum*—to fight the usurer *qua* instigator of
parricide—no longer arises.

Here a slight digression may be permissible. Marcian in Digest
12.6.40 pr. says that the *senatusconsultum Macedonianum* gave the debtor
a defence *in odium* of the lender, while Pomponius in Digest 12.6.19 pr.
employs the less striking term *poenae causa*.[22] The use of *in odium* for "in
order to thwart," "to spite," to vex," may be paralleled from Ovid, *Metamorphoses* 14.71: Scylla, who had been ruined for ever by Circe, the friend and
protectress of Odysseus, *in Circes odium sociis spoliavit Ulixen*, "robbed
Odysseus of his fellows in order to thwart Circe."[23] None the less, *in odium*
in this sense is uncommon enough to make one suspect that Marcian, in
choosing the expression, was influenced by the tradition, preserved in Gaius 4.4 (and Institutes 4.6.14), that *condictio*, as an alternative to *vindicatio*

22. Similarly, Ulpian in Digest 14.6.9.4, *ob poenam creditorum*.
23. The question how *in odium* acquired this sense need not here be settled. Perhaps there was a stage when it signified "in order to give expression to one's hatred";
gradually it came to mean "in order to vex." But it may from the outset have been capable
of denoting "in order to produce disgust in somebody," "in order to vex."

in the case of theft, was introduced *odio furum*. (This is not pronouncing on the question whether Marcian used Gaius.)

It is true that *odio furum* in Gaius 4.4 is nearly always translated by some phrase like "out of hatred of thieves."[24] That is to say, it is interpreted as referring not, like Marcian's *in odium*, to the purpose of the institution concerned, but to the emotions of those who created it. However, apart from the fact that there would be nothing strange in Marcian having given the idea a somewhat different turn, quite likely, the current rendering of *odio furum* in Gaius 4.4 is inadequate. To quote a little more of that passage, we are told that *condictio furtiva*, as an alternative to *vindicatio*, was recognized *odio furum, quo magis pluribus actionibus teneantur*. If we translate "out of hatred of thieves, in order to multiply the actions in which they are liable," the statement is almost ridiculous.[25] It seems to imply that the jurists, when they allowed the victim of theft to choose between *vindicatio* and *condictio*, were merely demonstrating their indignation with the offender in a pedantic manner. The explanation becomes far more sensible if we translate it by "in order to thwart, to penalise, thieves, to wit, in order that they should be liable in more actions."[26] On this basis, Gaius is expressing the view that the recognition of *condictio furtiva* as an alternative to *vindicatio* was a well-considered penal measure, designed to compel restitution even in cases where, for certain technical reasons, the latter action would not succeed—a view in all probability historically correct.[27] It may also be observed that the clause *quo magis pluribus actionibus teneantur* unquestionably has a final sense, not a causal. As it looks like standing in

24. See e.g. De Zulueta, *The Institutes of Gaius* 1 (1946), 233. Poste, *Gai Institutionum Commentarii Quattuor*, 3rd ed. (1890), 456, translates "for the prevention of theft," which is hardly warranted; and his reason why *condictio furtiva* was introduced is not convincing.

25. Buckland, *Text-Book*, 582, discussing *condictio furtiva*, remarks, justly so long as we proceed from the traditional rendering: "Gaius has no better explanation to give than that it was allowed *odio furum*."

26. The phrase *odio esse alicui*, "to be disgusting to somebody," is to be found as early as in Plautus (*Menaechmi* 1.2.2). From here to *odio alicuius aliquid facere*, "to act to somebody's disgust, vexation," is not far.

27. See Buckland, *Text-Book*, 582: "Possibly it lay at first only where the thing had ceased to exist."

apposition to *odio furum*, it is natural to assign a final sense to this phrase also, i.e. to take it as equivalent to *in odium furum*.[28] Again, the Veronese text has *quo magis pluribus actionibus teneant*, and, although all modern editors prefer Justinian's *teneantur*, the more difficult reading may be right. If so, Gaius's point comes out even more clearly: *condictio furtiva* was established "in order to thwart thieves, to wit, in order that they (namely, the upholders of justice) might catch (*scil.* them—*fures*, "thieves," understood from *odio furum*) by more actions." We might compare Digest 47.10.15.13, from Ulpian: *Si quis astrologus... consultus aliquem furem dixisset qui non erat, iniuriarum cum eo agi non potest, sed constitutiones eos tenent*, "If an astrologer, consulted, declares a person a thief who is not a thief, the *actio iniuriarum* does not lie against him, but the imperial constitutions catch him." And last but not least, if the rendering here suggested is accepted, there is complete agreement between the use of *odio furum* by Gaius and that of *in odium eius cui debetur* by Marcian.

One source of danger at least to the life of a father the *senatusconsultum* deliberately and successfully removed. Is it correct to say that its general effect was to render parricide more rather than less frequent? It is submitted that this, too, is a mistake. The *senatusconsultum* made it difficult for a *filiusfamilias* to secure a loan. Hence, the critics of Theophilus claim, parricide would no longer be confined to the case where, after years of extravagance, the patience of usurers with a debtor was completely exhausted: it would have to take place every time extravagance was only intended. The conclusion drawn is that the decree had nothing to do with the repression of parricide.

For one thing, however, we must not forget that even under the regime of the *senatusconsultum*, there was no interference with what might be called open, forthright extravagance. The decree, as we have seen, spoke only of *mutua pecunia*, "money loans," and the jurists were careful not to extend the ban to other transactions on credit. Digest 14.6.3.3, 14.6.7 pr. and Code 4.28.3, quoted above, are all perfectly clear on this

---

28. Muirhead, *The Institutes of Gaius and Rules of Ulpian* (1904), 267, seems to have felt the lack of a real parallelism between *odio furum*, interpreted in the traditional fashion, and the *quo magis* clause. He separates the two by "and," translating: "in detestation of thieves, and to make them responsible in a greater number of actions."

point: the latter text, for example, says that *si filius familias aliquid mercatus pretium... cum usurarum accessione spondeat, non esse locum senatus consulto... nemini dubium est,* "If a *filiusfamilias*, buying something on credit, promises the price and interest as well, nobody doubts that the *senatusconsultum* does not apply." A *filiusfamilias* was free to squander all his prospective wealth, and more—provided he obtained the credit from ordinary business men, in an honest manner. He might even stand surety for a prodigal friend: that was not a dirty, underhand arrangement. (Dodges of course, were not tolerated.) What the senate was out to prevent or at any rate render harmless was the pure money loan from a usurer. It was this transaction which so easily led to crime, or, as Ulpian explains in Digest 14.6.3.3, *perniciosa parentibus eorum visa est,* "was considered dangerous to their fathers." Beseler and his followers have declared this reason a Byzantine interpolation. But the strict limitation of the enactment to pure money loans is indeed best explicable on this ground.

Honest extravagance was not interfered with. Yet this alone, it must be admitted, would not be a sufficient reply to the view here combated. For it was, of course, the *filiusfamilias* decidedly not content with what he might get by dealings with ordinary business men who was a potential murderer of his father. A son prepared to put up with his limitations thought neither of usurers nor of parricide; he thought of them neither before nor after the introduction of the *senatusconsultum Macedonianum*; and this enactment did not affect his life very much. The type chiefly contemplated by the decree, if Theophilus is right, was a man desiring the wildest luxury, far beyond his resources present or prospective. It is a *filiusfamilias* of such a disposition whom the critics of Theophilus have in mind. He, they contend, before the *senatusconsultum* was in force, could go to the usurers, when parricide would be at least staved off. Under the *senatusconsultum*, he could not go to the usurers, so that he would have to consider the other solution of his dilemma from the outset.

The point sounds plausible—very plausible, or it would not have been so widely accepted—but, like the argument that a usurer had no means of becoming troublesome to a *filiusfamilias*, it is a piece of abstract, academic speculation. It entirely disregards the familiar experience that a deed as horrible as that in question is far more readily committed by a person who has gradually accustomed himself to ever more despicable courses than by one as yet a novice in crime—however intense his craving for an unhampered pursuit of pleasure. A man who had been in the hands of usurers for a long period was capable of anything, but not a man who kept, or was kept, away from them and the mode of life which they encouraged. "We are not worst at once," says the motto of one of the chapters of *The Fortunes of Nigel*, reminiscent of Juvenal's *Nemo repente fuit turpissimus*. Gaspardo, whose exploits are recorded in *Gil Blas* 10.11, for years stole from, and cheated, his father; and only when, after a particularly wild spell of gambling and ever more expensive love-making, he suddenly found himself deprived of his usual source of income, he decided on killing the old man. It is this elementary psychological datum on which the senate relied. It was enough to see to it that there should be no more cases of utterly corrupted *filiifamilias*, pressed by moneylenders: that was the situation to be feared and fought. That a *filiusfamilias* who had never had the means for a career of vice and illegality, and was under no duress, should murder his father in order to acquire those means was regarded as a thing not likely to happen very often.

But let us again turn from *a priori* arguments to the sources. All Roman writers dealing with the art of prosecution and defence in criminal cases take it for granted that a person long inured to wicked doings will commit a serious offence more easily than a person whose life has so far been virtuous. It is the task of the prosecution to shew that the accused is of a worthless disposition, and, more particularly, that his way of life was bound to lead him to the specific crime with which he is charged; and the task of the defence to represent him as never having deviated from the straight path. Quintilian, who was about thirty-five years old when the *senatusconsultum Macedonianum* was enacted,[29] writes in *Institutio Oratoria* 7.2.28, 33:

> Accusatoris autem est efficere ut, si quid obiecerit, non solum turpe sit, sed etiam crimini de quo est iudicium quam maxima conveniat... Probi vero mores et anteactae vitae integritas numquam non plurimum profuerint.

29. Or fifteen, if it goes back to the reign of Claudius; see below, section VII.

The prosecution ought to see that, if it mentions anything against the character of the accused, it should be not only discreditable, but also as consistent as possible with the crime for which he is arraigned. But honest conduct and blamelessness of his past life always help the accused most.

Certainly, the orators would have been deficient in the technique of *in utramque partem disputare* [arguing the other side] had they not seen that there were exceptions to the rule; and Quintilian, for instance, in 7.2.33, advises the prosecution, in case the past life of an accused is free from reproach, to insist *neminem non aliquando coepisse peccare*, "that every criminal must at some time commit his first offence." But this does not alter the fact—rather it underlines it—that the rule, in the eyes of the Roman psychologists, was as just stated: a hardened sinner will have less hesitation to commit a grave offence than a man so far innocent.

The principle is fully applied by Cicero in *Pro Sexto Roscio*, where he defends a man accused of parricide. Two illustrations only need be given, though there are more. In 39—part of which has already been adduced— he dwells on his client's simple life on the farms of his father and puts the rhetorical question: *Luxuries igitur hominem nimirum et aeris alieni magnitudo et indomitae animi cupiditates ad hoc scelus impulerunt*, "Revelry, doubtless, the magnitude of his debts and the unbridled desires of his soul drove the accused to this crime?" Excessive debts as a motive for parricide we have considered above. The point here to be made is that it was continuous debauchery, producing an ever more insatiable appetite, which counted as likely to result in parricide. It may be repeated that the relevance of this is not diminished by the existence of exceptions, cases of persons committing an atrocious crime as their very first offence. No doubt the prosecution, in trying to refute Cicero, laid stress on these exceptions. But the idea made use of by Cicero in his client's interest was evidently a commonplace, the truth of which in the majority of cases was considered as established—as it still is today.

It is highly suggestive that three of the terms employed recur in the text of, or comments upon, the *senatusconsultum Macedonianum*. Parricide is described as a *scelus*, "crime," in the decree, and prominence is given to the *aes alienum*, "debts," contracted by Macedo; while both Suetonius, in

Life of Vespasian 11, and Justinian, in Institutes 4.7.7, refer to the danger of *luxuria,* "revelry," of a *filiusfamilias* to be combated by the *senatusconsultum.* In addition, Quintilian, in *Institutio Oratoria* 5.10.47, in discussing a theme from parricide, speaks of *reus luxuriosus,* "the accused debauched by revelry," though he does not need the attribute in this particular context: he puts it simply because thorough familiarity with vice and wild luxury is the typical quality of one who murders his father. There was, it is manifest, a uniform teaching on the subject.

Again, in 68, Cicero says that parricide is so fearful a thing that it appears incredible *nisi turpis adulescentia, nisi omnibus flagitiis vita inquinata, nisi sumptus effusi cum probro atque dedecore, nisi prorupta audacia, nisi tanta temeritas ut non procul abhorrent ab insania,* "unless a man's youth has been disgraceful, his life polluted with all vices, his lavish extravagance accompanied by shameful and indecent conduct, his audacity unrestrained, his rashness such as to be hardly distinguishable from insanity." And he goes on: *Accedat huc oportet odium parentis, animadverionis paternae metus, amici improbi, servi conscii, tempus idoneum, locus opportune captus ad eam rem,* "In addition to this, there must be hatred of his father, the fear of parental punishment, wicked friends, slaves as accomplices, a favorable moment, a suitably chosen place for the purpose." So once more Cicero avails himself of what was a commonplace of criminal psychology, the notion of parricide as the conclusion of a long progress through the various stages of loose living. Actually, even the dread of what the father may do if he gets to know of his son's conduct and the moneylender urging the deed have a place in this sketch: the former motive is included in *animadversionis paternae metus,* "fear of parental punishment," and the moneylender might safely be classed among the *amici improbi,* the "wicked friends."[30]

It may not be superfluous, at this point, to interject that the *senatusconsultum Macedonianum* adopted not only the current ideas concerning

---

30. The favorable moment and suitable place for the deed mentioned by Cicero at the end of the passage cited are also part of a fixed scheme of proof, a system of definite factors, that is, the presence or absence of which makes a charge appear more or less plausible. See *Partitiones oratoriae* 34: *Verisimilia reperiuntur ex partibus...narrations; ea sunt in personis, in locis, in temporibus...,* "Probabilities are derived from the several parts of a statement of a case; these consist in persons, places, times."

the factors making for a crime, but also the forensic categories and arrangement usual in this connection; in other words, that it adopted not only the substance of the criminal theories then recognized, but also their recognized form of presentation.

1. The decree refers to the *causae sceleris*, "Macedo's causes for his crime." In every criminal case, according to the orators, the question whether there were sufficient causes, motives, for the deed is of the utmost importance, the prosecution trying to prove that there were, the defence denying it. *Proxima est ex causis probatio*, "The next type of proof is that from causes," is the beginning of Quintilian's section on this topic, in 7.2.36.

2. More remarkable is the notion to be found in the *senatusconsultum* of causes for a crime springing from a man's nature: Macedo, we are told, had acted from causes *quas natura administrabat*, "which his nature furnished him." The meaning of this also becomes clear when we consult the rhetorical systems. Besides the type of proof based on causes for the crime, there is, in these systems, the proof from *persona*, "the person of the accused" and this aspect includes a person's *natura*, his "natural qualities." Quintilian in 5.10.23 says, *In primis igitur argumenta a persona ducenda sunt*, "Firstly, then, arguments may be drawn from the person" and in 5.10.27 he mentions *animi natura*, "the nature of a person's soul." Now the proof from *persona*, "the person of the accused," is more general than the proof from *causae*, "his causes for the crime." The former, Quintilian observes in 7.2.39, is concerned with the question an *ullum crimen credibile*, "whether any crime can credibly be imputed to the accused," the latter with the question ad hoc, "whether the specific crime for which he is arraigned is credible." Moreover, between some natural qualities of the person and some causes, motives, for a crime, there exists a close genetic connection. For example, Quintilian, in 5.10.27 ff., not unreasonably treats *iracundia*, "angry disposition," as belonging to *animi natura*, the natural qualities," but *ira*, "anger," as a *causa*, "a cause for a crime." He adds, however, that, for some authorities, both are characteristics of a person. It is here that we must look for the background of the notion of a cause for a crime—such as the passion of anger—being furnished by a man's nature—his irascibility, for instance. Cicero, it should be noted, in *Partitiones oratoriae* 35, entirely suppresses the type of proof from *causae*, "causes

for a crime": no doubt he takes the view rejected by Quintilian that, as most causes for a crime have their roots in natural qualities, the latter may be regarded as covering the former.[31]

3. A further striking detail in the *senatusconsultum* is the division—the apparent division at any rate—of causes for a crime into two kinds, such as spring from the nature of the accused and such as do not. The text says that *inter ceteras sceleris causas Macedo, quas illi natura administrabat, etiam aes alienum adhibuisset*, "to the other causes for his crime, which his nature furnished him, Macedo added also debts." There seems to be intended a contrast between the other causes—say, anger, greed, fear etc.—which sprang from Macedo's nature, and his debts which did not, which he incurred in the course of his career. If this is so, we have before us an illustration of the traditional division of personal character into natural qualities and position in life. *Partitiones oratoriae* 35, just quoted, says:

> In personis, naturae primum spectantur valetudinis, figurae...atque haec quidem in corpore; animi autem quaemadmodum affecti sint virtutibus, vitiis, artibus, inertiis, aut quemadmodum commoti cupiditate, metu, voluptate, molestia. Atque haec quidem in natura spectantur. In fortuna genus, amicitiae... affines, opes... divitiae, et ea quae sunt eis contraria.

> In proofs from persons, we first consider their natural qualities of health, figure, which things concern the body; while as to their souls, we consider how far they are influenced by virtues, vices, culture, lack of culture, and to what extent they are impelled by desire, fear, pleasure, annoyance. All these are natural qualities of a man. His position in life involves birth, friendships, connections, resources, riches, and the opposites of these.

Evidently, where a system like this is followed, a distinction between anger, greed, fear etc. as in *natura*, "natural qualities," or at least as resulting from "natural qualities," and debts as in *fortuna*, as an element of

---

31. It may be connected with this attitude that, in his actual speeches, as a rule he discussed "causes" first and "person" second (as observed by Quintilian in 7.2.39). For him, "causes" were the results of "person" and, therefore, convenient signposts by following which one might arrive at the latter.

"position in life," is to be expected. Nevertheless, a different interpretation of the opening of the *senatusconsultum* is just conceivable. It is just conceivable that what Macedo added is thought of as of the same kind as that which was already present; that the relative clause *quas illi natura administrabat*, "which his nature furnished him," is not meant to refer exclusively to *ceteras causas*, "the other causes," as distinguishing these from the debts; in other words, that no contrast is intended between the other causes, anger, greed, fear etc., and the debts. On this assumption, the opening of the *senatusconsultum* might be paraphrased thus: "To the other causes for his crime which his nature furnished him, Macedo added one more such cause, namely, debts." Macedo's debts would be classed, not as in *fortuna*, but as in *natura*. This interpretation is far less likely than the one given above; but the result it gives us could be explained. There is nothing absurd in a subsumption of Macedo's debts under those causes for his crime which sprang from his nature, provided we take into account the real setting in a case of parricide. In a case of parricide, debts are not simply an external circumstance, an unfortunate incident: they are, we saw, of the very essence of the crime, implying, as they do, profligacy, illicit dealings, surrender to usurers and so on.

Regarded from this angle, their place is indeed with the causes for the crime originating in natural qualities. Actually, Cicero, in *Pro Sexto Roscio* 39, may well be so regarding them, when he asks: *Luxuries igitur hominem nimirum et aeris alieni magnitudo et indomitae animi cupiditates ad hoc scelus impulerunt*, "Revelry, doubtless, the magnitude of his debts and the unbridled desires of his soul drove my client to this crime?" However, as remarked, the probability is that the decree does oppose the other causes, as "natural qualities," to the debts, as belonging to "position in life."

(4) Having dealt with Macedo's causes for his crime, the *senatusconsultum* proceeds to the role of the usurer: he frequently stands behind the actual deed, says the lawgiver. This is a perfectly logical arrangement, and it, too, may be paralleled from the orators. In *Pro Sexto Roscio* 68, already cited, Cicero makes mention of the *amici improbi*, the "wicked friends," after causes for the crime such as hatred of the father and fear of punishment.

Is it too rash to suggest that the text of the *senatusconsultum Macedonianum* echoes the speech of the prosecution at the trial of Macedo, or at least the speech of the magistrate introducing the matter in the senate? Admittedly, until we recover that speech, this must remain a guess. But it is supported by a little point of syntax never so far accounted for, the curious position of the name "Macedo" in the text of the decree. In English, such a hyperbaton would be unheard of: "Whereas to the other causes for his crime Macedo, which his nature furnished him, added also debts." In Latin, though ordinarily out of place, it is quite possible both in poetry and in prose—in the latter where very special emphasis is wanted; and when we remember that this is the only *senatusconsultum* called, not after the proposer, but after the criminal whose act occasioned it, i.e. Macedo, it becomes evident that the senate did intend to give very special prominence to that name, or at any rate, that the public did interpret the text as giving it very special prominence. Yet the ultimate source, one would like to think, was a phrase coined in a speech. A Roman orator declaiming to a jury, or a magistrate declaiming to the senate, might well find this hyperbaton highly effective. True, a similar one, which occurs in Vergil,[32] is condemned by Quintilian in 8.2.14. But, first, the fact remains that Vergil uses it. Secondly, Vergil's hyperbaton is even more artificial than that in the *senatusconsultum Macedonianum*. Above all, from Quintilian's discussion in 8.6.62 ff. and 9.4.26 ff., we may see how usual it was for speakers to avail themselves of the device, with or without particular reasons. Some, indeed, made it almost a rule to deviate from the natural structure of a sentence. Of Domitius Afer, Quintilian, in 9.4.31, records that *adeo refugit teneram delicatamque modulandi voluptatem ut currentibus per se numeris quod eos inhiberet obiiceret*, "to such an extent did he avoid the soft and delicate satisfaction to be derived from regular measure that, where the rhythm, in the natural way, would have run smoothly, he interposed obstacles to break it." Domitius Afer was perhaps the most popular advocate of his generation, and it was the generation flourishing about the time of the *senatusconsultum Macedonianum*. (Who knows but that he might have conducted the prosecution in the affair of Macedo?) However, the whole question is only

---

32. *Aeneid* 1.109: *Saxa vocant Itali mediis quae in fluctibus aras*, "Which rocks in the midst of the sea the Italians call altars." The queer sequence of the original cannot be imitated in English.

loosely connected with the main thesis of this article.

To return to the latter, as the evidence adduced testifies, the Romans were fully aware that parricide was more probable after a long and intimate familiarity with excesses of all kinds than in a milieu of strict legality. It is, therefore, wrong to doubt Theophilus's veracity because the senate would not have reacted to parricide by putting fresh obstacles in the way of loans to *filiifamilias*. The truth is that that was precisely the reaction dictated by experience.

This second objection against the "Byzantine legend," then, has no force—no more than the first, resting on the postulate that a moneylender had no means of worrying a *filiusfamilias*. The *senatusconsultum*, by rendering loans to *filiifamilias* unattractive, not only eliminated the sinister character of the usurer inciting his debtor to parricide, but also made it less easy for a *filiusfamilias* to embark on a life of shady dealings and reckless intemperance; and this latter, general effect was as wisely planned as the former, more specific one. To stop *filiifamilias* from following Macedo's fearful example thus emerges as a principal object of the law.

As a matter of fact, when we put the law in its wider, historical context, we shall find that the senate, once it decided to act at all, had little choice as to the direction in which it was to go. Theoretically, it is obvious that an alternative method was open: the senate might have laid down say, that a *filiusfamilias*, so soon as he reached the age of twenty-one, should be free from his father's power and capable of owning what he earned. That would certainly have removed the basis for situations like that in the case of Macedo. But the time was simply not yet ripe for the shedding of the entire system of *patria potestas*. That system was still sacrosanct. To propose its abolition in the first century A.D. would have been like proposing today that a son, on coming of age, should automatically become joint owner of all his father's possessions. What, then, was the senate to do? Those underhand loans had proved disastrous. The regime of paternal power was to be upheld. There was no way but to strike at the loans.

It was just said that the system of *patria potestas* was still sacrosanct, but this is a slight exaggeration: for a definite measure of reform had been put into force not so long before the *senatusconsultum Macedonianum*. Augustus, as is well known, had granted *filiifamilias* certain rights over property acquired as a result of military service; such property, the *peculium castrense*, was to a large extent withdrawn from the father's control—an important regulation, affecting large numbers of *filiifamilias* and certainly, on the whole, the most active and resolute ones. Actually, it would not be surprising if the closeness in date between this step and the *senatusconsultum Macedonianum* were no mere coincidence. It is quite conceivable that, during the social and political upheavals towards the end of the Republic, the pressure for greater financial independence of adult *filiifamilias* had strongly increased. Augustus made the concession outlined, which was step by step extended in the following centuries:[33] that was the official solution of the problem. (This is far from denying that Augustus may have had other reasons as well.) All *filiifamilias*, however, were not satisfied with it, and the dealings between them and usurers became ever wilder: that was the solution of the problem by self-help, so to speak, and it threatened chaos. The *senatusconsultum Macedonianum* checked the latter development, while the jurists' all the time carefully went on with the former. This seems to be the connection between the two dates.

But whether this particular conjecture is correct or not, certain it is that, by the first century A.D., some implications of the system of *patria potestas* were no longer borne with equanimity by the middle-aged *filiusfamilias*. This we may safely conclude from the introduction of the *peculium castrense*: such concessions are not made unless they can no longer be avoided. We have also to remember that, if by the *peculium castrense* a father's exclusive right to his son's earnings began to be restricted, his power over the son's person, too, was rapidly curtailed from the close of the Republic—another sign, surely, of the tension created by the old regime.

One cannot help feeling that, in our legal histories of Rome, too little attention is being paid to the actual working of *patria potestas*. That system is taken for granted almost as if it were perfection itself, notwithstanding a few general remarks about its archaic character to be met with here and there. But the system must have given rise to much dissatisfaction on the part of *filiifamilias*. *Emancipatio*, it is true, voluntary release of a son by his father, provided a safety valve from very early times, but only a most im-

---

33. See Buckland, *Text-Book*, 280 f., on reforms by Hadrian and Constantine.

perfect one. It is also true that, when we examine the serious lay literature of the Romans, we come across extremely little complaint regarding that side of *patria potestas* with which we are here concerned, i.e. the financial subordination of a son. There are reasons for this, but it would lead too far afield here to go into them. In the comedy, we do find the problem treated again and again; and one scene out of a multitude may perhaps be quoted, as particularly pertinent to the principal subject of this inquiry, *Phormio* 2.299 ff.

A father here, on coming home from a journey, finds his son married to a penniless beauty. A slave who helped the son tells the father that, under a certain complicated statute, his son was compelled either to marry the girl, or to supply her with a dowry and give her in marriage to somebody else. The father asks why the latter course was not adopted, to which the slave replies that the son lacked the money for it: he could not give her the necessary dowry. Father: *Sumeret alicunde?*, "He might have borrowed it from someone?" Slave: *Alicunde? Nil est dictu facilius*, "From someone? Nothing is more easily said." Father: *Postremo, si nullo alio pacto, faenore*, "At the worst, if he obtained it under no other conditions, he might have borrowed it on interest." Slave: *Hui, dixti pulchre! siquidem quisquam crederet to vivo.* "Phew! Fine words! He might have done so if anyone would give him credit while you are alive." No matter how far Terence's plot is Greek or Roman, his Roman audience can have had no difficulty in understanding this dialogue; and even the impudent suggestion at the end—of considerable interest in the present connection, and the nearest thing to parricide we can get in a comedy—that the father's existence did not make things easier for his son was hardly lost on them.

In any case, quite apart from the fact that the rejection of Theophilus's version of the origin of the *senatusconsultum Macedonianum* is wholly unjustifiable on narrow, critical grounds—from the wider, historical point of view, the attempt to explain away the one case recorded in the sources of serious trouble resulting from the denial of property rights to *filiifamilias* seems to indicate a complete failure to correlate legal institutions with the social and economic data determining, and determined by, them.[34]

34. Ihering would have regarded it as an illustration of the ability *ein Rechtsinsti-*

This section is mainly recapitulation. It may be useful, however, once again to list the major objections against the modern theories set up to replace the account of Theophilus, and to demonstrate that none of them can be raised against that account.

1. The modern theories, we saw, are in conflict with the text of the *senatusconsultum*. The account of Theophilus is not.

A. The term *scelus*, for Theophilus, does not denote a mere lack of delicacy, but a serious crime, parricide.

B. The term *aes alienum*, for Theophilus, does not denote a claim of the moneylender, but a debt of the *filiusfamilias*.

C. The debts referred to in the decree Theophilus takes, not as themselves having been the whole crime, but as having been among the causes, motives, for the crime, the murder, committed.

D. What the decree declares to be the reasons for the legislation— Macedo's crime and the fact that such loans had often led to transgressions—Theophilus takes, not as having been a matter of indifference to the senate, whose true object was the protection of the young, but as really the reasons for the legislation.

E. What the decree first ordains and then, in the part giving the wider purpose of the lawgiver, says the usurers had better take note of— denial of an action even after a father's death in the case of a loan to a *filiusfamilias*—Theophilus takes, not as a secondary matter in comparison with the exclusion of the *actio de peculio*, but as the true meaning of the decree. There is no reference in the decree to the *actio de peculio*—nor is there in Theophilus.

2. The modern theories are in conflict with the effects of, and the ancient comments on, the *senatusconsultum*. The account of Theophilus is not.

A. First, for the theory that the decree was intended to protect thoughtless youngsters.

α) This theory does not explain why the *senatusconsultum* applies

---

tut ohne Anschauung der realen praktischen Bedeutung desselben rein aus den Quellen oder dem Begriff heraus aufzubauen. See *Scherz und Ernst in der Jurisprudenz*, 12th ed. (1921), 254.

precisely to *filiifamilias*. It applies to *filiifamilias*, however old, and to no one else, however young. If a man becomes a *paterfamilias* between the promise to repay the loan and the actual receipt of the loan, the *senatusconsultum* does not apply; if he becomes a *filiusfamilias*, it does. The holding of high office by a *filiusfamilias* makes no difference. There is no difficulty if we follow Theophilus: the decree was intended to avert parricide, most likely in the case of a depraved *filiusfamilias* acting under the guidance of a usurer.

β) This theory does not explain why the *senatusconsultum* applies precisely to money loans, but to no other transactions on credit, however unreasonable. There is no difficulty if we follow Theophilus: the decree was intended to avert parricide, most likely in the case of a depraved *filiusfamilias* acting under the guidance of a usurer.

γ) This theory does not explain why the law refuses a remedy to him who, having become a *paterfamilias*, repays an old loan in ignorance of his defence. There is no difficulty if we follow Theophilus: the decree was intended to avert parricide, and it is unnecessary, for that purpose, to admit a remedy in the particular situation put.

δ) This theory is contradicted by texts stating in so many words that the decree was not intended to protect the borrower, but to fight the lender. There is no difficulty if we follow Theophilus. The decree was intended to avert parricide, most likely in the case of a depraved *filiusfamilias* acting under the guidance of a usurer: there was, on this basis, no reason to be tender to the former, and all that needed to be done was to make it impossible for the latter to enforce his claim.

B. Secondly, for the theory that the decree was intended to protect the father against the *actio de peculio*.

α) This theory is contradicted by Suetonius who says that the gist of the decree was to deny the usurer an action after the death of the borrower's father. Tacitus, in dealing with a similar law of Claudius,[35] says the same. There is no difficulty if we follow Theophilus, who agrees with the two.

β) This theory does not explain why the Roman jurists never treat

---

35. If he does not also mean the *senatusconsultum Macedonianum*: see below, section VII.

the exclusion of the *actio de peculio* as the primary, or even a major, aim of the decree. There is no difficulty if we follow Theophilus, who makes no reference to this action.

γ) This theory does not explain why the *senatusconsultum* applies precisely to money loans, but to no other transactions, however unreasonable. There is no difficulty if we follow Theophilus: the decree was intended to avert parricide, most likely where a depraved son acted under the guidance of a usurer.

C. Lastly, for the theory that the decree was intended to avert murder of any third person, not parricide.

This theory does not explain why the *senatusconsultum* applies precisely to *filiifamilias*. There is no difficulty if we follow Theophilus: the decree was intended to avert parricide, most likely where a depraved *filiusfamilias* acted under the guidance of a usurer.

The upshot of all this is, the writer regrets to say, that Macedo's appeal must be dismissed. He did murder his father.

VII.

To conclude, two points may be noted. The one concerns the exact date of the *senatusconsultum Macedonianum*. This must be inferred chiefly from Suetonius, *Life of Vespasian* 11:

> Libido atque luxuria coercente nullo invaluerat. auctor senatui fuit decernendi, ut quae se alieni servo iunxisset ancilla haberetur; neve filiorum familiarum faeneratoribus exigendi crediti ius unquam esset, hoc est, ne post patrum quidem mortem.

> Wantonness and revelry, as no one had curbed them, had assumed larger dimensions. Vespasian proposed the *senatusconsulta* that a freewoman cohabiting with another person's slave should herself be considered a slave; and that those who lent money to *filiifamilias* should never become entitled to exact the debt, that is to say, not even after the fathers' death.

However, a similar, earlier step by Claudius has been adverted to several times; it is recorded in Tacitus, *Annals* 11.13.2:

> Et lege lata saevitiam creditorum coercuit, ne in mortem parentum
> pecunias filiis familiarum faenori darent.

> And by means of a law he checked the ruthlessness of creditors, re-
> straining them from making loans to a *filiusfamilias* recoverable at
> the father's death.

Now in calling this Claudian *lex* "a similar, earlier step," we are following the current teaching. It is very possible, however, that it is nothing
else than the *senatusconsultum Macedonianum*. Admittedly, Suetonius as-
cribes this decree to Vespasian. But he may be wrong, half or wholly.

In favor of assuming one measure only behind the two statements
are, for one thing, the striking similarity, both in substance and language,
between what Tacitus has to say about the Claudian *lex* and what Suetonius
has to say about the *senatusconsultum*; and for another, the absence of any
reference anywhere to two separate regulations dealing with loans to *filiifamilias*—though indeed this latter argument is merely from silence. But
the most significant fact seems to be this. Suetonius, in the passage cited,
couples with the *senatusconsultum Macedonianum* another decree, commonly called the *senatusconsultum Claudianum*. It was directed against
cohabitation of freewomen with slaves. This decree also he assigns to Vespasian, but, in this case, we know for certain that it was enacted under
Claudius. Its name alone, occurring many times in good sources (e.g. Gauis
1.91, 160), would be adequate evidence; and Tacitus, in *Annals* 12.53.1,
furnishes unambiguous confirmation, giving a detailed account of some
circumstances connected with its introduction. It is tempting to think that
the ascription to Vespasian of the *senatusconsultum Macedonianum* rests
on no stronger foundation.

Supposing, then, the *senatusconsultum Macedonianum* was passed
under Claudius, can we explain Suetonius's version? Maybe he attributed it
to Vespasian because Vespasian modified the rules. To be sure, we are nowhere told of such modifications. But some modifications by Vespasian of
the rules relating to cohabitation between free persons and slaves—though
not necessarily the rules of the *senatusconsultum Claudianum*—are referred to in Gaius 1.85, and they seem to account for his regarding Ves-

pasian as the author of the *senatusconsultum Claudianum*.[36] The cause of his error respecting the *senatusconsultum Macedonianum* may be similar.

It may, however, be worth reviving an ingenious solution of the discrepancy suggested by Peter Faber: he discovered a way of completely harmonizing Suetonius with Tacitus.[37] By speaking of Vespasian as the author of the *senatusconsultum Macedonianum*, Suetonius, or at any rate, his source, might mean that it was proposed by Vespasian when he was consul under Claudius. If we proceed from this assumption, then either description of the decree would be justified: that chosen by Tacitus, who speaks of it as a *lex* of Claudius—it dates from this emperor's reign—and that chosen by Suetonius, who speaks of it as the work of Vespasian—he initiated it. A small detail rather supporting this conjecture is that the date at which we should arrive would be very near that of the *senatusconsultum Claudianum*, with which the *senatusconsultum Macedonianum* is put together by Suetonius. The *senatusconsultum Claudianum*, according to Tacitus, was enacted in A.D. 52. Vespasian was consul towards the end of 51—it was one of those brief consulships which had become a normal institution by that time.

The final observation is about the history of the problem examined in the present article. Most of it was written when the writer discovered that the story of Theophilus was declared a clumsy Byzantine invention over 200 years ago. There arose a lively and long drawn-out controversy, which, about the middle of the last century, died down, virtual agreement having been reached that Theophilus was sound.[38] So Beseler, in 1920, was only re-opening an old case. The present writer would be satisfied if the foregoing remarks were again to settle the question for another 75 years. And his heart goes out to him who, when after that interval the attack on the traditional version is renewed, will perform the same task and a third time refute any doubts as to Macedo's guilt.[39]

---

36. See Buckland , *The Roman Law of Slavery* (1908), 412 n. 5.

37. See Glück, *Ausführliche Erläuterung der Pandekten*, 14, 2nd ed. (1868), 308.

38. See Glück, 306 f., and Windscheid, *Lehrbuch des Pandektenrechts* 2, 9th ed. by Kipp (1906), 583, n. 1.

39. The writer is indebted to Professors Last of Oxford and Duff of Cambridge for valuable suggestions and criticism.

The Preponderance of Intestacy at Rome

As most of the sources of private law represent the point of view of the haves, historians of this subject tend to forget the existence of the have-nots. A glaring illustration is furnished by the fantastic theory that, at Rome, from very early on, testacy was the rule and intestacy the exception. Actually, since Maine,[1] this is looked on as expressive of one of the most profound and characteristic compartments of the Roman psyche; and the "horror of intestacy" has become a stock phrase in discussions of the Roman law of succession. In reality, the theory is not true even for the classical period, when nine persons out of ten had nothing to make a will about. Or are we seriously to believe that the soup-kitchen proletariat instituted, disinherited, bequeathed and fideicommitted for the fun of it? They would not have achieved a first interview with a pettifogger: that required cash and there was no legal aid. If it were my sole object to refute the theory mentioned, I could indeed stop here. No detailed inquiry is needed to prove the contrary. It is safe to sum up that, from beginning to end, intestacy was the rule and testacy the exception, and both very much so.

However, what I now wish to go on to contend is that even if we confine ourselves to the haves, the position is very different from what it is generally held to be. More precisely, not one of the arguments commonly adduced in favour of the preponderance of testacy has any weight whatever. As regards the earlier times, there is every reason to assume an enormous preponderance of intestacy (even among the haves). But even in the late Republic and Empire, though wills were very frequent, it is by no means certain that the majority of people (even among the haves) did not still die intestate. My guess is that testacy did preponderate in the very highest

[*Tulane Law Review* 39 (1965), 253–62]
1.   Maine, *Ancient Law*, ed. Pollock (1920), 233.

property bracket: immense wealth is invariably attended by complications as well as special desires and duties. Of the comfortably-off, a sizeable proportion no doubt wanted to leave legacies to friends and relations, and not a few will have deemed distribution on intestacy unsatisfactory in one way or another. Victorian England might be comparable—not the present period, when an unprecedentedly large part of the population has joined the bourgeoisie.

Here are the arguments, five in all, relied on by the prevalent theory:

(1) Latin has only a negative word, *intestatus*, for a person not leaving a will, so this situation must be rare. The present writer attacked this reasoning nearly thirty years ago,[2] but it still crops up.[3] If it were correct, it would follow, since *intestato* is used by the XII Tables, that testacy was the norm prior to that legislation or at least from the very moment of its being passed. Surely few of the authorities who invoke the argument in question would find the implication acceptable. But this being so, they should cease repeating the argument. It is indeed of a nature highly disrespectful of Roman womanhood, considering a phrase like *virgo intacta*.

Words are coined to designate the striking, not the ordinary; and the striking is often the less frequent, in fact, it may be striking precisely because it is exceptional. *Testari*, "to make a will" (to pick out the meaning here relevant—we shall come across another under (3), below), *experiri*, "to try out," *auspicari*, "to take auspices" (there is also *auspicare*, however), draw attention to remarkable and, to begin with at any rate, unusual actions. There were no verbs for the unremarkable situations: without a will, without a try out, without auspices. Hence, while there is a positive past participle for the doer of the unusual, *testatus*, *expertus*, *auspicatus*, if the abstainer, who represents the ordinary, is to be described, it can only be done by negativing this participle: *intestatus*, *inexpertus*, *inauspicatus*. Basically, language gives an inverted reflection of reality; it is a laughing mirror in which the small appears large and the large small. We do not notice the mighty, continuous, harmonious diapason of the spheres, we only

---

2. Daube, "Intestatus," *Nouvelle Revue Historique de Droit Français et Étranger* 15 (4th ser. 1936), 341.

3. It is retained, of course, in the Italian translation of Schulz, *Prinzipien, I principii del diritto roman*, trans. Arangio Ruiz (1946), 136.

hear the petty interruptions.[4] In a way, ancient statutes, not yet suffering from completomania (Beseler's coinage), are comparable: they are apt to be restricted to the problematic. We shall see under (2) that the very regulation concerning the *intestatus* offers an example.

However, there are too many linguistic complications to establish a reliable criterion. To name just a few, a phenomenon may begin by being rare and end up by being common, or vice versa, yet our knowledge may be very slender. In the case of "literate" the development is clear (originally, the negative "illiterate," like *intestatus*, being applicable to the vast majority), but in other cases it is far less so. Again, the rarity of a phenomenon is only one of a number of features which may render it striking enough to deserve a word: even in tropical regions there are terms for "hot," "thirst," "sun." Further, owing to the variety of life, often a phenomenon and its opposite will each be equally outstanding in different circumstances—"friendly" and "hostile," "clean" and "dirty," "to eat" and "to starve." Lastly, in a particular context, what is otherwise usual may appear the opposite: "health" in the midst of plague, "to live" after a battle. Here it should be added that a negative word, with the prefix *in*, is likely to grow up where the peculiar circumstances would lead one to expect the positive phenomenon. *Auspicari* is an unusual action; yet in certain circumstances it is the done thing, and if omitted in these, one speaks of *inauspicato*. At one time, to be "literate" was a distinction, nearly everybody being "illiterate"; yet the latter attribute probably first came into existence as denoting one who, in view of his background or company, ought to have done better.[5] I shall suggest under (2) that *intestato* in the XII Tables is possibly expli-

4.   Aristotle, *De caelo*, trans. Guthrie, Loeb Classical Library (1939), 193: "To meet the difficulty that none of us is aware of this sound [of the planets], they [the Pythagoreans] account for it by saying that the sound is with us right from birth and has thus no contrasting silence to show it up; for voice and silence are perceived by contrast with each other, and so all mankind is undergoing an experience like that of a coppersmith who becomes by long habit indifferent to the din around him."

5.   It does not seem to have been realized that negatives are formed more freely of desirable qualities than undesirable ones. We find "unfriendly" but not "unhostile," "unclean" but not "undirty," "unbeautiful" but not "unugly," "unfreedom" but not "unslavery." The good tends to be taken for granted; disappointment strikes us more forcibly than materialization of the agreeable that we expect.

cable along these lines.

Evidently, it would be rash to assert that any negative must be the rule compared with the corresponding positive. Each case must be judged on its merits, and not infrequently[6] the result will be a *non liquet*. As far as *intestatus* is concerned, however, at least for the time of its initial appearance, we may safely assume the development outlined above: *testari* designating an extraordinary action, *testatus* its doer, *intestatus* the abstainer. If the nature of the term is to serve as an argument at all, it points to testacy as the exception, intestacy as the norm.

(2) The XII Tables treat testacy before intestacy: Digest 38.6.1 pr., Ulpian 44 *ad edictum, Posteaquam praetor locutus est de bonorum possessione eius qui testatus est, transitum fecit ad intestatos, eum ordinem secutus quem et lex duodecim tabularum secuta est* [After the praetor discussed *bonorum possessio* where there is a will, he turned to those who die intestate, following the same order as the Law of the Twelve Tables followed.][7] Hence, it is concluded, testacy must be preponderant.

This argument is found, for instance, in Jolowicz's *Historical Introduction*.[8]

Like argument (1), from *intestatus*, this one, from the sequence of the XII Tables, implies that already prior to that legislation, or at the latest from the very moment it was conceived, the majority of people made wills. It is not to be supposed that many of the advocates of the prevalent theory would care to defend this position. The proper thing, then, is to drop the argument.

Indeed, how do we know that it was a habit, an invariable habit, of ancient Roman lawgivers to start with the regular and append the less frequent? In the *lex Aquilia*, as we have it at any rate, chapter 1 deals with

---

6. The double negation has its own history.

7. The doubts thrown on the authenticity of this text by Pringsheim are refuted by Berger, "Vi sono nei Digesti citazioni interpolate della legge delle Dodici Tavole?" *Studi Riccobono* 1 (1936), 636. However, should we have before us a piece of Byzantine speculation, the support drawn from it by the prevalent theory would be worthless also on this ground.

8. Jolowicz, *Historical Introduction to the Study of Roman Law*, 2nd ed. (1952), 125.

the killing of another man's slave or beast, chapter 3 with the wounding or, in the interpretation of the classics, with any damage to property not covered by chapter 1. Is killing commoner than wounding or commoner even than any other kind of damage? Table VIII 24 may well have had the order *membrum ruptum, os fractum, iniuria,* of which offences the first, one hopes, occurred less often than the second and the second less often than the third.

The truth is that we have very little idea of what determined the sequence in early legislations, and it would not be surprising if, on examination, a multiplicity of factors turned out to be of relevance, the relative frequency of cases being one of them. But even where the latter was determinant, there might be good reason for preferring the arrangement (a) exception (b) norm, to (a) norm (b) exception.

The most plausible reconstruction of the portion of the XII Tables in question is as follows.

V 3: *Uti legassit super pecunia tutelave suae rei, ita ius esto;* V 4: *Si intestato moritur, cui suus heres nec escit, adgnatus proximus familiam habeto;* V 5: *Si adgnatus nec escit, gentiles familiam habento.*

V 3: As he has provided by will concerning his property or guardianship, so let the law be; V 4: If he dies intestate without a direct descendant, the nearest agnate is to have the *familia* [family property]; V 5: If there is no agnate, the *gentiles* [extended family] are to have the *familia.*[9]

It will be noticed that, as indicated above under (1), the regulation of intestacy, in V 4–5, contains no direction (except by implication) as to the very simplest case—where there is a *suus* to inherit. That he inherits is taken for granted, goes without saying; V 4 plunges straight into the contingency where a *suus heres* is lacking. It is incongruous to claim that the same lawgiver who, in V 4–5, omits the by far commonest case, must, in arranging V 3–5, inevitably be according pride of place to the more frequent of two situations.

9. [Thanks to David Johnston for the translation].

This is not the place to go into the history and meaning of V 3. Amidst a great deal of controversy it is agreed that, in some way or other, this law constituted an innovation—even though, conceivably, the innovation consisted in no more than that a custom which had grown up was formally sanctioned. Surely, whatever other factors might be thought of as influencing the sequence, one possibility (no more than that: a possibility) is that V 3 was placed at the head precisely because of its novelty and, indeed, in order to get this special case out of the way. First, recognition of the overriding validity of dispositions; then, the regular situation, intestacy—with the most obvious case, the *suus*, skipped.

So far I have proceeded from the current punctuation of V 4, which gives something like this translation: "If a person dies intestate, as for him who has no *suus heres* (or, no *suus* to be *heres*) let the nearest agnate have the family." The provision begins by stating the general area to be considered—"if a person dies intestate"—and then goes on to carve out from it a particular case—"he who has no *suus heres*." The sense would not be greatly affected if we were to replace the second clause, the *cui* clause, by another "if" clause: "If a person dies intestate, if he has no *suus heres*, let the nearest agnate have the family."

There is nothing to be said against this current punctuation—except that there is an alternative. We might suppress the comma between *moritur* and *cui*, regard the relative clause *cui suus heres nec escit* as the subject of the first clause *si intestato moritur*, and translate: "If a person who has no *suus heres* dies intestate, let the nearest agnate have the family." The bit *cui suus heres nec escit*, that is, would be deprived of its independence, would be made part of the *si* clause. Whether this construction accords better or less well with the style of the XII Tables as a whole is a question too vast to pursue here.[10]

The difference from the current reading is more than formal. On the basis of the alternative punctuation, with some exaggeration, we might say that the legislator does not treat intestacy as such at all; or with less exaggeration, that it is the novel confirmation of dispositions which leads him

---

10. Some observations made in Daube, *Forms of Roman Legislation* (1956), 6, on the respective roles of the "if" form and the relative form may be of use.

to affix a paragraph or two about a certain problem from intestacy. V 3 validates dispositions. It is in the absence of a *suus heres* that a man is most likely to make use of this now fully sanctioned power. The code, therefore, adds V 4 and 5 to declare what is to happen if, nevertheless, he fails to do so. We cannot (on this basis) speak of a sequence testacy-intestacy as if there were two themes of equal standing. The main weight attaches to the innovation of V 3, whereas V 4–5 are subordinate.

The coinage of *intestato*, if we accept this alternative, would be closely analogous to that of numerous words with the negative prefix. I instanced (under (1), above) *inauspicato* and "illiterate." *Auspicari* signifies an unusual action, and *auspicatus* its doer; "literate" (originally) an unusual quality. The vast majority of things happen *inauspicato*, yet this term, I pointed out, doubtless originated where, in the peculiar circumstances, the taking of auspices would have been the right course; in the peculiar circumstances, then, it was their omission which was striking. Similarly, though illiteracy (originally) preponderates, the term was surely first employed where, for special reasons, something better was anticipated. If we adopt the alternative construction of V 4, *intestato* was put because, though intestacy was the rule, in the exceptional case without a *suus heres*, it would be natural for a man to make a will. This does not mean that even in this exceptional case testacy necessarily predominated; we have no statistics.[11] But at least this was the most reasonable occasion for a will, and maybe the case for which the recognition enunciated in V 3 was principally intended—enough to render the absence of a will remarkable, enough to produce the formation *intestato* in the way found with *inauspicato* and "illiterate."

For my thesis it matters little whether we follow the current punctuation or that here proposed as equally feasible. In either case, the order of the provisions furnishes not the slightest evidence for testacy as the norm. It is neutral—and if a bias must be discovered, it is in favour of intestacy.

(3) This argument as well as the next, (4), though not, like (1) and (2), carrying back the predominance of testacy to the XII Tables or before, still would make it rather early, middle of the third century B.C. at least. While

---

11. And remember that all this discussion has exclusive reference to the haves—there was no testacy ever among the have-nots.

predominance of testacy in the epoch of the XII Tables is quite unbeliev-
able, it is implausible in my opinion even two hundred years later (and even
though I am thinking only of the haves). As a matter of fact, arguments (3)
and (4) will turn out misconceived, and, let it be said, amusingly so.

In Plautus's *Curculio*, the lover wants to institute proceedings against
a captain and, as a first step, attempts to summon him to court in the
presence of witnesses, *antestari*. The captain, however, refuses to accept
the summons. Whereupon the lover curses him:[12] *intestatus vivito*. This,
if rendered "mayest thou live without having made a will," proves that
intestacy was a disaster—so testacy the norm. The argument is invoked,
for instance, by Buckland[13] though, interestingly, he does note that Maine
overdoes the "horror of intestacy." Maine's description is really lurid—"no
evil seems to have been considered a heavier visitation... no curse appears
to have been bitterer."[14]

The correct rendering is, of course, "mayest thou live incapable of
calling witnesses" or "of being called as a witness," and there is a *double
entendre*, "without testicles."[15] *Intestatus* signifies "incapable of calling
witnesses," without pun, in another line of the same play.[16] Probably it
signifies the same here: the lover wishes on the captain for ever his own,
momentary, infuriating position—as the captain refuses to cooperate,
the witnesses are no use to the lover, he cannot do anything with them.
Kornhardt, in the *Thesaurus*,[17] translates "incapable of being called as a
witness," the usual meaning of *intestabilis*, and this interpretation is also
tenable: the captain, not behaving as a decent citizen, summoned, ought
to behave, shall be infamous. There is a line in the *Miles gloriosus* where
intestatus seems to have the sense of *intestabilis*—and the pun reappears,
too.[18] *Intestabilis* itself, "incapable of being called as witness," "infamous,"

12. Plautus, *Curculio* 622.
13. Buckland, *A Text-Book of Roman Law*, 3rd ed. (1963), 365.
14. Maine, *Ancient Law*, at 233.
15. The pun can be imitated in English and German, but it is advisable to forbear.
16. *Curculio* 695.
17. Kornhardt, in *Thesaurus* 7.2, fasc. 1 (1956), col. 5.
18. Plautus, *Miles gloriosus* 1416. The word *intestabilis* is found in 1417. Strangely,
Kornhardt and others (Hammond, Mack and Moskalew, *Miles gloriosus* [1963]) assume
the sense "incapable of calling witnesses" in 1416 rather unlikely.

occurs twice in Plautus, both times with a play on the improper meaning; Plautus, or his audience, was inordinately fond of this pun. One of the two passages is again from the *Curculio*.[19]

The Plautine usage of *intestatus* or *intestabilis*, then, speaks very much against explaining the curse as having regard to the absence of a will.[20] But, quite apart from this, why ever should the public watching the play think of wills in this scene? There is a frustrated *antestari*, followed by the curse *intestatus vivito*. No difficulty in associating the latter with the calling of witnesses or the bearing of witness in similar circumstances or even in general—but how should wills specifically come in? And whatever one's view of testacy or intestacy, would the captain mind one way or the other? And the curse says *vivito*: it must contemplate something affecting his life, not his death. It cannot be objected that *vivito* may constitute a further playful twist within the main pun, intended to be a distortion of *morito*. That would be too much of a strain on the audience's receptiveness. Moreover, it would not suit the *double entendre*, which definitely requires *vivito*. In addition, there is the parallel from the *Miles gloriosus, vivam semper intestabilis*,[21] on which I shall say a little more presently. The whole idea of connecting this curse with wills is impossible. It reveals a touching overestimate of learning (erroneous learning, as it happens) to imagine that a captain in a comedy by Plautus might be frightened by the prospect of failing to make a will. No doubt the misunderstanding of a statement by Cato, to be the subject of (4) below, has something to do with it, but it remains an astonishing notion.

Vivo with the double nominative, incidentally, is frequent in Plautus—and later—and is employed both where it is a question of somebody

---

19. *Curculio* 30. The other is *Miles gloriosus* 1417, next door to 1416 with *intestatus*.

20. Kornhardt, cols. 2, 5, actually distinguishes between an *intestatus* from *testari* and an *intestatus* from *testis*, assigning the curse to the latter. However, I am not convinced that there is a strict distinction, and further, I do not quite understand her criteria—for example, why she places *Curculio* 695 under the former and *Miles gloriosus* 1416 under the latter though she translates in both cases "unsupported by witnesses." Perhaps it is the pun in *Miles gloriosus* 1416 which in her view points to derivation from *testis*. But, then, the absence of the pun is hardly adequate proof of a different derivation. I incline to derive all cases from *testari*.

21. *Miles gloriosus* 1417.

living an unhappy man, as in this case,[22] or a happy man.[23] I wonder
whether perhaps legal or semi-legal pronouncements are behind the curse
intestatus vivito. In the *Miles gloriosus*, a soldier protests that if he does not
stand by his word, *vivam semper intestabilis*;[24] in the "Trinummus" we find
the comment *omnes mortales hunc aiebant Calliclum indignum civitate ac
sese vivere*;[25] and centuries later, a constitution by Gratian, Valentinian and
Theodosius ordains that a dangerous Manichaean *intestabilis vivat*.[26] (The
law goes on: *nihil vivus impendat illicitis, nihil moriens relinquat indig-
nis*. So here "intestability" indeed specifically denotes "powerlessness to
dispose of one's estate." But, then, the context could not be more different
from that of the lover's exclamation in the *Curculio*.)

(4) The elder Cato, according to Plutarch,[27] declared that he was sor-
ry about three things he had done, one of them being that he had remained
without a will for an entire day. Schulz criticizes v. Woess for not using this
statement as evidence for the preponderance of testacy.[28]

But v. Woess is right. We have to do with one of Cato's eccentricities
or extremisms—otherwise, why should it have been found worth recording? It is not even safe to infer (though that would leave my thesis unaffected) that, while few would have lived up to it, this attitude represents the
general ideal of the time. The other two things Cato said he regretted are,
one, that he once told his wife a secret, two, that he once voyaged by sea
when he could have travelled on land (or it may mean, that he paid a ship's
fare when he could have walked it).[29] He also boasted, when he expelled
Manlius from the Senate for kissing his wife by day in front of their daughter, that his wife never came into his arms except when there was violent

---

22. Or, e.g., Plautus, *Casina* 403 (*tu vives miser*).

23. E.g., Plautus, *Captivi* 828 (*nemo vivit fortunatior*); *Trinummus* 390 (*lepidus
vivis*).

24. *Miles gloriosus* 1417.

25. *Trinummus* 212–13 (reading *ac sese* controversial).

26. Codex Theodosianus 16.5.9 pr.

27. Plutarch, *Lives*, trans. Perrin, Loeb Classical Library (1914), 329.

28. Schulz, *Principles of Roman Law*, trans. Wolf (1936), 156.

29. The latter interpretation is adopted by Perrin in his translation of Plutarch, 2,
329.

thunder.[30] At any rate it is naive to reconstruct historical reality on the strength of such idealizing descriptions. Titus is reported to have lamented *diem perdidi* when he allowed a day to pass without a gracious act, and my student friend E.G. at Freiburg applied the phrase when no new girl had been charmed. A collection of the one, two or three errors great men have felt they committed in their otherwise perfect lives would indeed be revealing—but not in the simple way in which the anecdote about Cato is nowadays thought to be.

Finally, let us recall that the very rendering of this passage is extremely dubious. The Greek is *hoti mian hemeran, adiathetos emeine.* Certainly, this can have the nowadays accepted sense. In that case, either, when his father died and he became a *paterfamilias*, capable of owning property and making a will, a day elapsed before he had completed the formalities; or, at some date an existing will of his was in need of alteration or was accidentally destroyed, and a day elapsed before a fresh one was substituted. No details are supplied; and, with the exception, perhaps, of the alteration of the will, it is not easy to see how Cato could have helped these matters. Still, this interpretation is not unattractive. I incline to that which held exclusive sway prior to the first half of the last century and even after that found defenders until not very long ago, and which takes *adiathetos* as signifying "not purposefully engaged." Cato reproaches himself for having remained a whole day without serious, planned business. A slightly different nuance is equally plausible: he reproaches himself for having remained a whole day "in disorder," "with his affairs not tidily arranged."

(5) From Cato's saying Schulz concludes that to make a will "was as much the duty of every self-respecting Roman as to keep proper accounts." This goes much further than the claim that testacy was the rule; nearly every Roman, we may presume, at one time or another borrowed an object (this includes even the have-nots), but it does not follow that there was a moral obligation to that effect. In point of fact, none of the countless texts in Roman literature dealing with ethical or civic duties hints at the making of a will.

The reference to accounts is puzzling; it looks as if it were meant

30. Ibid. 353. This was hardly true of his second wife.

as an argument—that is why I am adding this separate section (5). The anecdote about Cato does not mention accounts. Schulz quotes a passage from Cicero's *In Verrem*.[31] This passage, however, does not mention wills. It does not even say, or imply, that it is usual to keep proper accounts. What it does say (and even this, we should bear in mind, is part of an advocate's case) is that a citizen whose dealings are honest does not start recording a transaction and then break off in the middle; where that happens, there must be something fishy.

Anyhow, accounts and wills have absolutely nothing to do with one another. One can conceive of a society in which the keeping of accounts is compulsory though wills are unknown.

31. Cicero, *In Verrem* 2.1.23.60, in *The Verrine Orations*, trans. Greenwood, Loeb Classical Library (1928), 1.

What Price Equality?
Some Historical Reflections*

I should state at the outset that I am not concerned with the plain, literal admission fee into a community. In antiquity no less than today there are associations and even states and subdivisions of them membership of which is available for money, whether officially or by way of bribe. Take Rome. As the apostle Paul invokes the rights of a citizen, the military tribune in charge, a naturalized subject, remarks that he paid a huge sum for them.[1] Assignment to a desirable class or order may depend on how much tax or other contributions you can afford.[2] To some extent the slave allowed by his master to purchase freedom with the *peculium* belongs here.[3] No doubt a modern re-examination of this area would be interesting. What I here understand by "price," however, is a more indirect *quid pro quo* (admittedly, at times, bordering on the direct): the duties, restraints, losses of all sorts, consequent upon equality attained if not already upon equality sought.

[*Rechtshistorisches Journal* 5 (1986): 185–208 (*BLL*, 535–53)]

* To Ed and Sandra Epstein. The Gail A. Burnett Lecture in Classics at San Diego State University, 1983.

1. Acts 22:28. See G.E.M. De Ste. Croix, *British Journal of Sociology* 5 (1954), 41 f.; D. Daube, *TR* 47 (1979), 237; J. T. Noonan, *Bribes* (1984), 717.

2. See B. Kübler, "Classis," in *Pauly-Wissowa's Realencyclopaedie der classischen Altertumswissenschaft*, vol. 3, 2 (1899), cols. 2630 ff.; T. Mommsen, *Römisches Staatsrecht*, 3rd ed., vol.1 (1876; rpt. 1952), 498 f., vol. 3, pt. 2 (1888; rpt. 1952), 876 f., 882 f., 899 f.

3. See A. Watson, *The Law of Persons in the Later Republic* (1967), 178 f., 201 ff.

I. Me

Let me describe the occasion in my own life in England when it struck me that, from being a refugee, I had become U—as far as I ever could. I stepped ashore there in the thirties, a student, penniless, totally unacquainted with the language. For the first couple of years, William Warwick Buckland, who got me into Caius, and I conversed in French. In that era, even foreigners of wealth and standing were looked down on, and not only by the *haute volée*. Yet if you were young, intense and soulful, you had extraordinary leeway precisely because, *au fond*, you were dirt. Damsels who would never have gotten involved, except for good, with a guy of their set were responsive to an outsider. A touching experience on a different level was a ring of the doorbell, early one morning, and out there stood Buckland, President of the College, deep in his seventies, having made his way, on foot and by bus, from the high-class sector he lived in to my shabby one: his sister, the only surviving member of his original family, had died. Surely, some of his colleagues were as capable of sympathy, deep down, as I; but to come to them with this would not have done. So he came to me: I was sympathetic—and did not count. (There are, of course, innumerable analogues to my then position. The servants of grandees come to mind or, say Heathcliff of *Wuthering Heights*.) Three decades later, when the Queen was opening a new hospital wing at Oxford, as Regius Professor I was invited to the lunch at Trinity (whose Master, that year, happened to head the University government). It was a relatively small party, about twenty, and at one point four bodies were lying on the floor. Harold Macmillan presided, being Chancellor of the University. This is a purely honorary office, for just such events only; by chance, though, he was also Prime Minister at the time. At his right hand was placed the Queen, at his left the Duke of Edinburgh. It was very hot and midway through the meal the wife of the Lord Lieutenant of the County, a lady of advanced age, fainted and sank to the ground. Her husband, mortified, rose, stretched out an arm toward the servants and exclaimed: "Take her away." But he, too, poor fellow, was around eighty, clad in his full regalia, with a heavy sword dangling from his belt. So he, too, swooned and fell down. At this, Macmillan lifted himself up a fraction, to show concern. The page behind him assumed he meant to get up to walk over to the victims and helpfully withdrew the chair. Alas, it was a miscalculation. Macmillan, his gesture completed, was going immediately to sit back again. Instead he landed at the royal couple's feet, flailing monstrously: he was huge. Apparently in a playful mood, fate finished up with someone quite different. Trinity, in order that everything at this important lunch should go off flawlessly, had recalled from retirement its butler of pre-World-War-II days, who knew all the lore pertaining to a gala with such high guests. This venerable—even he, needless to say, thickly costumed—had indeed done very well up to this scene. But with three persons prostrate, he did not know where to turn and himself collapsed. Through it all, I behaved as if nothing out of the ordinary were happening. Nobody could have noticed that I noticed. Without a moment's pause, without the slightest change of inflection, I continued discussing with the Master of Balliol, my neighbor, the metres of T. S. Eliot's "Waste Land." Full marks. Yes—if you leave out of the reckoning the suppression of all the promptings deriving from my South-German Jewish upbringing and greatly at variance with the etiquette superimposed. Why, by then, an old dignitary who lost his sister might prefer calling on a newcomer from Hungary.

II. WOMEN

Turning now to the past, I must prefix a caveat: I shall not bother about the veracity or exactitude of the sources. This is not to belittle the problem. But for the purpose of a brief survey, when we hear, for example, about a plebeian leader wresting parity from the patricians and the ensuing incapacity of both his opponents and himself to handle his success, or, in the Rabbinic field, about the entrapment of an outstanding woman scholar, what counts is less the factual details than the experiences and feelings revealed by the reports.

In deference to the spirit of the times, I shall consider women first.[4]

---

4. See D. Daube, *Archiv Orientální* 17 (1949), 93 [*BLL*, 83 f.]; *Civil Disobedience in Antiquity* (1972), 31 ff., *JR* 90 (1978), 177 ff. [*NTJ*, 231 ff.]; *ZRG, RA* 99 (1982), 27 ff. [*TL*,

In many cultures, to begin with, adultery is a private affair, in the sense that it is up to the husband to deal with the offending couple. Gradually, the community takes over punishment of the intruder while his wife still remains under the *iudicium domesticum*. The whole of Greece goes to war against Paris and his abetters and razes their city. Helen's fate is decided by Menelaos alone—who reinstates her as Queen of Sparta. The adulterous David, secular justice being powerless, is at least called to account by a prophet. His partner in sin, Bathsheba, escapes any censure: her husband perished before being informed.[5] In this period, the situation resembles today's when your spaniel is lured away by a thief. The state provides remedies against the latter. As for the former, you may do nothing, kick him or—if so inclined—improve his treatment. In the Bible, Deuteronomy represents a new stage: the two culprits equally incur the death penalty. Indeed the same regulation applies to the seducer of a maiden affianced to another man and the maiden. In Rome, it is Augustus who has both adulterer and adulteress exiled (to different places!). The woman has been promoted from pet to person. Nor is the gain merely ideological: she is assured of an orderly procedure, need no longer fear condemnation out of hand by an oversuspicious husband or, in the Jewish orbit, fiancé. At the same time—here we come to the crux—once her misconduct is public knowledge, she can no more rely, like Helen of Troy, on pacifying her master.

Here are two vastly different episodes, separated by some twenty years only, one from Judaea,[6] the other from Rome.[7] When Mary, betrothed to Joseph, was found pregnant, he could have brought a capital charge,[8]

---

149 ff.]; *Sons and Strangers* (1984), 14 ff. [BLL 166 f.]; and the contribution to *The Legal Mind: Essays for Tony Honoré*, ed. N. MacCormick and P. Birks (1986), 2 ff., below 234–243.

5. Or, who knows?, perished pretending ignorance.

6. Matt 1:18 ff.

7. Tacitus, *Annals* 2.85.1 ff.; Suetonius, *Tiberius* 35.2.

8. The contention by H. L. Strack and P. Billerbeck, *Kommentar zum Neuen Testament aus Talmud und Midrasch*, vol. 1, 5th ed. (1926; rpt. 1969), 51 f., that Rabbinic limitations made such a charge impossible takes no account of their relatively late origin. A similar backdating causes the *Kommentar* difficulties with John 8: see D. Daube, *The New Testament and Rabbinic Judaism* (1956; rpt. 1973), 307, and "Origen and the Punishment of Adultery in Jewish Law," *SP* 64 (1957), 111 f. [*NTJ*, 621; *TL*, 167–71].

thus making an example of her.[9] However, being of a charitable, selfless disposition,[10] he decided to dismiss her quietly; whereupon a higher truth was revealed to him. What we have before us, throughout, is a throwback to the "house trial," in this case of obvious advantage to the woman.

Under the Roman system, as the incident to be presented shows, in certain circumstances, a husband refraining from prosecution might get into serious trouble. The punishment for adultery introduced by Augustus was not meted out to professionals. In A.D. 19, Vistilia, a lady of high rank, registered as one of them. She did not indeed intend to ply the trade; all she wanted was to cultivate her liaisons unmolested. She was hauled before a court, which held that she was not a *bona fide* whore and relegated her to a desolate island. Her husband narrowly missed being engulfed: he had not initiated proceedings and was suspected of condoning her doings. He does seem to have been a maverick. It is probably he whom the elder Pliny castigates for painting miniatures. At any rate, Vistilia manifestly thought little of the enhanced standing of wives: the old dispensation suited her better.

Often the cost of advancement is to be defrayed in coin of the heart. A little intermezzo in the *Ecclesiazousae*[11] illustrates Aristophanes's tender side. The wives of Athens have resolved to wrest the government from their foolish husbands. Disguised as men, they are gathering for a legislative session. One of them, however, brings along the equipment for carding wool and, when told off, asks what is wrong with it so long as she listens; the point is that "my children go naked." Plainly, she is reluctant to sacrifice motherhood. Alas, they warn her that the work might cause her cloak to

---

9. *Deigmatizo.* Jude 7 employs the noun *deigma:* "Sodom and Gomorrah, giving themselves over to fornication, are set forth as an example." *Paradeigmatizo* is met in Jer 13:22, "For the greatness of your iniquity are your lower parts shown as an example," and Ezek 28:17, "Your heart was lifted up because of your beauty, I will lay you before kings to become an example." We may also compare passages with synonyms, like Ezek 23:10: "These discovered her nakedness and slew her with the sword and she became a name among women." The Septuagint translates "name" by *lalema* which recurs, e.g., in 1 Kgs 9:7: "Israel shall be a proverb and byword among all people."

10. On this meaning of *ṣaddiq*, see D. Daube, in *Aufstieg und Niedergang der Römischen Welt,* ed. H. Temporini and W. Haase, part 2, vol. 25, 3, "Religion" (1985), 2346 [*NTJ*, 872 f.]. The interpretation of H. L. Strack and P. Billerbeck, op. cit., 50, is forced.

11. *Ecclesiazousae* 88 f.

shift and reveal her gender. As we are engaged on feelings, an aside about
the first-century A.D. biography of Aesop may pass.[12] The lady who owned
him, we are told, vowed to free him if he could perform coitus ten times in
a row. Nowadays, I guess, not a few readers will object to the crude male
orientation which takes it for granted that the male's orgasm automatically
pleasures the woman. They are right. Only, even in this sphere, progress
is attended by some loss. Before they broke their chains, doubtless women
might in fact derive a measure of sexual gratification simply from that of
their men.

The Old Testament regulation of succession is pertinent.[13] Originally,
a daughter did not inherit. Then she became entitled in the absence of
a son. To go by what we are told, the reform was requested by the five
daughters of one Zelophehad not from a feminist motive but in the interest
of their father: his name would be extinct if the estate went to someone not
his issue. Nevertheless the result was inevitably an increase in women's
power; and a Freudian might wonder whether perhaps the petitioners had
a subconscious inkling. However, this was not the end. There was now a
danger that an heiress might marry into another tribe and thereby alienate
the estate from its permanent base. The heads of Zelophehad's tribe, therefore, asked for and obtained supplementary legislation, to the effect that
an heiress must marry within her tribe. So the new benefit entailed a curb
on the choice of husband: not a small matter—remember the Danaids.
(Remember, too, the manifold strategies of men similarly restricted: concubinage, morganatic marriage etc.) In fact the Biblical author is evidently
conscious of its gravity. For one thing, like many laws past and present that
curtail a right, this one opens by diplomatically stressing, exaggerating,
what remains of it: "To whoever is good in their eyes they may become
wives." For another thing, the story ends by recording emphatically and
expansively the marriage of the five to their father's brothers' sons: for sub-
missive imitation.

Quite a few cases under this rubric are less civil. Deuteronomy, with

---

12. See B. E. Perry, *Aesopica*, vol. 1 (1952), 95, 127 f. On the relation of the anecdote to Balzac's *Contes Drolatiques*, see D. Daube, *Mnemosyne* 30 (1977), 176 ff.
13. Num 27:1 f., 36:1 ff.

one ruling for adulterer and adulteress, also places the mother of an incor-
rigibly rebellious son on the same level as the father: his arraignment, with
a view to execution, is the right and duty of both jointly. (A short verse
in Mark—and Mark alone—mentions an attempt, as Jesus is starting to
create a stir, to take the first steps then customary if a son embarked on
that route. Significantly, they are taken, not just by the head of the family,
but by "those near him.")[14] The priest-judge Eli incurs God's wrath for not
dealing with his depraved offspring as sternly as he ought to. Normally, a
mother will be even less inclined to cast off a child. Yet that is what, her
inferiority ended, she is expected to do.

A mother's special difficulty is, of course, recognized. The Maccabean heroine who encouraged her seven sons, one after the other, to undergo torturous death rather than be disloyal to God "nerved her weak
woman's heart with the courage of a man, was a wonder, to be held in
glorious memory." So imbued was she with her religion that "though a
mother's sympathy is deeper than a father's, she did not shed one tear."[15] In
Roman legend,[16] when Coriolanus, offended by his compatriots, was leading a Volscian army against them, his mother and wife went out to his
camp and persuaded him to raise the siege—saving the city and ruining
him. Brutus and Manlius, having their sons beheaded for crimes of state,
are certainly looked up to with awe. But the two women are celebrated in
the most outstanding fashion: by the erection of a temple to the Goddess of
Female Luck.

To go on to another facet, it is scarcely surprising that praise for unla-
dylike strength tends to surge up in crises, when men are badly in need of
help. We have just gone through two world wars typical in this respect. No
doubt wisdom, enlightenment and acknowledgement of the maternal role in
education do play a part in developments like the Deuteronomic one. But so
many concrete examples resemble those from Maccabees and Livy.

---

14. Mark 3:21. See D. Daube, *Das Alte Testament im Neuen—aus jüdischer Sicht*,
translated from the English by W. Schuller, *Xenia* 10 (1984), 23. The English text will be
found in "The Old Testament in the New: a Jewish Perspective," probably coming out in
Zeitschrift für die Neutestamentliche Wissenschaft (1987), section 5 [*NTJ*, 43–63].

15. 2 Mac 7:20 f.; 4 Mac 15:4, 20:2.

16. Livy 2.40.

Jael takes us back to an Israelite revolt against Canaanite oppression
in the second millennium B.C.[17] Right at the start, Barak, the leader, is
forewarned that, though he will succeed, the supreme triumph will be a
woman's. The prediction itself, it should be noted, emanates from a woman,
the judge-prophetess Deborah, his guide. It proves true. Sisera, command-
er of the Canaanite troops, is beaten and flees. On reaching the place of
Jael, wife of a Qenite, he hopes to be safe for the night. He is indeed received most hospitably but, when he is asleep, she drives a tent peg through
his head. She, then, wins the laurel. In passing, just as a woman is admired
for doing in a man, so her victim is disgraced: Abimelech, first king over
Israel, comes to mind, also Samson, Nabal, Haman.[18]

The tale is transmitted in prose and as a ballad—ascribed to Deborah and Barak, the oldest instance of explicit joint authorship known to me.
A line in the poem, by hinting at sexual commerce, goes to extremes in
bringing out the *contra naturam* character of the deed. "Between her legs
he bowed, he fell, he lay; between her legs he bowed, he fell; as he bowed,
there he fell—wrecked." Three parts. (1) "Between her legs he bowed, he
fell, he lay": heavily smacking of intercourse.[19] (2) "Between her legs he
bowed, he fell": keeping up, savoring, the image. Everybody in the audience, of course, already knows the outcome. (3) "As he bowed, there he
fell—wrecked": itself subdivided. First, a continuation of what precedes,
yet with a menacing undertone, that precise "there," suggesting "that was
it, with nothing beyond." Then the horrid disclosure, a single word, in radical contrast to the initial clues, hence all the more barbarously enjoyable. I
suppose the public was left free either to think of Jael as actually pleasur-
ing her guest or to take it all as sheer mockery, alluding to what a soldier
invited in by a woman would normally get but decidedly did not here. The

17. Judges 4 f.
18. Judg 9:53 f., 16:19 ff.; 1 Sam 25:36 ff.; Esther 5 ff.
19. "Between her legs" = "her genitals" in Deut 28:57, "The afterbirth that comes
out from between her legs." As for the verbs—"to lie" is common in this area. "To bow"
occurs in Job 31:10, "If I have loitered shamingly at my neighbor's door, let others bow
over my wife"; "to fall" in Esth 7:8, "The king returned and Haman had fallen on the bed
whereon Esther was, and the king said, 'Will he also rape the queen?'"

prose version has none of this entire excursus.[20]

Judith is modelled after a fair number of prior figures, female ones such as Rahab[21] and Esther[22] and male ones such as her ancestor Simeon,[23] Jonathan,[24] Job[25] and Daniel.[26] Obviously, her principal precursor is Jael: like her, she murders the enemy general in his sleep after a great show of affection. Holofernes' death at a woman's hand brings shame on the whole of Assyria.[27] She is hailed as the "exaltation of Jerusalem" and the like,[28] though in her own utterances the honour of achieving victory through so frail an instrument is attributed to God.[29] Strikingly, the question-mark attaching to Jael's exploit is erased: Judith, it is impressed on us, remains undefiled. She skilfully manages to inflame the tyrant's desire. Banqueting with her at his side, he drinks himself into a complete stupor and is despatched by her in this state; and when she shows his severed head to her fellow-citizens, she loses no time in affirming on oath that God did not allow him to commit sin with her.[30] In the circles to which this work is addressed, even when it is a matter of winning or losing a war, a woman's saving feat would be marred were she to compromise her purity in the process. Actually, in this domain, the fearless and ruthless deliverer of her people who are on the point of giving up is singularly faithful to the traditional feminine ideal: she is a widow who never re-marries, a *univira*.

---

20. Maybe, in the poem, even the milk she generously offers instead of the water he asks for stands for sweeter delights. In Cant 4:11, the lover finds "milk and honey under your tongue." But I do not wish to become like a psychoanalyst's client who, when the analyst sketched a house and asked, "what is your association?" replied: "sex." He gave the same reply when shown a garden, a book, a cupboard. Finally, the analyst remarked: "You know, everything seems to remind you of sex." To which the client retorted: "How can you say so? Who is drawing all these pictures?"

21. Jdt 11:12 f.; Josh 2:9.
22. Judith 10 f.; Esther 5.
23. Jdt 9:2 ff.; Gen 34:25.
24. Jdt 9:11; 1 Sam 14:6.
25. Jdt 8:13 f.; Job 11:7.
26. Jdt 12:2 ff.; Dan 1:8 ff.
27. Jdt 14:18.
28. Jdt 15:18 ff.
29. Jdt 9:10, 13:15, 16:6.
30. Jdt 12:20, 13:1 ff., 16 .

The Maccabean mother also, it may be observed, is a widow and, indeed, throws herself into the pyre before she can be seized—in order that no man touch her body.[31]

(Moralists throughout the ages have taken exception to Jael's and Judith's treacherous method. Admittedly, it is not nice. But one wonders whether the person most closely affected, if given a choice, might not prefer it to the honest way, whereby he would be brutally thrown into a wagon, driven to a secluded spot and there strangled or hacked to death.)

A comment by Livy on the homage paid to the disarmers of Coriolanus reveals yet a further risk accompanying a rise in status, one that applies not only to women but to almost any newcomers from below and, ironically, all the more the higher the merit by which the rise is earned: the resentment of the mean-spirited. In that epoch, he remarks nostalgically, people were not given to begrudging someone else's fame, hence the men felt no envy of these women. Evidently, by his time at least, the male ego was less tolerant.

Beruriah, of the second century A.D., daughter and wife of eminent Rabbis, is the only female scholar in the Talmud to discuss theology and law with male sages on equal terms. She makes no effort to hide her ability and mocks the stereotype downgrading of women as lightweight. Her husband, R. Meir, warns her that she is no exception; and he gets a young disciple to pay court to her. After a long siege, she relents somewhat—though not, of course, to the extent of permitting the slightest physical intimacy. However, she is now told of the scheme and how she has failed—whereupon, deeply mortified, she hangs herself.[32]

This brings me to another punishment befalling virtually every attainment of a goal. In fact, its role in daily life can hardly be overrated; and precisely for this reason I shall confine myself to a mere hint—otherwise it would absorb excessive space. I am thinking of the evaporation of the zest that animated the pursuit. Coupled, if the pursuit was a shared one, the concern of a group, with the discontinuance of the joy that was felt in being united with friends against a foe. Coupled also, often enough, with the letdown on finding out that the pastry looked sweeter than it tastes. In short,

---

31. 4 Mac 16:10, 17:1.
32. Rashi on *Babylonian Avodah Zarah* 18b.

the strike, the demonstration or the shootout while the oppressor rules is apt to be more rousing than the fifth anniversary celebration of his caving in. Tying up, somewhat, with the growing recognition among our health experts that there are positive elements in tension. I guess that before long the supermarkets will offer titles like "Stress is good for you" and we shall flock to classes where we are taught how to get into a state.

Before the *finis* of this section, I might raise the question what disadvantage would accrue to men if they became women's equals in departments where so far the latter have the upper hand. Say, their life expectancy were made to catch up. An oddly neglected datum; surely, if it were the other way round, it would be a major political issue nowadays. From time immemorial, it is not just strictly biological factors that account for it. Men rather than women fall in battle: Lysistrata knows about it.[33] Or when a city is captured, often while the adult men are put to the sword, the rest are spared. The Old Testament reflects this custom.[34] In Greek legend, Andromache, having seen Hector slain by Achilles and their son hurled from the walls of burning Troy, lives on for many years—with sad downs but also with happy ups.[35] One could readily make a long list of items were one to pursue my question.[36]

III. Slaves

As for slaves[37]—the early legislation in Exodus, admired, with good reason, for being more humanitarian than surrounding cultures, none the less puts

33. *Lysistrata* 589 ff.

34. Deut 20:13 f., cp. 21:10 ff.

35. See R. Wagner, "Andromache," in *Pauly-Wissowa*, vol. 1, 2 (1894; rpt. 1958), cols. 2151 f.

36. Not long after writing the above, I find in the *San Francisco Chronicle Review* of August 11, 1985, 11, a discussion of K. Chernin's *The Hungry Self* by R. T. Lakoff, entitled "The Rites of Over-indulgence." She enumerates conceivable solutions of the feminist plight, one of them being to "discard women's traditional roles in favor of men's." Her opinion: "while this might be immediately gratifying, it is ultimately unsatisfactory. Men's roles are really not much freer." Helen has expressed this view to me for years.

37. See D. Daube, *Archiv Orientální* 17 (1949), 96 ff.; id. with R. Yaron in *JSS* 1

its seal on a heart-rending dilemma. A Hebrew slave need serve no longer than six years. However, should his master have given him a slave-woman to wife, she and any children will remain behind. He may indeed choose to stay on with them but, if so, he continues a slave for ever.[38] There is a paragraph adding in so many words that the regular release thus ordained is confined to males: which suggests pressure the other way. (Females do obtain release in a few exactly circumscribed cases.) Obviously, if a female slave were equally entitled, no serious problem would ever arise for a male one: at the very worst, he would, on leaving, have to wait a few years for his wife to follow.

What stands out right away is that the statute reckons with no other motive for a slave's waiver of his due than attachment to his family: "I love my master, my wife and my children." The master, I guess, appears chiefly for appearances' sake though, as he supplied the wife, a modicum of substance may be conceded. Anyhow, the assumption is that the freedom is always craved except when it means losing your nearest: this price may be just too high. Of those who resolved to pay it many must have suffered excruciating pain; and it is hard to imagine greater love than a man's who, for its sake, on reaching at last the moment his chains are to be taken off, accepts them for the rest of his life. The importance of children is all the more touching when we consider that the eldest can be at most about five: namely, if the mother was donated as soon as the six years of servitude began. One is reminded of other notable instances of a father's affection for his brood of tender age: Hector's farewell, Jacob's reluctance to expose his toddlers to a strenuous march, David's prayer for the boy from his adultery.[39]

(1956), 60 ff.; *Typologie im Werk des Flavius Josephus*, vol. 6 of *Bayerische Akademie der Wissenschaften*, Phil.-Hist. Klasse (1977), 24 ff. (rpt. *Freiburger Rundbrief* 31 [1979], 66 f.), English trans. in *JJS* 31 (1980), 33 ff.; *Sons and Strangers* (1984), 3, 30 [*BLL*, 86 ff., 293 ff., 158 f., 177; *Ethics*, 277 ff.].

38. Exod 21:2 ff. On earlier Near-Eastern statutes comparable though with significant deviations, see R. Yaron, *Revue historique de droit français et étranger* 63 (1985), 139 f.

39. Homer, *Iliad* 6.466 ff.; Gen 33:13, where the concern extends to the sucklings among the flocks; 2 Sam 12:16 ff. How old the "tender" Solomon is supposed to be in 1 Chron 22:5, 29:1 is not clear.

It is safe, alas, to conclude that not a few masters would provide a wife precisely in order to finalize their ownership. Corroboration is furnished by the chapters on Laban and Jacob[40] whose relationship, while not that of master and slave, is not totally unlike it. The former brazenly uses his two daughters, plus their two handmaids, plus the children of the four, to keep hold of the latter—plainly an invaluable asset.[41] A seven years' indenture for one daughter and handmaid is followed by a further such for the other daughter (the really desired one) and handmaid; and even at the end of fourteen years, as Jacob wishes to quit, Laban balks at his demand to take his wives and children with him and yet a third rehiring is negotiated. We may indeed ask whether the ancient public was unqualifiedly sympathetic to the protagonist: perhaps he was looked on as a bit too soft. To be sure, the patriarchs all—and many other Hebrew leaders, from Adam on—are hugely influenced by their women. But Jacob comes near to being a *Weiberknecht* [subservient to women].[42]

At all events, the Exodus code arguably frowns on sacrificing liberty for sentiment. Its general trend, we should bear in mind, is somewhat comparable to that of the XII Tables, in that significant limits are set on power: henceforth it will not be so easy to get away with sheer murder or even severe harming of a slave, with indiscriminate killing of a thief, with

40. Genesis 29 ff.
41. Gen 30:26 f., 29 f., 31:15.
42. His supplanting of his elder twin was foreshadowed in Rebekah's womb as well as during birth and predicted to her by the Lord in answer to her enquiry (Gen 25:22 f., 26). Unlike Esau, he was born mild-colored and without hair (25:25). The ruse by which he obtained the blessing intended for Esau was thought up and prepared by his mother; in fact, he went along with it only after she promised to take upon herself the consequences should it miscarry (27:6). It was her idea that he take to flight from Esau and journey to Laban, her brother (27:42 ff.). He made a fool of himself for Rachel, mistakenly marrying her sister (29:21 ff.). He allowed himself to be hired by Leah from Rachel for the night (30:15 f.). He carefully got the two to agree to the escape from Laban (31:4 ff.); by contrast, Rachel carried off the latter's protective images entirely on her own (31:19, 30 ff.). He took no action against the handmaid who slept with his eldest son though he demoted the latter (35:22, 49:4). Joseph, born to him by Rachel when he was already aging, was his declared favorite (37:3), next to him Benjamin, also from Rachel (42:4, 38, 43:3 ff., 44:19 ff.). On his deathbed, he remembered her untimely end (48:7). Good thing his challenger at the Jabbok was not a female or he would have knuckled under.

seduction of a virgin.[43] It is not accidental that the provisions respecting
the release of slaves form the opening. More specifically—we are advised
that a slave deciding for family and lasting servitude shall have his ear
pierced with an awl in a public ceremony: cruel and, above all, producing a
mark.[44] It is conceivable that the lawgiver, hostile to greedy masters, hopes
a slave will think twice before going through with it. The proclamation in
Leviticus of universal freedom in the Jubilee deserves notice. It contains
an express condemnation of submission for good, on a theological ground
not met in Exodus: as in conflict with the supremacy of God. "For they are
my servants, they shall not sell themselves by a slave-sale."[45] Very likely,
this way of seeing it owes something to the doctrine preached by those opponents of the monarchy who blamed it not on the king but on the people
opting for it and thereby distancing themselves from their true sovereign:
"They have rejected me," says God, "that I should not reign over them."[46]
If there was some disapproval of a slave perpetuating his condition already
quite early on, the transfer to this area of that notion from the battle about
government becomes the easier to understand.

Johanan ben Zaccai, of the first century A.D., speculates as to why
the slave's ear rather than any other part of his body is singled out for mu-
tilation. His answer is that it is with his ear that he heard God's warning
from Sinai just quoted, "they are my servants." Unhistorical and tied to the
concerns of the Rabbi's period as this explanation is, it does capture a good
deal of the spirit of the Biblical development.[47]

I shall be brief about Deuteronomy.[48] In accordance with its policy
sketched above, both male and female slaves may claim deliverance after
six years. This effectively eliminates the complication of a marriage between two slaves dealt with in Exodus, hence Deuteronomy is silent on it.

43. Exod 21:20, 26, 22:1 f., 15 f.
44. It would lead too far afield here to investigate the role of slave-marks and similar identifications in the ancient Near East.
45. Lev 25:55
46. 1 Sam 8:7.
47. *Tosefta Baba Kamma* 7:5.
48. Deut 15:12 ff. On this and other laws in the Fifth Book of Moses, see C. M.
Carmichael, *The Laws of Deuteronomy* (1974), esp. 54 ff., 86 ff., and *Law and Narrative
in the Bible* (1985), 81 ff.

Much of the rest belongs to the idealized world of this author. The slave, male or female, may yet forgo his right and incur bondage for ever: the master and his household, it is explained, may be so wonderful. Since the very next paragraph imposes on the master the duty, if the slave prefers freedom, to equip him most liberally, so he will not set out with nothing, it is difficult to see why he should ever refuse this alternative; he could always keep up friendly relations. Enough.

Rome offers a wealth of material. As a rule, for obvious reasons, slaves were not allowed into the army. However, in critical situations they were. When Hannibal was about to conquer the city, thousands of them were recruited,[49] each one being separately asked whether he wished to serve:[50] an unwilling draftee was no use, and a Yes could not be taken for granted since, notwithstanding the prospect of being ultimately rewarded with freedom, the road to it would be thorny and risky. (It is one of the cases where we might almost speak of a direct purchase of freedom rather than the indirect price which is my theme.) A fable from the Aesopic corpus may have originated as a warning, passed around among the slaves—or other groups ordinarily not good enough for the military but appealed to in distress—to have a good look at the honour of going to war in behalf of your masters. The ass who envied a cavalryman's steed, prancing, well-fed, splendidly turned out, changed his mind when the poor thing was taken into battle to find a ghastly end.[51]

Separation from comrades of long standing or even the family was a regular consequence of manumission. Indeed, the tensions between slaves and freedmen, as also between slaves without hope and such as aspired to citizenship, must have greatly helped their betters to divide and conquer. Phaedrus introduces a cockerel digging for food on a dunghill and having no use for a pearl lying there which a connoisseur would eagerly restore

49. Livy 22.57.11 f., 24.14 ff.; Valerius Maximus 7.6.1. Gracchus' refusal to punish the less valiant ones on the day of victory (Livy 24.16.9) is reminiscent of Saul and David (1 Sam 11:13; 2 Sam 19:23).

50. Livy 22.57.11: "prius sciscitantes singulos vellentne militare."

51. C. Halm, *Fabulae Aesopicae Collectae* (1852), 161 f.; B. E. Perry, *Aesopica*, vol. 1 (1952), 468 f., and *Babrius and Phaedrus*, Loeb Classical Library (1965), 486.

to its exalted station.[52] Very possibly this fable was thought up by a slave of superior refinement—say a foreign artist or priest carried off when his hometown fell—as a hint to his owner to lift him above the rabble. In 1964, I conducted a Seminar in Political Science at U.C. Berkeley. Enthused by the movement on campus, towards the end of semester I asked the twelve participants to grade themselves. At the next session I was handed twelve straight A's. I said, I would stand by my word but, if I passed on this rating, the Department would just take no notice: so would they reconsider. In the course of the ensuing week, I received two personal letters, each setting forth reasons why the writer needed an A more than any of his fellow students. (This is the little twist because of which I report the episode here: the power of rivalry among underdogs.) When we met again, I still got twelve As. I did confirm eleven. To one member I could not bring myself to award this mark and gave a B plus. He had appeared for only a single session during the whole semester and even then was catatonic from LSD.

An incident from the Punic Wars is relevant. Scipio, having seized New Carthage, made two thousand mechanics into slaves of the State, with the promise of release if they excelled in manufacturing badly needed war equipment.[53] This group now worked with might and main against their former side. When some twelve years ago West Germany prepared legislation to give employees of big firms more seats on the decision-making bodies, my Konstanz colleague Bernd Ruthers feared too much influence from below; I feared too much compliance with on high.

Considering the, in general, less than whole-hearted acceptance meted out to freedmen by established society, theirs was hardly a bargain. Their isolation comes out precisely in the frequency with which eminent personages, including emperors, promoted them to important positions of trust: cut off from their old roots and as yet without fresh ones, they were not likely to join a conspiracy. Sulla freed hordes of slaves of his proscribed opponents in order to secure an absolutely reliable following.[54] There are, it goes without saying, other types whose good or bad fortune is tied up with

52. B. E. Perry, *Aesopica*, 573, *Babrius and Phaedrus*, 278 f.
53. Livy 26.47.2; Polybius 10.17.9.
54. Appian, *Civil Wars* 1.100, 104.

the patron's. One of them is the *Hofjude,* court-Jew, whom we meet from the Book of Genesis on and on whom I have commented in a discussion of Josephus, himself a specimen and aware of it.[55]

Unfortunately, a freedman may not even love his sole benefactor. The opposite occurs. That indebtedness for a boon can engender hatred is hoary wisdom; the hatred serves to disprove the indebtedness, says Seneca.[56] Additionally, a subtle, specific element feeds into the perverse response where the boon consists in the entrée to a nobler segment of the community. Demosthenes exaggerates in the interest of his case but, long before psychoanalysis, has a point when he propounds the axiom that freedmen hate their ex-masters who share their knowledge of their former condition.[57]

Fables about the problems of upward movement abound. In one that indubitably focuses on the step from slavery to freedom, a crocodile claims ancestry holding the distinguished rank of gymnasiarch, Director of a sports academy. No need to mention this, the fox assures him: his hide shows that he has been through many exercises.[58] Other similes are of wider application: the ass donning a lion's skin which falls off when a wind comes up[59] or which cannot mislead the fox after he hears the wearer's braying;[60] the oversized wolf who looks like a lion to his kinsfolk but not to the true breed he tries to join;[61] the mule elated when thinking of his mother, a horse, but relapsing into depression when thinking of his father, an ass.[62] A penetrating depiction of what, tragically, a parvenue may deem incumbent on him is furnished by the tale of an asp, so perfectly tamed that she dines with the family. In due course she has young ones and brings them with her. One of them, however, not yet quite adapted, inflicts a poi-

55. See D. Daube, *Typologie im Werk des Flavius Josephus,* n. 37, 59 ff. [*Ethics,* 277 ff.].

56. *On Benefits* 2.41.1. In 3.1.1. he explains that people may turn against others, not just after a kindness (say, when going on to other interests), but because of a kindness.

57. *Orations* 24 (*Against Timocrates*), 124

58. C. Halm, *Fabulae,* 19; B. E. Perry, *Aesopica,* 329, *Babrius and Phaedrus,* 424.

59. Halm, *Fabulae,* 163; Perry, *Aesopica,* 469, *Babrius and Phaedrus,* 182 f.

60. Halm, *Fabulae,* 165 f.; Perry, *Aesopica,* 395, *Babrius and Phaedrus,* 457.

61. Perry, *Aesopica,* 462, *Babrius and Phaedrus,* 128 ff.

62. Halm, *Fabulae,* 76; Perry, *Aesopica,* 446, *Babrius and Phaedrus,* 78 f.

sonous bite on her patron's son. She immediately, in front of all, kills her guilty child, then—almost worse—retreats in shame to her hole, never to reappear again.[63]

IV. PLEBEIANS

Greek designers of an ideal constitution exhibit much interest in the cost-benefit analysis of equality. In the Books of Judges and Samuel, it is the people who tire of equality as productive of weakness and ask for a king.[64] By contrast, according to Livy,[65] a fable discrediting equality is recited to the restless plebeians of the fifth century B.C. by an emissary of the patricians. The resultant truce, however, does not last; and by the later Republic, most discrimination has gone—on paper, that is. In reality, only the wealthy plebeian families genuinely share in the government: shoulder to shoulder with their previous oppressors they hold down the masses, now worse off than before.[66] It is not unimaginable that black liberation in the U.S.A. will unfold along the same lines.

The figure of Licinius Stolo—fourth century B.C.—is archetypal.[67] Member of a rising plebeian clan, he married a patrician who made no se-cret of her dissatisfaction with life among such as were precluded from the top honours. He threw himself into the battle for reform and got one statute passed prohibiting any person from renting above 330 acres of profitable State land—so the bidding would no longer be open only to the mightiest—and another stipulating that one of the consuls should be a plebeian—so political clout would be more widely distributed. He was indeed elected to this office himself. After a decade or so, he had grown as greedy as those

63. Perry, *Aesopica*, 651, *Babrius and Phaedrus*, 557.

64. Judg 8:22 f.; 1 Sam 8:3 ff., 19 f. See D. Daube, *Sons and Strangers*, 4 ff., 29 ff. [*BLL*, 158 ff., 176 ff.].

65. Livy 2.32.8 ff. See D. Daube, *Civil Disobedience in Antiquity*, 130 ff. [*BLL*, 664 ff.].

66. See M. Cary, *A History of Rome*, 2nd ed. (1954), 242.

67. See R. Münzer, "C. Licinnius Stolo," in *Pauly-Wissowa*, vol. 8, 1 (1926; rpt. 1972), cols. 464 ff., and "Tib. Semperonius Gracchus," in *Pauly-Wissowa*, vol. 2A, 2 (1923; rpt. 1972), cols. 141 f.

he once berated. In order to double his holding, he emancipated a son and procured for him a separate tract. As this son at the time did not own one cent (Roman law concentrates all property in the *paterfamilias*) he was totally dependent on the father; i.e. in economic reality, the latter was in sole control. Now the defeated patricians' hour for vengeance was come. He was tried under his own *lex Licinia,* his deal discounted as a feint and a heavy fine inflicted. It took over a hundred years for his house to make a comeback in public affairs. Nevertheless H. Siber is probably wrong in stating that the son also was found guilty.[68] In that period, he would scarcely have been expected the moment after his emancipation to disrupt a scheme imposed on him while under *patria potestas* and, indeed, the very reason for his emancipation. The wording of the sources, too, speaks against this proposition. Livy, for example, puts it thus:[69] "Stolo was sentenced under his own statute because he held 660 acres with his son and by emancipating his son had done fraud to the statute." No hint at proceedings against the tool.

That Stolo resorted to a dodge, in the sense of "an attempt to thwart an irksome restriction by means which will stand up to judicial scrutiny," is significant. This method is the preserve of the haves. The have-nots break the law, the haves skirt it, hoping that, if they are charged, they will be held to be just within.[70] He was unlucky: he was held to have "perpetrated fraud on the law," "disguised the crime."[71] That in different circumstances he might have won is demonstrable. From Appian we learn[72] that, despite his conviction, his maneuver became popular and at least semi-legal. Actually, it was not only sons but also less close poor relations through whom the rich took to cultivating more than the permissible maximum; and when

68. *Römisches Verfassungsrecht* (1952), 59: "wobei auch sein Sohn als mitschuldig genannt wird." A brief paragraph on a *filiusfamilias* contracting an illicit marriage at his father's bequest may be found in D. Daube, *The Defence of Superior Orders in Roman Law* (1956), 17 (rpt. in *LQR* 72 [1956], 508).

69. Livy 7.16.9.

70. See D. Daube, *Proceedings of Classical Association* 61 (1964), 28 ff., and the *Festschrift for Tony Honoré* (n. 4 above), 1 f. [233–234 below].

71. Livy 7.16.9, "fraudem legi facere"; Valerius Maximus, 8.6.3, "dissimulare crimen."

72. *Civil Wars* 1.1.8 f.

Tiberius Gracchus in the second half of the second century B.C. revived the Licinian statute, he did allow a half-portion for each son (perhaps without emancipation?).

There are, of course, various types of dodges. That here employed is the man of straw, to whom the juristic texts from the middle of the second century A.D. on attach the label *persona interposita* or *supposita*. A close approximation occurs in the elder Pliny[73] precisely in connection with Stolo who, he writes, possessed excessive acreage *cum substituta filii persona,* "account being taken of the deceptively inserted person of his son." By this time at the latest, the nature of the straw-man dodge is fully understood. How far analysis had proceeded when they cracked down on Stolo I leave open. It may be worth mentioning, however, that we seem to have before us in this case the oldest extant judicial repudiation of the use of a straw-man, if not—but here I am becoming more hesitant—of any dodge.

Two comments ascribed to him sound authentic.[74] The patricians fiercely resisted the bill concerning the consulship, endeavouring to appease their antagonists with that concerning State land. But he saw through this seduction and prevented the enactment of the latter apart from the former: the people, he quipped, "ought not to drink without eating."[75] In his eyes, access to large-scale farming was luxury, access to the consulate substance. That was at the height of his campaign; eventually he himself sacrificed meat for wine. The other remark dates from the end. His prosecution before an assembly of citizens was managed by a plebeian-scion, however, of an older family than his, ever zealous in patrician causes. A clever arrangement, though by then it was easy anyhow to whip up animosity against a power-broker of such long standing. After his condemnation he observed that "there is no wild beast more blood-thirsty than the populace, which does not spare those who feed it."[76] A great deal of truth in this. Yet

73. *Historia Naturalis* 18.4.17.

74. See F. Münzer, "C. Licinnius Stolo," col. 469.

75. Dio Cassius 7.29.6. See E. Cary, *Dio's Roman History,* Loeb Classical Library, vol. 1 (1914), 225.

76. Dionysius of Halicarnassus, *Roman Antiquities* 14.12.33. Translation by E. Cary, *The Roman Antiquities of Dionysius of Halicarnassus,* Loeb Classical Library, vol. 7 (1951), 279. I suppose it has been seen that this inspired Burke's formulation which

one cannot fail to notice a deep-rooted contempt for the majority as well as the assumption that, having been good to them, you are entitled to immunity whatever misdeeds you may commit—even if it be betrayal.

V. CHILDREN

All children, if living long enough, in a sense attain equality with the preceding generation—though, to be sure, they never catch up in years. Obviously, however, conditions, form and substance must vary immensely according as we have to do with a survival culture, a sophisticated aristocracy or plutocracy, a slave camp and so forth.

Here are a few data which may be of interest.

I have already adduced the Deuteronomic law[77] which requires a regular trial if a son proves unamenable to parental discipline. The father can no longer kill him on his own—but, on the other hand, once the judges find him guilty, he will be shown no mercy as he may under the old dispensation. Again, having discussed slaves in the Roman army, I need not dwell on a *filiusfamilias*'s sacrifices for whatever freedom he wins by joining up or, say, by helping to found a colony.[78]

Luke's prodigal son[79] exemplifies the consequences if the shackles are thrown off before the necessary prudence is acquired. Just so, many a hippie of the sixties has in the meantime moved back into the parental home. The evolution of a Roman youngster's standing in legal transactions is worth looking at in this connection.[80] Whereas he could enter into a marriage with his *paterfamilias*'s consent from puberty on, commercial

---

became proverbial. In *Thoughts and Details on Scarcity* of 1795 (*The Works of Edmund Burke*, 3rd ed. [1869], vol. 5, 156), he warns against state-guaranteed relief: "And having looked to government for bread, on the very first scarcity they will turn and bite the hand that fed them." He actually refers to Rome modern and ancient in this very paragraph.

77. Deut 21:18 ff.

78. See A. Watson, *The Law of Persons in the Later Roman Republic* (1967), 101.

79. Luke 15:11 ff.

80. See A. Berger, "Minores," in *Pauly-Wissowa*, vol. 15, 2 (1932; rpt. 1965), 1860 ff.; W. W. Buckland, *A Text-Book of Roman Law*, 3rd ed. by Peter Stein (1963), 169 ff.; A. Watson, *The Law of Persons in the Later Roman Republic* (1967), 157 f.

dealings would normally come much later since, while his *paterfamilias* lived, he had no property, not one cent. However, if the *paterfamilias* did die exceptionally early, the law simply applied the starting-point familiar from marriage and held the orphan to any undertakings as soon as he had reached puberty. (Prior to that, in the absence of a *paterfamilias,* he had a guardian to look after his affairs.) In a close-knit, modest community, this low age-barrier was acceptable. But it led to trouble as the city grew more populous and wealthy; and in the second half of the Republic measures were taken to penalize exploitation of one under 25. That made people chary of doing business with the protected group—unless a third party of judgement and repute gave his blessing, thereby more or less forestalling future charges. In the principate, for this reason and no doubt also in order to secure good advice and to avoid coming to grief, minors between puberty and 25 would themselves ask the magistrate to appoint a *curator:* a voluntary abdication of equality.

At this juncture we should remind ourselves that, once the "primitive" period was over and Rome a world power, the entire set-up under which a *paterfamilias* alone was capable of ownership needed a great deal of just that.[81] Imagine: if, for instance, he was an octogenarian, his three sons in their fifties—maybe a praetor, an aedile and a governor of Lower Germany—and his grandsons in their twenties (not to mention the females) had to beg him for the money for cornflakes and cigarettes. The arrangement endured because it defined an elite. It did not embrace the poor. It did not embrace foreigners. It was a status symbol comparable to the miseries proudly undergone up to not long ago by the pupils of English Public Schools. The *filiifamilias* really affected by these rules judged that the loss incurred by ridding themselves of their subjugation would be too heavy. When watching their Greek, Egyptian, Jewish, Spanish counterparts, of whom Rome was now full, buy, sell, make gifts, to their hearts' content, they were comforted by the thought that precisely such licence became the rabble. This is not to suggest that there were not those desperate to break out, and be it by parricide—which receives fairly frequent mention in the sources. In a way, cases of this kind make the prolonged upholding of the

81. See D. Daube, *Roman Law* (1969), 85 ff.

grotesque system all the more impressive.

Let me go on to an aspect less tied to a particular civilization. In a different context,[82] I remarked on the gigantic scope of unwanted salvation throughout history, all over the globe, and suggested that genetics helps to understand it. (I do not say it is the whole explanation.) From the dawn of the human species, natural selection would favour those who, regardless of whether they were welcome or not, fed their babies, carried or dragged them along when moving, restrained them from running into a fire, falling over a cliff or stroking an adder and, as soon as feasible, forced them to be co-toilers. Parents equipped with this instinct would have far more progeny reaching procreative age than others; in fact, those quite devoid of it would have none, it being so essential. Again, when we look at the other side, the young recipients of these efforts, plainly those capable of accommodation—kissing the hand that strikes them—must reach procreative maturity in far higher numbers than those incapable. The system resulting was a paradoxical collaboration, each party loving and hating at the same time, one of them a ruthless rescuer, the other putting up with a painful boon. Certainly, contemporary cultures are in many aspects gentler than their predecessors, but the main data are not subject to change. Unwanted salvation, then, is a universal mechanism, starting on day one of our lives—if not before—and indispensable for a good while. No wonder it has an impact well beyond its original setting. We are still fairly close to the latter in, say, Wisdom's praise for the father not sparing the rod and his grateful son[83] (with substitution, in religion, of God and his people);[84] the relation between the prophet and the imperfect king or nation;[85] Protagoras' dictum that an unruly child needs straightening with threats and blows;[86] our compulsory schooling and vaccination. Yet the same mindset contributes

---

82. See *Humanities in Society*, vol. 2 (1979), 74 ff. [*BLL*, 692 ff.].

83. Prov 12:1, 13:1, 24.

84. Deut 8:5; Prov 3:12.

85. Of which the fable of Balaam's ass (Num 22:21 ff.) constitutes the earliest recorded analysis; see D. Daube, *Civil Disobedience in Antiquity*, 65 ff.; *Ancient Hebrew Fables* (1973), 14 ff. [*BLL*, 615 ff., 704 f.].

86. Plato, *Prot.* 352D.

to Socrates' advice to keep the insane in fetters for their benefit;[87] to Lysistrata's determination to save the hidebound males from their wars "even if you do not consent";[88] to Verginius' stabbing of his daughter in danger of being dishonored;[89] to the Jews' killing of their children about to be compulsorily baptized;[90] to the Rabbinic doctrine that if one cannot stop a would-be murderer otherwise, "one saves him at the cost of his life";[91] to the laws compelling a person in incurable, excruciating pain to live on; to any missionary activity, whether theological or political, whether relying on violence or on pressure of persuasion; to my youngest son's anti-smoking crusade; and, yes, to my urge to enlighten you by the present Lecture. All these instances, and countless others, are off-shoots, in part, of the primitive process ensuring continuance of the race.

What is pertinent to my theme is the child's masochism, the falling in, more and more wholeheartedly, with an *au fond* detestable oppression. It is this element which considerably affects his or her feelings about equality. Before going into it, however, let me advert to three results of the foregoing argument. First, in anyone's growing-up, masochism, operating from birth, precedes sadism. Second, more than that, it precedes any "normal" state, free from either. Third, one root at least of virtually all manifestations of masochism doubtless lies in this absolutely basic experience of unwanted salvation. I am reminded a little of G. W. Groddeck's observation that masturbation, widely branded as unnatural, comes earlier in life than the twosome, a substitute for it, so does not deserve the pejorative.[92] Correct—only it needs to be added that, fertility being confined to intercourse, the make-up supporting this inclination during the period of generativity will prevail overwhelmingly in transmission. Once propagation by cloning became established, things might take a new turn. Till then, pairing is bound to remain the choice of most people between 15 and 55. His the-

---

87. Xenophon, *Memorabilia* 1.2.50
88. Aristophanes, *Lysistrata* 499.
89. Livy 3.48.5.
90. See H. H. Ben-Sasson, *Encyclopaedia Judaica*, vol. 10 (1971), 984.
91. *Mishnah Sanhedrin* 8:7.
92. See *The Book of the It* (1923), English trans., 30, 46 ff., 93 f., 130 ff., 139 f.

sis that homosexuality precedes heterosexuality in the individual[93] strikes me as less convincing. But even were it true, a similar proviso would be called for: prior to the advent of cloning, since homosexuality is infertile, heterosexuality during the procreative years cannot but remain dominant by a colossal margin. This is not to deny that abandonment of ugly and stupid prejudice would make a worthwhile difference. Hopefully, indeed, appreciation of the genetic security of heterosexuality's preponderance may render its champions more peaceable.

Now as for my actual topic. There are few situations of dependency which, however much resented, do not afford a trace of comfort. (Just as there are few which, however comfortable, do not produce a trace of resentment.) After what was said above, it will not surprise that dependency on parents—the model, up to a point—is cherished deep down even when burdensome or past any practical usefulness and its termination never constitutes sheer gain.

Isaac's willingness to be offered up by Abraham is still being extolled. In Genesis, too, we find Joseph, right-hand man of Pharaoh, crave his moribund father's blessing for his sons. Aeneas would have stayed on in burning Troy with all his had his lame old father Anchises not finally agreed to flee with them, mounted on his son's shoulders. An elaborate illustration is furnished by 1 Samuel.[94] Jonathan, serving in Saul's army, undertakes a foray which develops into a major victory. However, he does so without authorisation and, worse, in the course of the exploit, violates a solemn taboo imposed by the king. It is the people's protest which keeps the latter from exacting the ultimate penalty. Again, Jonathan consistently plots for David, dear to him, hateful to Saul. On one occasion, when he speaks openly in his friend's defence, Saul, enraged, throws his spear at him; and for once, the son also allows himself to display anger. None the less he does not leave his father, accompanies him into a hopeless battle "and in their death they were not divided." Three generations of Manlii in the fourth century B.C. are Roman counterparts.[95] Lucius banished his

93. 195 ff.
94. 1 Samuel 14.
95. Livy 7.4.4 ff., 8.6.16 ff. See F. Münzer, in *Pauly-Wissowa*, vol. 14, 1 (1928; rpt. 1965) 1176 ff.

son Titus, who seemed retarded, to a dungeon in the country, for which cruelty a tribune proposed to arraign him. Titus heard of this, made his way to Rome and, having obtained a private interview with his well-wisher, drew a knife and threatened to murder him unless he swore that he would halt the proceedings. Now Titus set out on a brilliant career. An early feat of his bears striking resemblance to David's slaying of Goliath.[96] But what interests here is a gruesome incident some twenty-five years later, recalling Saul's reaction to Jonathan's irregular achievement. Titus and his fellow-consul, fighting the Tusculans, had given order that no soldier might leave his assigned place. His own son, however, called Titus like him, could not bear not accepting the challenge of one of the enemy nobles. He triumphed and, amidst an admiring crowd, brought his father the spoils stripped from the victim's body. The general—with no public outcry to stop him—had him immediately beheaded, convinced that "if you have a drop of my blood in you," (he had indeed set a mighty precedent of filial self-effacement), "you will not object to restore by your punishment the military discipline

---

96. Livy 7.9.8 ff.; 1 Samuel 17. As in the Bible a contrast is drawn not only between the huge size of the ogre and the middling one of the youngster who takes him on but also between two kinds, or stages, of equipment: splendid, vain, knightly—modest, purposeful, popular. (In the David story, the popular is represented by sling and stones, in the Titus story by a footsoldier's handy sword and shield.) The lesson conveyed by this joint consideration of stature and outfit is that a little guy intelligently armed is a match for a giant impeded by unwieldy apparatus. The two kinds of equipment are, of course, continuously paralleled through the ages: Agincourt is a large-scale instance, at this moment we have guerillas versus armies. The German nursery rhyme *Hoppe, hoppe, Reiter* cruelly mocks the horseman's helplessness once he is thrown to the ground. I do not mean to belittle other no less significant points of the David-Goliath encounter highlighted by the commentators. Still, quite likely, it is the feature here noticed, the superiority of the commoner's gear, which largely accounts for David displacing one Elhanan (2 Sam 21:19) as conqueror of Goliath. It ties in with his role of, in contradistinction to Saul, being one of the people. Saul, it will be recalled, puts his armor and helmet on him for the duel and he discards them: an act with a political message, showing where he stands. Much later his wife Michal, Saul's daughter, who once loved him and sided with him but now, her exalted heritage re-asserting itself, despises him for his unkingly conduct, is silenced by him with the sneer that he won out against her father and his house and is proud amidst the vile and base (2 Sam 6:20 ff. See D. Daube, *NT* 24 [1982], 276 ff., and a contribution to the forthcoming *Essays on Aggadah and Judaica for Rabbi William G. Braude*, ed. B. Braude) [*BLL*, 716 ff., 727 ff.].

relaxed through your fault." As one might expect, the Greeks come nearest to a philosophical grasp of the matter. Socrates (or Plato) clearly senses the far-ranging influence of infantile conditioning when, among his reasons for not escaping from prison, he cites his duty, as a child of the city, to submit to punishment by that parent even though it is undeserved. The case probably has some weight yet; it can be used to bolster up the dogma that, to qualify as civilly disobedient, you must take your glass of hemlock.[97]

A complex forbiddingly large and intricate I dare not embark on: the innumerable cases where a child draws level, not with the adult world, but with siblings previously superior. We may think of disliked by parents vs. favoured, younger vs. elder or vice versa, illegitimate vs. legitimate or vice versa,[98] half-brothers and half-sisters from different wives or husbands, and so on. Actually, somebody in my position has an easy excuse. My brother Benjamin was my senior by two years. He has been dead for four decades. Yet to this day equality has eluded me,[99] so I have no experience of its costs.

VI. DESIDERATA

Perhaps some time I shall append a survey of the dire side effects when a minor nation joins the big league. For the moment, it may suffice to note what happens, before our eyes, to a state acquiring the atom bomb: it has the atom bomb.

And yet a further section dealing with the price we are all paying for having become, just as the serpent said we would, "like God, knowing good and evil." Goethe's Mephisto predicts to the stupid hopeful disciple: *Folg'*

97. Plato, *Crito* 12.50E ff. See D. Daube, *Civil Disobedience in Antiquity*, 3 f., 67, 76, 78 [*BLL*, 569 f., 616, 623, 624 f.]; F. Olsen, *Georgia Law Review* 18 (1984), 959 ff.

98. On circumstances in which the initial advantage attaches to illegitimacy, see D. Daube, *Sons and Strangers*, 8 f. [*BLL*, 162 f.].

99. Others seem no more successful. I have had many students with just one brother, a few years ahead or behind. It takes a five minutes' talk on any subject—often simply an exchange in the elevator—to enable me to say whether my interlocutor is the firstborn or the second.

nur dem alten Spruch und meiner Muhme, der Schlange. Dir wird gewiss einmal bei deiner Gottähnlichkeit bange! "Just follow the old saw and stay with the serpent, my aunt. One day your god-like show for sure will cause you to pant!"[100] One of the more memorable graffiti I have come across at Boalt Hall sums it up thus: I wish I were what I was when I wished I was what I am.

100. *Faust* I, Studierzimmer, towards the end.

Princeps Legibus Solutus

In his *Europa und das römische Recht*,[1] Koschaker lays emphasis on the coolness with which the maxim *princeps legibus solutus est* [The emperor is not bound by statutes], to be found in Digest 1.3.31, from Ulpian, was treated in the Middle Ages. It may be worth while to draw attention to a Rabbinic source which throws light on an early stage in the development of this famous rule.

As is well known, throughout the Principate the emperor was not considered to stand above the law. There were a number of laws from which he was exempted, and in particular, a number of laws from which the Senate might exempt him. But even by Ulpian's time, the jurists hardly recognized him as *legibus solutus* in a general sense; and we may assume that in the work from which the fragment *princeps legibus solutus est* is taken, the context provided some restriction. It was only the compilers who, by omitting the context (one of their favorite methods of generalization), made the words into a slogan of absolutism. At the same time there is no doubt that, from Domitian onwards, less and less respect was shewn for constitutional restraints. Above all, the right to exempt the emperor from a law was gradually usurped by the emperor himself, and in any case he gained almost complete control of the Senate.[2]

Both the changes initiated by Domitian and their limitations come out clearly in a Rabbinic sermon. Towards the close of his reign, as he was

[*L'Europa e il diritto romano: studi in memoria di Paolo Koschaker* 2 (Milan, 1954), 463–5]

1. (1947), 177.

2. See H. F. Jolowicz, *Historical Introduction to the Study of Roman Law*, 2nd ed. (1952), 336 f.

taking or contemplating anti-Jewish measures, the Palestinian Jews sent a delegation to Rome. It comprised Gamaliel II, Joshua ben Hananiah, Eleazar ben Azariah and Akiba. We are told[3] that, while at Rome, they preached that God's ways were unlike man's: whereas a man issued a decree, enjoining others to act in this or that manner, and did not abide by it himself, God did abide by his commandments.

This must be directed against Domitian, otherwise there would be no point in the notice that the sermon was delivered at Rome. That the charge should have been preferred in a veiled form—"a man issues a decree and does not abide by it" instead of "the emperor issues a decree" etc.—can cause no surprise. It is, however, conceivable that, originally, the accusation was quite open and that some of those who transmitted it had reason to render it inoffensive.

The idea that God follows his commandments is older in Judaism than the date of this delegation. So is the idea that wicked people often love to tell their fellow-men to be good; it occurs, for instance, in the Epistle to the Romans.[4] What was novel in the sermon under discussion was the combination of the two ideas with a view to attacking Domitian's practices. Very probably, among the circumstances inducing the Rabbis to contrast his government with the divine government was his habit—equally hateful to Jews and Christians—of having his laws referred to as laid down by *dominus et deus noster.*[5]

In an anonymous passage immediately preceding the story about the sermon at Rome,[6] God's ways are said to differ from man's: the latter teaches others what he himself is not prepared to act upon, whereas God does not do so. If this passage is earlier than the incident at Rome, the Rabbis at Rome applied a traditional saying to the mode in which Domitian ruled. It should be observed that the anonymous passage does not speak of a man "issuing decrees," but of a man "teaching;" it is not concerned with government. In all probability, however, priority should be accorded to the incident at Rome. The anonymous passage is later. It generalizes a saying

3. Exodus Rabba on 21:1.
4. Rom 2:21 ff.
5. Suetonius, *Domitian* 13.2.
6. Exodus Rabba on 21:1.

that had at first been uttered with regard to a very specific situation.

The four Rabbis, then, reproached Domitian for disregarding his own laws. They may have thought chiefly of his dissolute life, most unbecoming for one who revived the Augustan laws designed to encourage marriage and improve morality. Significantly, Juvenal's arraignment of this emperor is somewhat reminiscent of the Rabbinic one:[7] "But worse are those who, after discoursing on virtue, practise vice. Such a man was the adulterer (Domitian) who revived the stern laws to be feared by all." Manifestly there was a common source: Juvenal and the Rabbis were all acquainted with popular jibing at the discrepancy between Domitian's words and deeds. One difference is that Juvenal wrote when Domitian was dead and disgraced. Again, whereas Juvenal hardly went beyond the simple notion of a scoundrel telling others to behave—he said it would be the same if Clodius had disliked adulterers or Milo murders—the Jewish scholars were distinctly interested in the public law aspect of the matter, in the relation between a ruler and his legislation. This is obvious from their comparing the attitude of the emperor with that of God.

It is noteworthy, however, that they did not accuse Domitian of putting himself above the law as a matter of principle; they did not, that is, accuse him of claiming to be *legibus solutus*. What they accused him of was his actual, arbitrary violations of the laws and also, it can scarcely be doubted, his abuse of the possibility of obtaining exemption from certain regulations. That the latter point played a part is probable from various considerations. We need only recall that it was in the field of the Augustan marriage laws that senatorial dispensation from the outset became of particular importance for the emperors (though, of course, they would never be authorized to commit adultery). Indeed, the sentence *princeps legibus solutus est* comes from Ulpian's discussion of these laws.

Still, the fact is that the Rabbis preaching at Rome did not yet know of a maxim according to which the emperor was above the law. It is questionable whether, had such a rule existed, they could have opposed human government and divine government at all from this angle. For surely, despite the doctrine that God prized and observed his laws, and despite even

---

7. *Satires* 2.19 ff.

the identification of the Law with Wisdom,[8] the Rabbis would not have denied in so many words that God was *legibus solutus*.

8.   See W. D. Davies, *Paul and Rabbinic Judaism* (1948), 165 ff.

Fraud No. 3

As I am going to inspect a certain dodge, I had best start by declaring what I understand by the term: the attempt to thwart an irksome restriction by means which will stand up to judicial scrutiny. It is an attempt. Strictly, my dodge is a dodge only so long as the courts have not spoken, have not put "objective" truth in the place of "subjective" groping, testing. Once upheld—as "avoidance" in today's nomenclature—then, though it was aimed against a law, it has always been within it, a tenable construction, not essentially different from any other courses open. Once rejected— "evasion"—it has always been off, a misinterpretation, essentially like any other courses ruled out. (Why not enliven the vocabulary a little and add the pairs "strategy" v. "stratagem," "circumnavigation" v. "circumvention," "adjusting" v. "twisting"?) One is reminded of hope in Greek myth, right at the rim of Pandora's box, alive only till either realized or disappointed. A dodge indeed by my definition involves a peculiar hope—that it will pass muster when challenged. The retrospective judicial determination of legality or illegality ushers in an entirely new phase.

There is about a dodge something entrepreneurial—of a special nature: a champing at the bit and risk-taking on the one hand, a wary underhandedness on the other. In a paper "Dodges and Rackets in Roman Law"[1] I pointed out that, by and large, dodges are the preserve of the haves (which is corroborated rather than contradicted by the fairy-tales where the little guy gets the better of the big guys by using one). The have-nots break the law, the haves skirt it. The former steal and perjure themselves: in order to obtain a handout offered to starving families, they will swear they are mar-

[*The Legal Mind: Essays for Tony Honoré*, ed. N. MacCormick and P. Birks (Oxford, 1986), 1–17]

1. Summarized in *Proceedings of the Classical Association* 61 (1964), 28 ff.

ried though they are not. The latter, under less pressure, and with access to expert advice, aspire to eat their cake and have it too, set the law at naught while keeping on the right side of it: if you are entitled to a legacy provided you are married and you loathe marriage, you marry—on the understanding that divorce is to follow without delay. Now and then a statute expressly nullifies its circumvention (a clause not quite futile though, obviously, whoever was trying on a dodge would deny that it was covered by it). The *lex Fufia Caninia*, limiting the number of slaves that may be released by will, is one example,[2] the part of the *lex Tarentina* laying down property qualifications for councillors another.[3] Neither is addressed to the street people.

No wonder an enormous amount of ingenuity goes into the thinking up of ploys from hoary antiquity. My previous paper, however, suggested that the countless forms assumed by them are reducible to a few basic models and their combinations. I discussed two. (1) Where a law prohibits a certain transaction—sale or gift or interest—an alternative transaction is substituted which will produce the nearest effect—gift plus countergift for sale, sale at a nugatory price for a gift, a late-repayment-penalty with an impossibly early repayment-date for interest. (2) Where a law debars a certain group from a transaction—a governor from money-lending in his province—an *interposita persona* is used—he does business through his cousin. Here I propose to look at a further scheme: (3) Where a law attaches an advantage or disadvantage to a certain quality, this is indeed acquired or shed but in a fashion that drains the change of substance.

II.

The punishment for adultery introduced by Augustus was not meted out to professional whores:[4] in olden times, we hear from Tacitus,[5] to figure on the aediles' list of them was considered punishment enough. However, early in Tiberius's reign, he narrates, one Vistilia, highborn and highwed,

---

2. Gaius 1.46.
3. *Lex Tarentina* 29 ff.
4. See T. Mommsen, *Römisches Strafrecht* (1899), 691.
5. Tacitus, *Annals* 2.85.1 ff.

inscribed herself in that list. Whereupon the senate decreed that no woman whose father, grandfather or husband was a knight might take up this occupation. So far, so good. What is puzzling is that she was tried, convicted and exiled to Seriphos, "the island having everything one doesn't need."[6] On what ground, seeing that her indiscretions preceded the decree?

C. S. Rogers comments:[7] "Probably no defence was possible; her conduct was a matter of record on the aediles' books." Not satisfactory. It is this record which, far from explaining the verdict, creates the problem. In its absence, there would be none; whereas, at first sight at least, the orderly advertisement of her doings ought to have afforded immunity.

The answer lies in the authorities' refusal to recognize her registration, which was a blind. She never meant to provide the indiscriminate, base, paid services of her co-registrants. She chose a lover, or lovers, like any lady of her standing. The sole purpose of her entry was to ward off the criminal sanction she deserved. In short, she was not a *bona fide* prostitute, and the judges pronounced accordingly. Additionally, in order once for all to close this loophole, the senate passed the resolution already mentioned: a woman of rank must not trade in her body. What about an untitled one? No need to bother *de minimis*.

Support is furnished by Suetonius.[8] To go by him, a fair number of women in that epoch avowed themselves madams or procuresses, the point being that these facilitators were no more punishable for adultery than outright sluts. No doubt in this case, too, the members of the *haut monde* in question were selective, not at all like the brothel-keepers or lessors of rooms by the hour at Sankt Pauli. They would have their friends over for wild parties and the like. And in this case, too, exile was the consequence, though exactly who inflicted it is not made clear. The women's aim, we are told, was "to escape the penalties of the laws." It is tempting to translate *evitare* by "to evade" and, conceivably, it does in this passage carry

6. Plutarch, *On Exile* 7, *Moralia* 602B; see L. Bürchner, "Seriphos," in *Pauly-Wissowa, Real-Encyclopädie der classischen Altertumswissenschaft*, 2nd ser., II.A.2, (1923), 1732.

7. See C. S. Rogers, *Criminal Trials and Criminal Legislation under Tiberius* (1935), 31.

8. Suetonius, *Tiberius* 35.2.

a trace of the crooked. But generally, the verb as such is still neutral in
this period. (So is *evadere*—in contradistinction to *eludere*, as we shall see
further on. It would be interesting to pursue the development of these and
related terms leading up to their present roles.) However, Suetonius goes
on to report that the government reacted so fiercely "lest such fraud should
provide shelter to anyone." A direct reference to fraud on law, of the sort
I am postulating: they were "madams" or "procuresses" in inverted com-
mas, it was not real. He assigns to the same category those youngsters of
the senatorial and equestrian orders who, chafing under a regulation which
kept them from the stage and the arena, deliberately got themselves defeated in a court case of the kind where defeat brought with it infamy—and
thereby removal from the higher orders and their shackles. Once again,
they did not genuinely leave their class. On the contrary, they would earn
the admiration of their dissolute clique. Tiberius did not put up with the
sham. If they became actors or gladiators, their ruse did not make them any
less accountable. A recently unearthed inscription with more detail will be
briefly introduced below.

In Republican Rome, as in many cultures, an adulterous wife was
dealt with by her husband or father, who might be assisted by other male
relations. They had ample discretion and could be brutal or friendly.[9] Augustus's ordinance, oppressive and male-chauvinist as it was, by bringing
her before a public tribunal did inch towards her treatment as a person
rather than as an object. Plainly, for those who would have managed well
under the old dispensation—with Helen of Troy as patron saint, lovingly
reinstalled by Menelaus, *un mari épique* —the price of progress was high.
Vistilia was unwilling to pay it. She resorted to a dodge—wanting to have
it both ways, be accounted law-abiding and defy the law. To be more concrete, the system so far prevailing reckoned with an elite faithful to the
tenet *noblesse oblige*. She was not, but neither had she any inclination to
mingle with the rabble. Her nominal enlistment was meant to safeguard
the *noblesse* unencumbered with the obligation. From a slightly different

9. See D. Daube, *Juridical Review* 90 (1978), 177 ff. [*NTJ*, 231–33]. Tiberius
restored the *iudicium domesticum* for cases which the new one did not cover: Suetonius,
Tiberius 35.1

angle: the hookers were enjoying a *privilegium odiosum,* a liberty that is really a disability.[10] (One may think of a court jester's licence to speak out or a medieval Jew's to practise usury.) Vistilia craved the privilege without the *odium.*

We can now say a little more about the sensatusconsult Tacitus mentions. So long as matrons of rank were practically all of them jealous of their reputation, an occasional misuse of the exemption from prosecution granted to professionals would not be alarming. From Suetonius it is evident, however, that at a certain juncture indifference to official censure became widespread among the jet set. Quite apart from general, moral considerations—to have to investigate in each case whether the label of prostitute did or did not correspond to lifestyle was too much. A complete exclusion from this trade of females belonging to the aristocracy cut the Gordian knot. Time was, in the USA, when to be kept out of the army because of homosexuality or schizophrenia constituted a fearful disgrace. During the war with Vietnam that changed. Strange no one thought of a senatusconsult prohibiting men from being homosexual or schizophrenic. The Roman lawmakers cannot have been happy being forced into explicitness as to the reservation of the aediles' list for the lowly majority. At the time, whenever possible—for example, in getting more progeny out of the well-to-do minority—less overt means of discrimination were preferred. (Which did not prevent Pliny, under Trajan, from noticing it: "Massive rewards and corresponding penalties urge the rich to rear children.")[11] Only in many cases, as in the present one, plain language was unavoidable. I cannot here enter into the tangled fortunes of this distinction.

Women, it appears, bravely continued wrestling with the spoilsports. Justinian's Digest contains an excerpt from Papinian[12]—around A.D. 200—to the effect that she who, "in order to escape the penalty of adultery," goes in for procuring or hires herself out to the theatre can still be charged under that head and sentenced. A few details may be noted. First,

10. See D. Daube, *Harvard Theological Review* 68 (1975), 371 ff., *ZRG, RA* 99 (1982), 27 ff. [*TL*, 137–42, 143–52].

11. Pliny, *Panegyric* 26.5. See D. Daube, *The Duty of Procreation* (1977), 32 [*BLL*, 965].

12. Digest 48.5.11.2, Papinian II *de adulteriis.*

the text presupposes that, like a harlot and a procuress, in principle, a
professional actress is exempt from the Augustan reform; hence, here is
yet another opening for a fake alibi. It is arguable that this part is interpolated: the subjunctive *fecerit* is followed by the indicative *locavit*. I prefer to
ascribe the switch to abbreviation. Secondly, here as in Suetonius, *evitare*
as such may be free of any derogatory connotation. The phrase "to escape
a penalty" recurs in quite different fields in the Digest,[13] not once alluding
to trickery. That we have to do with it in the fragment before us is shown by
the accompanying data; the verb itself is not needed for it. Thirdly, Papinian says that where procuring or acting is intended to neutralize the legislation, the latter will none the less operate "by virtue of a senatusconsult."
Possibly, he has in mind the decree cited by Tacitus, which may have done
more than deal with a pseudo-whore, or at least have been rendered more
widely useful by a vigorous exegesis. Or, possibly, he is thinking of a supplementary measure. Anyhow, his *evitandae poenae adulterii gratia* and
Suetonius's *ad evitandas legum poenas* are similar enough to warrant the
guess that some such expression was employed by the first-century senate.

A tablet found near Larino, south of the Abruzzi, preserves a senatusconsult of A.D. 19, the very year of the Vistilia scandal, combating public
performances by nobles. Its edition by Barbara Levick is provided with so
magnificent a commentary, philological, legal, historical and cultural, that
I may confine myself to some selective observations.[14] On the whole, the
decree does the same about these deviations that Tacitus's does about adultery: it makes them illegal even where a noble has lost his or her status as
a result of becoming infamous. The motivation, too, is no doubt analogous.
The senate is perturbed by a fashion of advisedly incurring infamy—for
example, by getting oneself condemned in a *famosum iudicium*,[15] a method
we came across in Suetonius. In default of a countermeasure, each time

13. See *Vocabularium Iurisprudentiae Romanae*, ed. Preussische Akademie der
Wissenschaften, 2 (1933), 619. I had been unable to locate 325,11 when Alan Rodger
informed me that it ought to read 315,11 = Digest 10.2.25.13.

14. See B. Levick, *Journal of Roman Studies* 73 (1983), 97 ff. When first writing
this paper, I was unaware of the discovery. I am greatly indebted to Alan Rodger, whom I
asked to comment on my draft, for drawing my attention to it.

15. Line 13.

an ex-noble acts or fights, there will have to be a preliminary inquiry as to whether he or she is truly disreputable—entitled to perform—or only a pretender—having engineered the infamy and therefore not entitled. The solution: a once-for-all debarment, outlasting the loss of status. The law-giver is indeed aware that the daredevils in question might not be overly impressed. That is why a major portion of the pronouncement is addressed not to them but the impresarios: henceforth they must hire no one who ever belonged to the upper classes."[16] Parallels abound through the ages. At this very moment, there is controversy over here about a paragraph in a proposed Immigration Act which would penalize not only the permitless alien employee but also—and more effectively—the employer.

Suetonius, we saw, notes that, in the eyes of the powers-that-be, both the fake madams and the youths sacrificing their name for stage or arena were seeking "shelter in a fraud," in a reprehensible dodge. In conformity with him, the senatusconsult from Larinum charges the latter group with "applying fraud by which they impair the majesty of the senate": they de-ceitfully get out from under an anti-performances regulation of this body.[17] Several lines after this, the purpose of their dodge is said to be "to elude the authority of their order."[18] In the Digest *eludere* invariably signifies "to ward off an obligation or punishment by misuse of the law."[19] Tacitus informs us that exile was the fate of one who planned by procedural fi-nesse and deals with the prosecution "to elude the retribution" threatening friends of his for the forgery of a will.[20] The senatusconsult, then, is char-acterizing the culprits as disengaging under a pseudo-legal cover from the demands of their position.[21]

Vistilia's husband, Titidius Labeo, we gather from Tacitus, narrowly missed being engulfed. The statute concerning adultery reserved the hus-

16. Lines 7 ff.

17. Line 6.

18. Line 12.

19. Digest 4.8.30, Paul XIII *ad edictum*; 9.4.26 pr., Paul XVII *ad edictum*; 42.8.10.8, Ulpian LXXIII *ad edictum*; 49.5.12.9, Papinian *singulari de adulteriis*; 48.19.1.3, Ulpian VIII *disputationum*; 49.19.6 pr., Ulpian IX *de officio proconsulsis*.

20. Tacitus, *Annals* 14.41.

21. See B. Levick, op. cit., p. 103; "the burdens imposed by membership of a high class."

band the exclusive power of arraignment for the first sixty days. The senate
demanded an explanation from Labeo why, though his wife had displayed
conspicuous indications of the offence,[22] he made no move. His plea that
the sixty days—"granted for deliberation," he emphasized—had not yet
gone by in the end got him off the hook. Since K. L. Nipperdey,[23] the consensus is that the senate exceeded the bounds set by the statute. In C. S.
Roger's words, owing to "the public indignation, the husband's sixty-day
privilege was transformed into an obligation." I am not sure. In the circumstances, his passivity may have seemed to be the tip of the iceberg
indicative of actual aiding and abetting. Thus the interrogation would be
designed to find out whether the evidence sufficed to proceed against him
for this—not at all for the waiving of the right itself. We are in the dark
about other particulars. C. S. Rogers considers it "a little more likely" that
Labeo did finally prosecute than that he did not. I like to think that, notwithstanding his peril, he left it to others though I am aware that people,
men with a position to guard especially, will do a great deal to save their
necks—and weep when the cock crows.

The elder Pliny, writing in the seventies A.D., in a chapter of his
Natural History which treats of art, introduces a Titedius Labeo, possibly
Vistilia's ex-husband.[24] He is described as recently deceased at an advanced age, which would fit: if he was, say, thirty-five when she acted out,
he would now be well into his eighties. He had once been a praetor, we
learn, and then governor of Narbonne. It is not divulged when, but it was
hardly after the rumpus though, who knows?, perhaps he worked his way
back like politicians in our century. Pliny is silent on the affair which he
must have remembered. Nevertheless Labeo does get a black mark: he
painted miniatures—a contemptible specialty, *contumeliae erat*. How different cultures or individuals rate miniatures would make a fascinating

22. This is what *delicti manifesti* signifies. It does not mean "to be caught in the
act." Compare "displaying recognizable signs of distaste or fear" in Tacitus, *Annals* 4.53,
"displaying clear signs of life" in 12.51, "displaying obvious indications of ambition" in
14.29.

23. K. L. Nipperdey, *Tacitus*, 11th ed., 1.226.

24. Pliny, *Natural History* 35.7.20. See M. Fluss, "Titidius Labeo," in *Pauly-Wissowa*, VI.A.2 (1937), 1536 f.

study. The buyers of miniatures at a London or Munich auction are not mainstream, those at a Tokyo or Kyoto auction are. In the former places, as at Rome, this interest does not quite befit a self-respecting male. Labeo, despite his frightening experience, remained a maverick.[25]

He has, of course, nothing to do with the famous jurist. Yet by an odd coincidence, a striking idea which Tacitus voices in outlining the case, and to which I have already called attention, is reminiscent of Marcus Antistius. When Vistilia sought freedom from the anti-adultery enactment by enrolling as a harlot, she was relying, Tacitus observes, on a practice established by the ancients: they regarded the shameless as sufficiently punished by this very publicity of their wretchedness. In other words, the overall degradation made it superfluous, illogical, to come down on any specific lapse. With this we may compare a statement in the Digest[26] with respect to the problem how far money paid out for an illegal or immoral purpose may be reclaimed. Labeo refuses such an action against a whore "on a new ground, namely not on the ground of immorality on the part of both (the customer and the whore) but on the ground of immorality on his part alone: for though she is acting immorally in being a whore, once she is a whore her acceptance of money is not immoral." It is the same distinction as above: the abject condition *in toto* is a bar to the enforcement of purist directives in each single incident. The authenticity of the text has been attacked.[27] But at least the portion here relevant is, in the main, exceptionally trustworthy. As for form, it is enough to single out the accusative and infinitive in the stretch "for though she is acting immorally," typical of the classical handing-on of an earlier teaching. And as for substance—surely, Labeo is applying by analogy a notion much talked of in his day in connection with Augustus's pioneering promulgation.[28] In fact, his method is precisely

25. I am not the only Oxford professor to indulge in fantasies about the characters in this drama. Vistilia had an aunt who married several times (without having to do so under the levirate as the woman in Matthew 22) and R. Syme wonders (*Tacitus* [1958], 1.373 f.) whether the niece's conduct was "perhaps a paradoxical protest against the matrimonial adventures of her aunt."

26. Digest 12.5.4.3, Ulpian XXVI *ad edictum.*

27. See P. Heck, *Archiv für die Civilistische Praxis* 124 (1925), 42 ff., G. v. Beseler, *Studia et Documenta Historiae et Iuris* 3 (1937), 377.

28. *Eine der eingreifendsten und dauerndsten strafrechtlichen Neuschöpfungen,*

that which Peter Stein has demonstrated to be characteristic of him.[29] The very term *ratio* is significant: "It is almost certainly he," says Stein, "who added *ratio* to the list of sources of law." In this instance, he approves of the prevalent opinion *nova ratione*. I have argued elsewhere[30] that, over a century later, Simeon ben Yohai, a leading Rabbi, seems greatly indebted to him. He displays enormous concern with the wherefore of a provision, and even the new ground crops up when he agrees with somebody else's decision "but the reason is not according to his words."[31] Maybe, after all, it is not a one hundred per cent coincidence to come into touch here with M. Antistius Labeo. The name Titidius Labeo might cause Tacitus to think of the jurist whose ethos he admired[32] and to recollect some pertinent reflections of his on the adultery statute.

Yet another fluke allows me to grant a walk-on to Labeo's rival Capito: having been honorary consul in A.D. 5, he appears as senior witness in the Larino decree.[33] One more illustration of his eager playing along with the new bosses.

Naturally, dodges such as depicted in these sources, with the object of earning infamy, are a rarity. The reverse object is the rule, and we do hear, for example, of pimping under the guise of managing an inn.[34] On the other hand, when I first came to England in the thirties, I met husbands striving to be branded as adulterers. Divorce (in old-fashioned lingo, revealingly, "matrimonial relief") was then not obtainable by agreement. When a couple resolved to split, the rational course was for him to enable her to allege adultery. He spent a night at a hotel with a call-girl and, as the law presumed that an adult man and an adult woman sharing a bed-

---

welche die Geschichte kennt: T. Mommsen op. cit., 691. But not a patch on Deuteronomy 22:22 (see my article quoted above, n. 9) with an impact on life and letters—for better or worse—extending from biblical era (Susannah, the pardoning of an adulteress in John 8:22 ff.) right into the present.

29. See P. Stein, *Cambridge Law Journal* 31 (1972), 14 ff.
30. See D. Daube, *Jewish Law Annual*, Suppl. 2 (1980), 59 f. [*TL* 227–29].
31. *Siphra on Leviticus* 23:20; *Mishnah Menahoth* 4:3.
32. Tacitus, *Annals* 3.75.
33. Line 2; see B. Levick op. cit., 100.
34. Digest 3.2.4.2, Ulpian VI *ad edictum*; 23.2.42.9, Ulpian I *ad legem Juliam et Papiam*. See L. Friedlaender, *Sittengeschichte Roms*, 9th ed. G. Wissowa, 1 (1919), 348.

room had sexual commerce—except if they were married—the expedient mostly worked. Mostly: not, that is, before a judge too upright to play ball. Few novels can have been as effective in helping on a law reform as A. P. Herbert's *Holy Deadlock*.

Why some dodges pass and others do not, or why the same dodge succeeds at a certain time and place and not at another, I leave unexplored. Under a luckier star, Vistilia's scheme might have prospered. Indeed, it might have grown into an acknowledged, formal transaction available to couples desiring an "open marriage." (Fiduciary *coemptio* comes to mind—to be touched on in the following section.) It was not to be. For all that, she may merit a niche in a pantheon of female resisters. She did fight back, in her way.

III.

Fiddling with time, more precisely, the substitution of a flash in the pan for solid duration, distinguishes not a few exploits of the variety here examined. Here is a selection.

The *lex Tarentina*, already adverted to,[35] required a councillor to be owner, "without evil machination," *sine dolo malo*, of a house roofed with at least 1,500 tiles; and imposed the same fine on one who did not own such a house and one who did but had bought it and taken it over by mancipation "in a manner doing fraud to this statute," *quo hoic legi fraudem faceret*. An aspirant to office unable to afford a good enough building might acquire one from a wealthy friend pro forma, paying nothing or very little, with a fiduciary clause accompanying the transfer to the effect that at the end of the councillorship the building was to be re-transferred. Pacts empowering each of the parties to rescind the sale would do the same trick.[36] The legislator wanted councillors of dependable substance and—doubtless wised up by experience—issued a warning that fleeting appearance would not be

35. 29 ff.; see above, n. 3.

36. On *fiducia cum amico*, see W. W. Buckland, *A Text-Book of Roman Law*, 2nd ed. by P. Stein (1963), 432, on pacts attached to sale, 495 ff.

accepted in lieu of reality.

In the same chapter in which Suetonius relates the discomfiture of those who reckoned they could circumvent the dictates of virtue, he tells us about two more jugglings, the first, it seems, designed, like this one, to hide inadequate funds. A senator whose fortunes declined risked being deprived of his seat by the emperor.[37] The one in question had to give up the superior house he owned at Rome and be content with renting a cheap one; and he sought to cover up the operation by a short withdrawal to the country just before 1 July, the general moving day, planning to take up his new abode a little later on. Tiberius expelled him from the senate.

The second subterfuge was provoked by Augustus's *lex Papia Poppaea* which, if of two magistrates running for the administration of two provinces one was married and the other unmarried, allowed the former to choose instead of submitting to the lot.[38] A quaestor took a wife the day before the appointment and divorced her the day after. Not only did he not get his province: he was stripped of his quaestorship. The Loeb translator's footnote, "The reason for his divorcing his wife is problematical,"[39] dates from the eve of World War I, the last moment it could have been penned.

In the Digest it is affirmed[40] that "a simulated marriage is of no force." This, from Gaius' work on *lex Julia et Papia*, originally had regard to just the type of phantasma produced by that quaestor—or, indeed, other victims of the anticelibatarian policy of the two statutes. For instance, a bachelor or spinster was prohibited from taking a legacy,[41] so when your uncle died you married, to resume your old ways as soon as the legacy was yours. Justinian, as often,[42] by dropping the limiting context, gains a comprehensive, over-comprehensive, rule. How undogmatic the statement was in its original setting, how narrowly oriented towards the Augustan

37. Suetonius, *Tiberius* 35.2. See T. Mommsen, *Römisches Staatsrecht*, 3rd ed. (rpt. 1952), 3.2.883, n. 3, not quite finding his way through this text. Mine is admittedly somewhat speculative.

38. See ibid., 2.1.254, 534.

39. See J. C. Rolfe, *Suetonius with an English Translation*, 1, (1914, rpt. 1920), 344 f.

40. Digest 23.2.30, Gaius V *ad legem Juliam et Papiam*.

41. See Buckland, *A Text-Book of Roman Law*, 292 f.

42. See D. Daube, *ZRG, RA* 76 (1959), 175 ff.

legislation, may be seen from the fact that, in a different area, virtually the same dodge enjoyed the status of an institution. From the later Republic on, *coemptio*, primarily a mode of establishing *manus* marriage, admitted of a fiduciary arrangement to have it immediately undone—by which tactics a woman might get out of an expensive family cult or achieve a change of guardians.[43] The casting off of the *sacra* is indeed given by Cicero—half-banteringly, to be sure—as an example of the corruptive ingenuity of the jurists;[44] and in expounding the change of guardians, Gaius speaks of *evitare tutelam*, "to escape from the existing tutelage."[45]

J. Partsch claims[46] that, as a Roman marriage was concluded by the setting up of a joint life, it could never be "simulated" in the sense of publicly going through one transaction while privately intending another. Hence the fragment must envisage a case such as where an alien woman was misrepresented as a citizen—not really "simulation." But it is difficult to see why at any time, classical or post-classical, it should have been necessary solemnly to point out that a downright lie will not do. Whereas the quaestor's procedure did pose a problem. One can imagine a huge wedding celebration (with the unmarried colleague as guest of honour), to all appearances, and indeed in respect of all tangible data at this hour, a perfect start; yet when its premeditated, short-lived nature emerged, a fake. I am far from denying that *simulare*, ripened or decayed into a highly technical concept, is frequently interpolated. But it looks all right here; and we shall soon come across further early evidence—not only from the Digest but also from Tacitus—for this application of the word.

Like marriage, divorce might be for a while only, an intermezzo staged with a view to meeting the demands, statutory or unwritten, of an austere regime. Domitian, we read in Suetonius,[47] removed a knight from the list of jurors for taking back his adulterous wife after dutifully divorcing and charging her. Marcian, in the Digest,[48] calls him who remarries the

43. See Buckland, *A Text-Book of Roman Law*, 119 f.
44. Cicero, *Pro Murena* 12.27.
45. Gaius 1.114.
46. See J. Partsch, *ZRG, RA* 42 (1921), 253 ff.
47. Suetonius, *Domitian* 8; see Mommsen, *Römisches Strafrecht*, 700, n. 4.
48. Digest 48.5.34.1, Marcian I *de publicis iudiciis*.

divorced adulteress guilty of "fraud." The excerpt has suffered at the hand
of revisers but definitely enshrines a genuine nucleus. G. v. Beseler holds
that Marcian spoke, not vaguely of "fraud," but more trenchantly of "fraud
on law," *fraus legi*:[49] not implausible, though the shorter phrasing is clear
enough. "Fraud" unqualified, we shall presently see, serves in an analogous case (a transitory adoption) in Tacitus—not to mention its occurrence
in connection with the flight into infamy in Suetonius and the Larino inscription.[50] Domitian's own shenanigans can fortunately be distinguished.
When his wife (whom he had snatched from her former husband) committed adultery, he had her paramour killed and almost killed her as well but
then only divorced her and, in fact, shortly took her back.[51] This divorce,
however quickly remedied, was serious, not a dodge. How far the resumed
relationship would or would not be looked on as continuing the old one may
be left open.

A temporary "divorce" was opportune also where the spouses felt
they must beat the ban on gifts between them.[52] This ban was quite possibly incorporated somewhere in Augustus's enactments, so its circumvention may have sprung up in the same climate as the cases just discussed.
Anyhow, the Digest contains an extract from a work by Javolenus—around
A.D. 100—on Labeo's posthumous writings,[53] with an opinion by Trebatius, Labeo's teacher, in a dispute between Maecenas and Terentia. As he
was ageing, she—much younger and having a liaison with Augustus (yes,
Augustus)—led him a dance. "She kept divorcing him," Seneca writes,[54]
obviously to return on her conditions: "he married a thousand times, all
the while having one wife."[55] On one occasion she left him,[56] came back on

49. See G. v. Beseler, *Beiträge zur Kritik der römischen Rechtsquellen*, 3 (1913), 90.
50. Suetonius, Tiberius 35.2; line 7 of the senatusconsult from Larinum; see above,
n. 17. I am not certain whether the same nuance attaches to *fraus* in Tacitus, *Annals*
13.26.1, cited by B. Levick, op. cit., 101.
51. Suetonius, *Domitian* 3.1, Dio Cassius, *Roman History*, Epit. 65.3.4, 67.3.1.
52. See Buckland, *A Text-Book of Roman Law*, 111 f.
53. Digest 24.1.64, Javolenus VI *ex posterioribus Labeonis*.
54. Seneca, *On Providence* 3.10: *cottidiana repudia*.
55. Seneca, *Epistles* 114.6: *uxorem milliens duxit cum unam habuerit*.
56. Not, of course, a *gerichtliche Scheidung*, "court-pronounced divorce," as A. Stein,
thinking in modern terms, has it: see "Maecenas," in *Pauly-Wissowa*, XIV.I (1928), 215.

receipt of a satisfactory inducement and then left him again. This time, he lost patience and sued, or prepared to sue, for restoration, on the ground that they were in fact husband and wife when he bribed her. It was Trebatius who first enunciated the idea that a leaving need not be taken at face value: "if it was a true divorce, the gift was valid, if a simulated one, the contrary," *si verum divortium fuisset, ratam esse donationem, si simulatum, contra.* That is to say, if her running away, the present and her rejoining were one manoeuvre, that was a foiling of the law, the divorce was "simulated" and the present void. Jurists later than Trebatius set down criteria of the genuine article: entry into another marriage or the lapse of a lengthy period—here we find a conscious grasp of the time factor referred to at the beginning of this section.

J. Partsch labels "if a simulated one, the contrary" as spurious and E. Levy follows him:[57] "this passage utterly distorts the Roman problem," he holds, in making everything dependent on the subjective will of the parties instead of their objective conduct. But this censure is based on the premise that "simulated" here has the same meaning as hundreds of years later in Byzantine doctrine. There is no evidence for this; and we are free to assume that Trebatius, Javolenus, and Gaius all judged the verb appropriate where a certain conduct—primarily objective though not devoid of pointers to the subjective attitude behind it—makes it look as if something had happened, yet before long the magic evaporates. As for style, J. Partsch finds fault with the clause as "superficially patched on."[58] To my ear, without it, the rest would sound lame: we want to hear, above all, that play-acting will not be accepted for real. At any rate, here are two *responsa* similarly structured in two parts, both found in the same work of Javolenus as that under review. The first[59] is from Servius, transmitted by his disciple Ateius. Somebody bequeathed "the silver which he would have been keeping on his country seat at the time of his death." Servius advised that "that silver also was owing which prior to his death was transferred from the city

57. See E. Levy, *Der Hergang der römischen Ehescheidung* (1925), 86 ff., 100 f.: *in der letzteren Stelle verschieben die Worte si simulatum, contra vollkommen das römische Problem.*

58. *Oberflächlich genug angeflickt.*

59. Digest 34.2.39.2, Javolenus II *ex posterioribus Labeonis.*

to the country seat at his, the testator's, bidding; the contrary would be the case if it was transferred without his bidding." No reason to cross out "the contrary" etc. The second parallel[60] goes back to none else than Trebatius. A testator freed his slave provided he paid Attia a certain sum. Attia died in the testator's lifetime. Labeo and Ofilius declared that the slave could not be free. Trebatius: "Attia died before the will was made, the same (the slave could not be free), if later, he would be free."

Not surprisingly, under the pressure of Augustus's regulations, people posed not only as married or divorced but also as parents. In the reign of Nero, according to Tacitus,[61] complaints about this mischief expressly invoked the time element, expanded on the contrast between the momentary and the lasting. In order to share in the advantages accorded to competitors for high office with children, childless candidates adopted children just before an election or distribution of provinces and emancipated them immediately after. Authentic fathers were enraged by these "fictitious adoptions" and opposed "the right founded on nature and the toils of rearing" to the "fraud, artifice and brevity of adoption." (Note "fraud" in the sense of "fraud on law" discussed above.) They, the true fathers, "waited years for the promises of the law"; and it was wrong if those others could "by a quick stroke catch up with their long cherished expectations." The senate thereupon decreed that "a simulated adoption should be of no avail," *ne simulata adoptio iuvaret,* anywhere in the public sphere, nor indeed—this was a rider going beyond the particular grievance voiced—in connection with inheritances, where the law also penalized the childless. So firmly has J. Partsch set his face against "to simulate" in healthy jurisprudence that he doubts the accuracy of Tacitus's quotation. As far as the tenor of this essay is concerned, the classicality or otherwise of the notion matters not. Still less (can that be?) whether it figured in the actual senatusconsult or only in Tacitus. None the less, for the record: the combined testimony of Gaius, Trebatius and Tacitus, all three treating of topics central since Augustus, and all three affixing the designation to the identical charade, strikes me as unshakeable.

---

60. Digest 40.7.39.4, Javolenus IV *ex posterioribus Labeonis.*
61. Tacitus, *Annals* 15.19. See Mommsen, *Römisches Staatsrecht,* 2.1.216.

A few more illustrations may indicate the enormous range of this variety of model 3. Alan Rodger has just gone into one of those maxims in the Digest which were much narrower in their native context:[62] "Things are not deemed to be given which do not become the property of the recipient at the time they are given." Paul, he shows, was discussing the *actio aquae pluviae arcendae* available where, as a result of a construction on your neighbor's land, yours was exposed to rainwater coming from there. In classical law, your remedy was stronger so long as he who erected the construction still owned the land. Hence, if he made a gift of it to someone, it was important to determine whether ownership had fully passed: it is this specific situation Paul has in mind.[63] Rodger goes on to transfers made for the very purpose to impede the action and calls attention to another Pauline disquisition mentioning "a simulated sale"[64]—manifestly, with an arrangement for re-transfer when the stormclouds have passed. I have nothing to add to his comment: "The particular clause is widely regarded as interpolated, and this may well be correct, or else the clause may reflect a somewhat more elaborate treatment of the same topic in the original Paul."

An altruistic dodge belonging here was invented to spare an insolvent debtor infamy.[65] We hear of the following debate among Republican lawyers. Owing me 1000, you hand me 100. I at once return it to you by way of a gift. You hand me 100 again, again to get it back as a gift. And so on, till you have handed me ten times 100—of which I keep only the last installment. Question: have you paid me 100 or 1000? When I first came upon this conundrum, I could not make head or tail of it; suddenly it became clear. In ancient Rome, infamy befell not only a debtor whose goods were auctioned off but also one who got his creditors to be satisfied with a percentage. By the procedure here described, it was hoped to forestall the

---

62. Digest 50.17.167 pr., Paul XLIX *ad edictum*; see A. F. Rodger, *Law Quarterly Review* 100 (1984), 77 ff.

63. It will be noticed that, as in many other instances, Justinian creates his maxim with the aid of a "free" text, i.e. a text which, because of changes in the law, is no longer valid in its original sense; see my article cited above, n. 42: 261 ff.

64. Digest 39.3.12, Paul XVI *ad Sabinum*.

65. Digest 46.3.67, Marcellus XIII *digestorum*. See, in addition to the summary cited above, n. 1, D. Daube, *Roman Law* (1968), 93 f.

consequences of such an arrangement: formally, payment was in full—
once more, a substitution of the vanishing for the enduring. To begin with,
legal reaction seems to have been hostile, but Servius decided in favour.
He saw through it no less than his predecessors. However, what is misinterpretation one day may be tenable the next. By his time, the views about
insolvency had become generally less harsh; and, probably, he considered
that a man for whom his creditors were willing to do that much despite the
loss he caused them deserved remaining a member of the club.

The primitive *fideicommissum*, i.e. before being legalized and tamed
in the Principate, exemplifies a combination of the three patterns sketched
above, in section 1.[66] Say, in the age of Cicero, when an alien could not
be an heir, a testator, wishing his possessions to go to his Greek teacher,
instituted a Roman friend, adjuring him to pass them on to the Greek. In so
far as this was a replacement of an invalid transaction by the nearest hopefully effective one, it was pattern 1. Actually, an extreme variant, since the
alternative resorted to altogether dispensed with the power of law in favour
of religion. It was also pattern 2: the Roman friend, though nominally heir,
was really a mere stand-in for the Greek, a *persona interposita*. In so far
as he was to play his part for the minimum time only, just long enough to
project an image, we have to do with pattern 3.

IV.

From outside Roman law, an instruction by Jesus concerning the temple
tax is surely worth adducing.[67] On the one hand, he and his, he contends,
are subject to it no more than the sons of an earthly monarch are to tribute. On the other, he stresses the importance of giving no offence. To solve
this dilemma, he must find a path around the imposition contemptuous of
their unique freedom. He sends Peter out to cast a hook: the first fish to
be caught will have in its mouth the appropriate coin with which to satisfy

---

66. See in addition to the summary, Daube, *Roman Law*, 96 ff.

67. Matt 17:24 ff. See D. Daube, *New Testament Studies* 19 (1972), 13 ff. [*NTJ*,
760–62, 771–810.

the authorities. Thus, they manage at the same time to pay and not to pay. From a narrowly formalistic point of view, the ownerless coin miraculously brought along does become their property, so can be used for a valid discharge—preserving some *modus vivendi*. But, plainly, it is theirs just for this very purpose, during a tightly circumscribed interval. Substantially, that is, by handing it over, they give up nothing of their own, they do not submit, they remain sons of the King. In this case, it is payment of a debt which is simulated (to draw on Roman terminology) in order to prevent hostility. The Talmud records an occasion when a Rabbi, in order to prevent hostility, simulates acceptance of a gift.[68] No need here to elaborate on it.

In conclusion, some personal reminiscences. Prior to 1933, a marriage entered into solely with an external aim and on the understanding that, as soon as that was attained, it would terminate was a pretty academic topic for me. That changed overnight when it became common, say, for an American to marry a German who badly needed to get out of Germany or into the States. From a talk with Auden, at Oxford around 1960—not world-shaking but unforgettable for revealing his wit, responsiveness and truly good nature—I received the impression that his marriage with Erika Mann was of this description. Others no doubt have precise information. Sad that the need for this dodge did not come to an end with the end of World War II. In fact it has hardly diminished.[69]

A less heavy item goes back to about the same time. Pensions began to be paid by West Germany to refugees in England. At first, though some tax was deducted at source, the Inland Revenue taxed them too. A few years later this stopped, maybe partly in view of the plethora of dodges that sprang up. One of them made use of a provision according to which a pension was not taxable if paid directly to a needy dependant (directly, that

68. *Babylonian Avodah Zarah* 6b.

69. A fortnight after completion of this paper I came upon the following report in the *San Francisco Chronicle* of August 4, 1984, 1, 10: "As many as 500 American disciples of guru Bhagwam Shree Rajneesh married foreigners solely to enable them to become citizens, according to an Immigration and Naturalization Service investigation of the sect. An Immigration service memo... says the government is cracking down on the marriage ploy... The sect's top attorney, Swami Prem Niru... said it is natural for members of a religious group to intermarry, and he accused the government of launching a systematic program to destroy Rajneesh and his church."

is, without ever reaching the pensioner). This was easily arranged: the German authorities did not mind making out their cheques to whoever those entitled named. There can have been few epochs in civilisation when aged parents and grandparents were shown so much solicitude as when knowledge of this method spread. Of course, whether the dependant retained what was addressed to him was of no concern to the Inland Revenue. An acquaintance of mine, a lawyer in general sternly moralistic, when I called it a farce, defended it by pointing out that, for however briefly each month or quarter, the dependant did in fact have the money and, suppose he had a falling-out with the pensioner, might refuse to transmit it. Well, it is the mark of a good dodge that some defence can be thought up.

However, my earliest memories of the flash in the pan dodge date from age 5 or 6. They are linked to Passover and Tabernacles. The sages took very seriously the biblical ban on leaven during Passover.[70] (Meticulous observance is presupposed by Paul's metaphorical warning of the danger of even "a little leaven".)[71] You might neither eat it nor have it in your possession nor derive any benefit from it; and their definition of "leaven" was extremely wide. However, in certain circumstances, they did condone a pre-Passover sale to a non-Jew, to be followed by a post-Passover resale.[72] How the dodge developed, who sponsored it, who disliked it, is not here material. My father and his youngest brother carried on an import trade including goods which were, or conceivably might be, classifiable as leaven. So regularly, two or three days before the festival, they made over their business to a non-Jew, with all the traditionally requisite formalities; and, of course, kept strictly aloof from it till re-acquisition. For the buyer, it was just a rigmarole, except that he received a gratuity. Let us pray that the heavenly academy will approve of the construction.

As also of a similar one, having regard to the biblical precept that, on Tabernacles, "you shall take you an Ethrog (a citrus), a Lulab (a palm-branch), myrtle and willow-twigs and rejoice before the Lord."[73] For the

---

70. E.g. Exod 12:15. See L. I. Rabinowitz, "Hamez," in *Encyclopaedia Judaica* (1971), 1235 ff., and H. Rabinowicz, "Hamez, Sale of," 1237 ff.

71. 1 Cor 5:6; Gal 5:9.

72. E.g. *Tosephta Pesahim* 1:24.

73. Lev 23:40. See D. J. Bornstein, "Laubhüttenfest," in *Encyclopaedia Judaica*

sages, the phrasing "take you," "take for you," instead of simply "take," implies that the plants over which joyful benediction was to be recited must be your own—not stolen, not borrowed etc.[74] An *exemplum* of how to mitigate this requirement, however, was set towards the end of the first century A.D. by an illustrious quartet: Gamaliel II, Joshua ben Hananiah, Eleazer ben Azariah and Akiba. They were travelling on a ship and only the wealthy Gamaliel had a Lulab, bought at 1,000 zuz. He could afford procuring one well ahead of the festival when the price would be exorbitant; the others had no doubt hoped to reach port in time, but voyages often took longer than expected. After reciting his blessing, he made a present of the branch to Joshua; Joshua in due course gifted it to Eleazar; and Eleazar did the same for Akiba who returned it to Gamaliel. What they did in an emergency in course of time became routine. In our little orthodox community at Freiburg, whenever anyone was without a Lulab, this ritual of transfer and re-transfer was scrupulously performed. Why do I not remember it in connection with the other three plants? For the simple reason that they were much cheaper—not 1000 zuz—therefore everybody had them: even small children brought their Ethrog along, the willow-twigs we usually gathered ourselves. In the evolution of juristic personality in Jewish law, by the way, some interesting reflections take off from a Lulab purchased by a congregation or—more recently—by a Kibbutz: may a member use it as his own?

The fourth model, Tony, I reserve for your seventy-fifth birthday.

(1934), 10.692 ff.; A. Kass, "Legal Person," in *Encyclopaedia Judaica* (1971), 10.1570; L. Jacob, "Sukkot," 15.501.

74. *Mishnah Sukkah* 3:13; *Babylonian Sukkah* 41b.

The *Lex Fufia Caninia* and King Arthur

In the year 2 B.C. a *lex Fufia Caninia* imposed severe restrictions on the number of slaves a man could free in his last will. Modern writers on Roman law, at least Western ones, without exception approve of this measure: it was directed, they say, against the conferment of citizenship on morally or racially worthless creatures, as well as against the selfish motive frequently actuating an owner—namely, to make a posthumous show of his benevolence by having a large number of freed slaves appear at his funeral. I have sampled some thirty textbooks, manuals and monographs in English, French, German and Italian, and they all take this line. Essentially they follow Dionysius of Halicarnassus who, some five years before the *lex Fufia Caninia*, recommended restrictive legislation in his *Roman Antiquities*.[1]

Far be it from me to judge in this matter. But it may be well to recall that Dionysius's sympathies were with the senatorial party. Moreover, it is clear, as far as the particular problem of manumission is concerned, that his attitude was by no means universally shared. For one thing, the very condemnation of an overgenerous owner's motive proves that his action was in fact likely to enhance his reputation for humanity; many people, then, did regard wholesale manumission as a noble thing. For another thing, the authors of the *lex Fufia Caninia* from the outset reckoned with resistance to their measure: the statute itself contained a clause invalidating evasions, i.e., manumissions which, though formally somehow compatible with the statute, went counter to its intention.[2] It makes no difference to my argument if, as is possible, this clause was put in because earlier laws had been

[*Law Quarterly Review* 80 (1964), 225–7]
1. 4.24.
2. Gaius 1.46.

got round by means of ingenious dodges. The fact remains that anything but cheerful, general compliance was anticipated. Nor were the pessimistic prognostications slow in being fulfilled. We hear of all sorts of stratagems to defeat the law. Indeed, the anti-evasion clause soon turned out inadequate: no doubt any inventor of a new dodge would plead that this was not a dodge and therefore did not fall under the clause. Time and again the Senate had to step in and issue special decrees against successive methods of circumvention.[3]

The statute provided that if a testator accorded freedom to more slaves than the permissible number, his disposition was to be cut down to the permissible limit and the gift was to be valid for those named first. For example, an owner of four slaves was allowed to release two. Suppose the will gave freedom to Stichus, Pamphilus and Sosia: Stichus and Pamphilus would be free, Sosia would remain a slave. A dodge that was thought up was to write the three in a circle, so that each might claim to be named first or among the first two. It was held, however, that this was precisely the kind of evasion ruled out of order by the statute itself; and that far from all three gaining freedom, none of them was to gain it.[4] It may be confidently assumed that this trick was not attempted more than once—if at all; maybe it never got beyond the stage of hopeful discussion, one of those things that ought to be tried on but never are. If it is reported on at length both in Gaius and the Visigothic Gaius, this is because of its remarkable nature; it is interesting, amusing, out of the ordinary.

It may indeed be worth a second look. The names are written in a circle, *in orbem* according to Gaius, *in circulo* according to the Visigothic Gaius. The purpose, according to the latter, is *ut qui prior, qui posterior nominatus sit non possit agnosci*, "that it cannot be recognized which of them is named before and which after." Gaius declares that the result is that *nullus ordo manumissionis invenitur*, "no order of manumission is discoverable." Evidently, the device is based on the notion, familiar to ancient science, that a circle has neither beginning nor end. As Heraclitus formulated it, ξυνὸν γὰρ ἀρχὴ καὶ πέρας ἐπὶ κύκλου περιφερείας, "For

---

3. Ibid.
4. Ibid. and *Gaii Epitome* 1.2.2.

common is beginning and end on a circle's periphery."[5]

The inventor of the dodge did not, however, do all the work. He was not, that is, the first to make use of the scientific notion for producing a list of names where top and bottom were indistinguishable. The link is a legend transmitted by Ausonius, of the fourth century A.D.:[6] when somebody asked the Delphic Oracle who was the first among the Seven Sages, he was told *ut in orbe tereti nominum sertum inderet, ne primus esset, ne vel imus quispiam,* "to wind a wreath of names around a polished circle, that no one should be either first or last." This legend was certainly known in the Rome of the *lex Fufia Caninia.* The inventor of the dodge was less original, therefore, than one might think at first sight; which is not to deny that the way he applied the idea to testamentary release was brilliant. Incidentally, while we know a good deal about Hellenistic elements in the legislation and legal writings of that epoch, here is a case of a private party, a slave-owner, seeking ammunition against a disagreeable statute in his—or his legal adviser's—elegant learning. Unless—see above—it was all just hot air, speculation among the livelier jurists.

The Delphic reply may well be responsible not only for this—unsuccessful—bid to evade the *lex Fufia Caninia,* but also for King Arthur's Round Table. It had been a question of precedence in the case of the Seven Sages: just so, it was in order to avoid jealousy and feuds about precedence that the Round Table was introduced. I am not indeed claiming that other factors did not contribute; the work of Loomis, Tatlock and others will retain all its value. For the roundness of the Table, however, and its purpose the oracle does seem to me a principal inspiration—"a wreath of names around a polished circle, that no one should be either first or last."

If this is correct, we may ask how the idea reached the romanciers. There may have been channels unknown to us; but the most likely is Ausonius, who, as a glance at Manitius will show, was popular throughout the Middle Ages. The *Ludus septem sapientium* in which the oracle is quoted is preserved both in the Vossianus, dating from the ninth century and writ-

---

5. Diels, *Herakleitos von Ephesos*, 2nd ed. (1909), 42 f., fr. 103.

6. *Ludus septem sapientium* 4 (Solon), 78 f., cited in the apparatus of Seckel and Kuebler's *Iurisprudentia Anteiustiniana* (1880), ad Gaius 1.46.

ten in Visigothic script, and in the Parisinus 8500, fourteenth century. Actually, increasing information as to the study of Ausonius will perhaps in time enable us to be quite precise about the period and region in which the Knights were first arranged like the Sages.

As this poet was a Celt, my solution of the problem of the Round Table ought to give particular satisfaction. I need hardly add that there are few authors with a greater and more continuous influence on history: to him are indebted all organizers of roundtable conferences as well as those society ladies who—vainly, since Heraclitus was, of course, wrong—try to avoid the dilemma of grading by placing their guests in a ring.

The Influence of Interpretation on Writing

I propose to comment on two aspects of this theme: first, on the feedback from exegesis to composition, and second, on the kind of writing in which interpretation is set forth.

I

First, the feedback. In addressing a person I automatically take account of the likely way he will understand me, which means, that I express myself with his reaction in mind. Communication links the two sides, provider and recipient, to such an extent that there is no total separation between them: the recipient, as perceived by the provider, takes part in the shaping. Thus the description of the Berkeley Campus which I give to a German boy of six will be very different from that which I give to a retired schoolmaster at Aberdeen.

This elementary fact is noticeable in law no less than anywhere else. Professor Milsom's *Historical Foundations of Common Law*, designed for a learned public, has little in common with a primer on the subject to be read the evening before the bar exam, or even with an after-dinner speech in which the same author submits his ideas to a wider circle; the formulation is adapted to the level of comprehension expected. In this illustration we have to do with expositions of law, but the same holds true of the legal texts themselves—statutes, treaties, contracts. It is usual for experts on interpretation to start from these and see what is made of them, and this is indeed the most important approach. Yet to inquire how what is made of them affects their framing may not be without interest.

[*Buffalo Law Review* 20 (1970–71): 41–59]

Let us inspect those Roman injunctions and agreements where near-synonyms are heaped two, five, ten, on top of one another: "I give and bequeath," "pierce, break, damage." For adherents to the doctrine that the initial phases of civilization are characterized by strange compulsions,[1] it may be tempting to see in this diction the earliest stage of drafting. But it is not. The primitive texts are simpler. The XII Tables impose a penalty on you if you break a bone of my slave; they say, if you do this "to a slave."[2] Some hundred-and-seventy-five years later, the *lex Aquilia* makes you liable if you kill "another's male slave or another's female slave."[3] The expansion is due to the manner in which statutes had come to be handled. In order to prevent a powerful aristocrat from succeeding with an arbitrary claim, it was made easy for a defendant to show that the provision under which he was sued did not cover the case. Hence the necessity for a law-giver to be very specific about what he did want to be covered: "another's male slave or another's female slave."[4] We can observe a similar evolution in the area of contract. A third stage was reached when such listings, by now a common feature of legal texts, developed a momentum of their own and no document would be respectable without some lengthy specimens—the phenomenon Professor Yaron has called *Herzverfettung*.[5]

It would indeed be astonishing if the piling up of synonyms sprang from some quirk of the archaic mind. After all, even in 500 B.C., there were daily dealings, and I cannot believe that a mother could not tell her child "to eat up" but had to say: "Eat up your bread, drink up your milk and suck up your honey." In the later Middle Ages, when many laws displayed the over-meticulous wording (as a result of a development analogous to the Roman), humorists celebrated hippies like Eulenspiegel treating ev-

1. Cf. on this school, D. Daube, *Roman Law* (1969), 172.

2. XII Tables VIII 3, *servo*. Cf. X 2, concerning delict "by a slave," *si servus furtum faxit*. VIII 3, to be sure, is not quite free from accumulation: it speaks of breaking a bone "with the hand or with a club," *manu fustive*.

3. D 9.2.2 pr., Gaius VII *ad edictum provinciale, servum servamve alienum alianemve*.

4. Possibily, in the case of this statute, there was a further, special factor contributing to the enumeration: at one time, the fine may have varied according to sex, and the *lex Aquilia*, by putting *servam servamve*, may be stressing its uniform regulation. See D. Daube, *Studi Solazzi* (1948), 155.

5. Adiposis, fatty degeneration. *Bibliotheca Orientalis* 15 (1958), 18.

eryday rules and orders as if they were of a juristic nature, to be taken *stricto sensu*. An apprentice requested "not to talk" while his master was praying would sing or whistle. Evidently, the matter was well understood.[6]

The near-synonyms in Roman injunctions and agreements are, then, of rational origin, brought about by the author's anticipation of a certain type of exegesis. This is confirmed by the senatusconsults, in which such phraseology is at no time the rule: they are addressed to high magistrates who can be trusted to get the meaning. Nothing could be looser than a *senatusconsultum ultimum* conferring extraordinary powers on the executive: "Let the consuls see that the State suffer no harm;"[7] and when towards the middle of the second century B.C. philosophers and rhetoricians were to be expelled, the praetor was advised to take care "that they should not be at Rome"[8]—as simply as that. Significantly, there are exceptions: some of those senatusconsults intended to function much like statutes. For instance, the senate, resolved to prevent a repetition of the Bacchanal conspiracy, issued a decree against "combining with another man by oath or by vow or by covenant or by promise, as also pledging one's faith to another man."[9] The decree was indeed sent to the consuls, but with the request to publish it at large by means of an edict.[10] Its language was determined by that eventual use.

Modern authorities on drafting, when recommending simplicity, brevity, intelligibility and accuracy, tend to assume that these necessarily go together, one involving the other. This is about as correct as the belief, in the moral domain, in the pre-established harmony between wisdom,

---

6. On a curious instance of over-literalism from which "the Parliament of Bats" has its name, see Daube, *Journal of Roman Studies* 30 (1940), 53 ff.

7. *Videant consules ne quid detrimenti res publica capiat*; e.g., Cicero, *Pro Milone* 26.70.

8. *Uti Romae ne sint*; Suetonius, *De rhetoribus* 1, Gellius 15.11.1. A solemn pair, however, appears in the clause bidding the praetor "take heed and arrange," *animadvertat curetque*, that they should be off.

9. Burns, *Fontes Iuris Romani Antiqui*, 7th ed. by Gradenwitz (1909), 165: *neve post hac inter se coniurasse neve convovisse neve conspondisse neve compromisse velet, neve quisquam fidem inter se dedisse velet.* An additional reason for scrupulous formulation lay in the fact that the matter reached into the religious sphere.

10. See D. Daube, *Forms of Roman Legislation* (1956), 43.

honesty and loving-kindness. Take simplicity and brevity on the one hand, intelligibility and accuracy on the other. Radbruch, having in mind the *Code Napoléon* and, I guess, some ancient laws, praises the "self-imposed poverty of the lapidary style" with "its utmost precision."[11] But in what sense are these lapidary pronouncements precise? "No costly sprinkling," the XII Tables ordain with regard to funerals,[12] and the *Code Civil* lays down: "In the case of movables, possession is tantamount to title."[13] Such apothegms decidedly indicate a direction, but they do not take you by the hand. They illumine like beacons in the night: but have you ever tried to find your way by the light of a beacon? Look at the commentaries on the possession-title paragraph and judge whether terseness equals clarity.

Piesse and Smith urge the draftsman to "study and practice, in addition to the methods of attaining exact accuracy of statement of fact, the various aids to clear statement and to brevity."[14] One wonders whether this sentence is a perfect model: "exact accuracy" at least could be shortened. Anyhow, again, brevity and accuracy are coupled. Sir Alison Russell does notice that a statute can have too few provisions to be definite: "A Bill must be no shorter than... is necessary to deal with all the questions which may arise under the Act when enacted.[15] Brevity when it means incompleteness is by no means a drafting virtue."[16] He does not, however, realize the extent to which the choice must depend on what the addressees of the Act are going to do to it. He subscribes to Sir George Jessel's criticism of Gulliver (or Swift), who approved the laws of Brobdingnag invariably of the most extreme economy and plainness.[17] Jessel and Russell think Gulliver was naive. But he was not. He points out that these laws were written for people "not mercurial enough to discover above one interpretation." A draftsman placed in such a happy world has no need to make many words.

---

11. *Die selbstgewählte Armut eines Lapidarstils... in seiner haarscharfen Genauigkeit; Rechtsphilosopie,* 4th ed. by Wolf (1950), 206.

12. XII Tables X 6, *ne sumptuosa respersio.*

13. *C. Civ.* art. 2279, *en fait de meubles, la possession vaut titre.*

14. Piesse and Smith, *The Elements of Drafting,* 3rd ed. (1965), 12.

15. At least, apparently, questions arising sooner may be left open.

16. A. Russell, *Legislative Drafting and Forms,* 4th ed. (1938), 16 ff. Cf. Plato, *Laws* 4.722A: "the best, not the shortest or longest, is to be valued."

17. J. Swift, *Gulliver's Travels* ch. 7 (Brobdingnag).

If we probe the traits considered desirable in a document one by one, further problems crop up. Of intelligibility, it is generally admitted that we must ask "intelligibility to whom?," so that the answer may differ according as you compose for the ignorant or for the educated. "The draftsman should bear in mind," Sir Alison urges,[18] "that his Act is supposed to be read and understood by the plain man," but he goes on: "Of course, in Acts of a technical kind, he may find it necessary to use technical expressions; but such Acts will usually only attract readers who are qualified to understand them." Piesse and Smith, after naming "the principal objects, exact comprehensiveness and clarity of statement," make the reservation that complex situations or ideas cannot be expressed intelligibly to everyone."[19] There are in fact endless gradations, and with up-to-date means of research a great deal could be found out. In 1948, Norway enacted a "Law of Housemaids," directed against the exploitation of domestics. Some fourteen years later sociologists conducted an inquiry and concluded that its language was too difficult for housewives, not to mention housemaids.[20] It is in the cards that in future legislation in this province an effort will be made to come within the mental grasp at least of the employers.

I would now voice a more fundamental doubt: these attributes, simplicity, brevity, intelligibility, accuracy—do the authors of legal texts really accept them as non-negotiable? Ought they to? To invoke once more a moral parallel, in many a treatise loving kindness figures as a never-to-be-neglected ideal. Yet not only do people in fact constantly dispense with it, but anyone who never did would soon be branded as intolerably anti-social. The truth is that those drafting standards are far from being universally applied, nor should they be.

Simplicity. Sir Alison declares that "the simplest English is the best for legislation," and indeed, "the modern Acts of the United Kingdom are, on the whole, models of clear, simple English."[21] Nonetheless, in another

---

18. Russell at 13.
19. Piesse and Smith, at 12.
20. Aubert, *The American Behavioral Scientist* 7 (1963), 16 ff.
21. Russell at 12 ff.

part of his book,[22] he warns us that "wherever" or "whenever" must not be used in an Act; the correct formulation is "when and as often as." I have never encountered the latter expression either in my low-class pub or in my high-class Common Room. Evidently, there are limits to a lawgiver's simplicity, and they are imposed to a large part by the attitude at the receiving end: so long as the masses are supposed to revere the law as a mysterious craft, some jargon is called for. It is interesting that Radbruch, in the same sentence in which he extols the supreme precision[23] of the lapidary style (a deceptive precision, I have just argued), also notes that this style "gives unsurpassable expression to the self-confident consciousness of power of the commanding State."[24] So simplicity—or rather, this type of simplicity, for there are many—has a purpose: to overawe. It will give way to complication (and I need hardly add that of complication, too, there are many types) when and as often as this achieves a more relevant object.

I shall not here go into the historical question at what date and against what background simplicity—or each of the other features usually listed with it—was set up as a quality to cultivate or pay lip service to. To answer, we should have to go far beyond law. Let me just say that in non-legal areas also, awareness of the two sides in communication is sometimes less than complete. In our day, liturgists eager to vulgarize the idiom may be insufficiently in tune with the consumer, keyed up to hear a sacred message, marked as such by its dress.

Intelligibility. Distinctly overrated. The sociological investigation of the Law of Housemaids adverted to above established that, though neither housewives nor housemaids understood it, its mere existence (doubtless in combination with other factors such as increasing scarcity of domestic labor) produced much of the desired effect. Mr. Namasivayam emphasizes that, as ignorance of the law does not protect, obscurities do great harm.[25] True enough, but the reality is that no matter how laws are drafted, the vast

22. Ibid. at 117.
23. *Haarscharfe Genauigkeit.*
24. *Der Unübertrefflich das selbstsichere Machtbewusstein des befehlenden Staates zum Ausdruck bringt.*
25. Namasivayam, *The Drafting of Legislation* (1967), 62.

majority of the populace have only the vaguest notion of the vast majority of them. In many societies, a few elementary criminal laws (about murder, for example, not, say, about extortion by magistrates in the Roman provinces or about tax evasion today) are relatively easy to get the gist of; though even here modern refinements result in full understanding being reserved for a tiny band. The ever-present possibility of differences or shifts of opinion as to the meaning of a law on the highest level must not be forgotten.

On numerous occasions, legal texts are deliberately couched in misleading terms. Hire-purchase or moneylending agreements, for instance, are sometimes drawn up with a view to keeping buyer or borrower in the dark on a point as to which the court will have no doubt. Here the different modes of treatment relied on, a careless one by the private party, a careful one by the court, may influence even the physical lay-out: the tricky bit is apt to be relegated to the bottom of the sheet, in small print. Again, it is not unusual for the person seeing a bill through the legislature to make the draftsman give prominence to items agreeable to the assembly and deemphasize unpleasant ones. Sir Courtney Ilbert in his discussion of this device[26] quotes Lord Thring: "Bills are made to pass as razors are made to sell."

A special case is that where you do not primarily intend to make use of the hidden clause. You may in fact hope it will never be needed; still, it is there for an emergency. I was caught in this way when I had bought a ticket to fly from England to the States, and a fortnight later, just before I set out, the pound was devalued. Under some stuck-away proviso I had to make an additional payment. This kind of thing often occurs in the admission and expulsion rules of colleges or clubs: the initiated know that, in the last resort, it will be possible to keep out or get rid of an unwanted individual or group who, on their part, will be nonplussed when the trap is sprung. But we find it even in legislation—camouflaged legislation is the designation I suggested for it.[27] Nor is it confined to the decrees of an absolute monarch or a close-knit, entrenched oligarchy. Incredible as it may sound, even in a

---

26. C. Ilbert, *Legislative Methods and Forms* (1901), 241. I owe this reference to Professor Peter Stein of Cambridge.

27. Daube, "Marriage of Justinian and Theodora: Legal and Theological Reflections," *Catholic University Law Review* 16 (1967): 394 [above, 124–25].

democracy where all proposed legislation is openly debated in parliament, it may be a handful among that body who are in the know and wink at one another. A few years ago I was told how, owing to public pressure, when the constitution of a certain state was being revised, the Governor's influence on the appointment of his officers was to be curtailed. So in a different section the drafting committee slipped in a few inconspicuous words which, in the event of a conflict between Governor and officers, would enable the former to assert himself. In the summer of 1967, the parliament of the Federal Republic of Germany gave the first reading to emergency laws, under which in a time of crisis the government could arrogate extensive powers. Among the criticisms made in the *Times*[28] was that "there is also a disturbing veil of secrecy over some sections."

A remarkable ancient piece of camouflaged legislation is a reform of about A.D. 523 by the Emperor of Byzantium,[29] designed to enable Justinian, then Crown Prince, to marry Theodora with whom he was in love but whom, as she had been an actress, the prevailing laws precluded from joining one of his rank. Under the new dispensation a penitent actress was no longer unacceptable. But in the particular circumstances, this was not the whole problem. Theodora was widely thought to have been a prostitute as well as an actress, so that there was a second, more serious impediment. The dilemma for the imperial draftsman was that, on the one hand, this blemish could not be admitted for one moment, quite apart from the fact that it was not intended to make things easier for prostitutes; while, on the other hand, something had to be done since, otherwise, after Justinian's death, the legitimacy of offspring from the union might be attacked. Accordingly, in the subtlest fashion—it would take too long to give details and in any case I have given them elsewhere[30]—four short words (sixteen letters altogether), barely noticeable, innocent-looking, with no apparent reference to this charge, were inserted which, at a pinch, would save the situation. The success of the camouflage can be gauged from the fact that for some fourteen hundred years commentators have indeed failed to mark the little clause, let alone see its point.

28. June 30, 1967.
29. Code 5.4.23, Justin.
30. Daube, supra note 27, at 386, 392 [above, 117–124].

II.

I go on to the kind of writing in which interpretation finds expression. It is easily demonstrable that the nature of interpretation will affect its formulation. We need only look, for Scripture, at the commentaries of the Dead Sea sect, Jerome, Gunkel, Strack-Billerbeck and the British Israelites to realize that diverse approaches are likely to lead to diverse literary structures. The same is true in law: just note the differences between the Accursian Gloss, Martin Wolff's *Sachenrecht* and Chalmers on his Sale of Goods Act, 1893. Little has been done on this subject: What, if a text is to be explained, is the plausible setting for a word-for-word commentary, or a paragraph-for-paragraph one, or for a paraphrase,[31] or for an epitome, an abstract, or for a treatise? So neglected is this field that for not a few genres and sub-genres we have not even got names.

I can here pick out only a few points. To start with an example from Biblical studies, the ancient Rabbis looked on all parts of the Old Testament as essentially one whole, inspired by God. For them, therefore, a passage from Genesis anticipated one in Chronicles, and what Isaiah said or did resumed a saying or action by Moses.[32] In fact, in a way, each statement in the Bible contained *in nucleo* each other statement. Two types of exposition which this attitude produced were the Haphtarah and the Prooemium. The Haphtarah: originally, on a Sabbath or holiday, a lesson from the Pentateuch only was read, but from a certain date one from the Prophets was added, meant to illumine that from the Pentateuch. Today there is a fixed Haphtarah for every service, but for a long time, in general,[33] you could choose your prophetic lesson—as Jesus did, in a scene described by Luke.[34] After all, in the Rabbinic view, any piece from the Prophets would

31. Or translation-paraphrase, like that Theophilus made of Justinian's Institutes, or, long before, some of the Aramaic Targumim of the Hebrew Bible.

32. Naturally, this position was reached by stages. The prophets attained this degree of recognition before the Hagiographa, and even within these groups some works attained it before others.

33. The fixed Haphtarah came in gradually: the Book of Jonah, for instance, became de rigueur for the Day of Atonement before many another prophetic lesson for an ordinary Sabbath.

34. Luke 4:17.

throw some light on the Pentateuchic portion (though, of course, this was more readily seen in some cases than in others). Here, then, is a strange sort of commentary: sections of an existing corpus the Prophets—are appended, without the least adaptation, to sections of another corpus—the Pentateuch—to help bring out the meaning of the latter. The Prooemium: a Sabbath or holiday sermon opening with a quotation from the Prophets or Hagiographa. This was treated in such a fashion that it was possible to finish up by bringing it into relation with and thus elucidating the principal lesson of the service.[35]

It is this interpretation of the Old Testament as absolutely unitary, with its components so closely interwoven as to constitute just several aspects of the same truth, which underlies those multivalent allusions in the Gospel of John analysed by Professor Barrett.[36] When for instance the Baptist says of Jesus, "Behold the lamb of God which taketh away the sins of the world, this is he of whom I said," etc.,[37] we are directed to a number of Old Testament chapters at the same time: the paschal lamb,[38] the Day[39] of Atonement, the near-sacrifice of Isaac,[40] the suffering servant of the Lord,[41] Jeremiah brought to the slaughter.[42] For this Evangelist, Jesus is the Word become flesh, hence at every moment comprising, living, the Scriptures in their entirety.

Schulz seems to believe[43] that Hellenistic commentaries, lay or legal, were invariably lemmatic. That is to say, a bit from the document to be expounded was cited and by some means—special spacing or the like—identified as the main text: this was the lemma, literally, what is taken for

35. See Bacher, *Die Proömien der Alten Jüdischen Homilie* (1913).
36. Barret, *Journal of Theological Studies* 48 (1947), 155 ff.
37. John 1:29; cf. 1:36.
38. Exodus 12.
39. Lev 16:21 f.
40. Gen 23:13.
41. Isa 53:7, 11.
42. Jer 11:18; and one may add Saul, the first King, 1 Sam 9:15. See D. Daube, *The New Testament and Rabbinic Judaism* (1956), 17 ff. [*NTJ*, 227–29].
43. F. Schultz, *Roman Legal Science* (1946), 183 ff. He refers to Faulhaber, *Byzantinische Zeitschrift* 18 (1909), 383, and Zuntz, *Byzantion* 13 (1938), 631 ff., *Byzantion* 14 (1939), 545 ff., but I can find in neither of these two a proposition going as far as his.

granted, premise, theme. Whatever the commentator had to say about this bit followed. Then a further fragment from the document was introduced, the next lemma, and provided with its exegesis, and so on. There was, then, no complete edition of the main document: all those parts which the commentator left unannotated were missing—they did not figure among the lemmata.

No doubt many expository works did show this structure. To represent it as the only one is an amazing simplification. Besides such cases as the Haphtarah and Prooemium which are understandably overlooked by scholars coming from the Classics and in any case for centuries belonged to oral rather than literary tradition, there is, for instance, Philo. In his writings on the Bible, he never, it is true, supplies an edition. But while, say, his exposition of chapters 2 and 3 of Genesis—*Allegorical Interpretation*—is lemmatic, that of the first chapter—*The Creation of the World*—is a continuous tract, not lemmatic at all. Neither of his two chief commentaries on legal matters, *The Decalogue* and *The Special Laws*,[44] is lemmatic. *The Special Laws* could not be since the discussion follows the order not of the Bible but of the Ten Commandments: each special law is assigned to one of them—for example, the various festival ordinances and the cancellation of debts in the seventh year to the Sabbath commandment,[45] damages if your cattle grazes in another man's field to the commandment Thou shalt not steal.[46] Several more types of commentaries are met in this one author: in some circles, obviously, it was sophistication, not uniformity, which prevailed.

There was less of the latter than might be supposed even among the Roman jurists. I am not even quite sure whether a commentary like Ulpian's on the Edict was strictly lemmatic. It may have been. But from some stretches,[47] it is conceivable that he systematically quoted in full each edictal provision or cluster of provisions before taking up noteworthy terms and clauses. If so, his work did contain an edition of the Edict. Anyhow, an undeniable instance of an edition accompanied by a commentary goes

---

44. I am aware that in a sense these two may be considered as one work.
45. Philo, *Special Laws* 2.10.39 ff.
46. Ibid. 4.1.1 ff.
47. Digest 21.1.1, LXXXII *ad edictum*; 47.10.15.25, LV *ad edictum*.

back to long before: the *Tripertita* by Sextus Aelius Paetus Catus, consul in 198 B.C. In this work on the XII Tables each provision, or group, is set out in full, followed by an explanation, in turn followed by the action suitable for enforcing the law. So we get provision, interpretation, action, provision, interpretation, action and so on—an exhaustive edition *cum* commentary *cum* procedural application.[48] Such is the blinding effect of prejudice that Schulz gives an account of the *Tripertita* in the same book[49] in which he upholds the exclusive existence of the lemmatic commentary, without an edition. The two topics are dealt with by him in different parts and never brought together.

We can guess at one of the stimuli affecting Sextus Aelius. If you write about a code in operation, you have the choice between an edition cum commentary, a lemmatic commentary without edition, an abstract, and so forth. But if you desire innovation and advocate a code of your own, manifestly, you must make an edition. No use picking out a word or two here and there, a lemma, from a code nobody could possibly have knowledge of. If you propose legislation for Utopia, you must state your laws: without them your comments on them would be in the air, absurd. Well, Plato did write such ideal laws, with preambles and argumentation. He was highly esteemed in the set in which Sextus Aelius moved, and the latter's plan to give the text of the XII Tables may well owe something to this inspiration. A mode of writing *de lege ferenda* [what the law ought to be] would have crossed over into writing *de lege lata* [the law as is].[50]

---

48. Digest 1.2.2.38, Pomponius *singulari enchiridii*. It is sometimes held that the *Tripertita* in its first part presents the entire XII Tables in one go, in its second the results of interpretation for the whole and in its third all actions. This is unlikely (see Daube, *Hebrew Union College Annual* 22 [1949], 263 [*TL*, 354–55]); but if it were correct, it would strengthen rather than weaken my case—there is here an edition of the text expounded.

49. Schulz at 35.

50. Little as we know about the *Tripertita*, it is very different indeed from Plato's *Laws*. This does not rule out borrowing. Cicero's *Laws* are unlike Plato's in numerous respects, but plainly indebted to them in some. It is not impossible that the title *Tripertita* is partly a response to Plato's description of laws giving no reasons as "simple" and laws giving reasons as "double": e.g. 4.721A ff. Sextus Aelius is adding a third division strikingly unrepresented in Plato: the actions. Even in Pomponius's report there seems to be preserved a vestige of the feeling (which to be sure need not originate in a contrast with

Admittedly, this thesis contradicts the picture Schulz paints of "honest Sextus Aelius" who looked down on the new learning.[51] Schulz concedes that the publication of a juristic book at all betrays Hellenistic impulse, but for the rest Sextus Aelius belonged to "the old school": he kept quoting a verse from Ennius, "Greek science? Yes, but only a dash of it, for on the whole I dislike its taste."[52] However, the opposite conclusion emerges if the verse is translated correctly and, moreover, attention is paid to the context in which Sextus Aelius quoted it. He took the view, Cicero informs us, that a character in a play by Pacuvius was too hostile to theory;[53] one of Ennius's characters, he held, hit the nail on the head in "wishing to philosophize, though in moderation, for he did not approve of doing so full-time."[54] There is no contempt here for the new learning. The idea that too much study is unbusiness-like or ungentlemanly recurs much later, in Tacitus, for example;[55] it is widespread in England. What is amusing—and distinctly in favor of my assessment—is that Ennius is drawing on Plato's *Gorgias*:[56] "Philosophy is charming if a man pursues it in moderation in his youth."

A most curious literary genre which grew out of interpretation is the cento.[57] Three hundred years ago as many of you would have been addicts to it as are to the detective novel today. Today, some may not even have heard of it, so let me explain what it is. Suppose you want to write a history of the United Nations in the form of a cento. You choose a poet, say, Longfellow, and you put lines or half-lines or quarter-lines of his together

---

Plato) that this third division is an extra. The law, we are told, is "placed at the head," *praeposita*, the interpretation is "joined on," *iungitur*, and the action is "then appended," *deinde subtexitur*.

51. Schulz at 38.

52. Ibid. at 36. Cicero, *De republica* 1.18.30.

53. *Doctrina.*

54. *Qui se ait philosophare velle, sed paucis, nam omnino haud placere.*

55. *Agricola* 4.

56. 484C, the speaker being Callicles. The affinity has long been seen: see, e.g., Cicero, *De republica* 54 (trans. Keyes, Loeb Classical Library [1928]). Incidentally, the character from Pacuvius whom Sextus Aelius finds too antiphilosophical is Zethus: in the Gorgias, Callicles quotes him with approval.

57. See Daube, "Zür Palingenesie einiger Klassiker Fragmente," *ZRG, RA* 76 (1959), 259 ff.

in such a way that they make up your history. "The gift of God:[58] the king-
doms of the world[59] set everything in order."[60] Needless to say, the longer
you make your unit the harder your task and vice versa: it is easier to
pick quarter-lines and combine them so as to give the requisite sense than
half-lines, not to mention whole lines. I ought also to warn you that proper
names have always caused trouble to writers of centos: you will not, for
example, find the name of U Thant in Longfellow, hence you must employ a
phrase which describes him: "A student of old books and days to whom all
tongues and lands were known,"[61] or "Who with grief has been acquainted,
making nations nobler, freer."[62]

Anyhow, the cento originated in a mode of interpretation: *anastrophe*,
interpretation by transposition. In Ptolemaic Alexandria, in the third pre-
Christian century, Homer was regarded by his worshippers as absolutely
flawless, much as fundamentalists treat the Bible. Now somewhere he mentions an enormous tankard the Greek heroes used at a banquet and says:
"Another man could scarce lift it, but old Nestor lifted it easily."[63] The
commentators were worried by this verse for, strictly, it represented Nestor
as stronger than even the most gallant youngsters like Ajax or Achilles—
which, well preserved as the aged warrior was, just was not the case. Of
course, the poet never meant this; he did not expect to be scrutinized in a
literalistic fashion, he wrote for a public that would make adjustments to
conventional presuppositions and to context. But the Alexandrian scholars
could not rest satisfied with such a vague excuse. Several of their attempts
to twist the verse into an accurate statement are extant. One day, however,
Sosibios, court philologist to Ptolemy Philadelphos (the king who commissioned the Septuagint) came up with a novel idea how to achieve the object:
he suggested transposition of the word "old"—"Another old man could

58. "Jacob's Well," chap. 6 in Part I: The Divine Tragedy: Second Passover, from
Christus: A Mystery.

59. "Mount Quarantania," chap. 2 in First Passover.

60. "At Bethany," chap. 9 in Second Passover.

61. *Tales of a Wayside Inn*, Part First, Prelude.

62. *Birds of Passage*, Flight the First, "Prometheus," changing Longfellow's
"have" into "has": the centoists allowed themselves such liberties; cf. note 70 infra.

63. Homer, *The Iliad* 11.636 ff. The treatment of this passage by the ancient critics
is narrated by Athenaeus in *Deipnosophists* 11.493B ff.

scarce lift it, but Nestor lifted it easily." Thus Nestor would be superior to his contemporaries only: perfectly correct.

It is reported that on the pay-day following this invention Sosibios's stipend was withheld and, when he asked and obtained an audience with the king, the latter told him that he had been paid and had indeed signed a receipt. To the astonished petitioner the king shewed receipts from the court physician Soter and the court philosopher Sosigenes. He said: "Let us transpose the syllable *so* from Soter to the syllable *si* from Sosigenes, so as to get *sosi*. Then we have here receipts from the court astronomer Bion, from whom we take the *bi*, and from the court costumier Apollonios, from whom we take the *os*. The result: your own tool of *anastrophe* furnishes me with a receipt from you, Sosibios." Formerly I was inclined to look on this anecdote as apocryphal, but in the meantime experts have assured me that Ptolemy Philadelphos had precisely the kind of wit that comes out in it. Whether true or fabricated, the story is evidence that the arbitrary nature of the new method was immediately seen. No doubt even modes of interpretation generally deemed reasonable can be used for the purpose of distortion;[64] indeed the very fact that they are reasonable may enhance the risk. Still *anastrophe* is extreme: once it is permissible to interpret a text by making its components change places, it is child's play to turn yes into no, no into yes, any thing into any other.

Nevertheless it took root. As may be expected, we rarely find it applied to legal texts; but it flourished as a means of solving problems in historical and religious accounts. Actually, where it suited them the interpreters of a piece would soon switch around not only words but entire clauses. My point is that it is this mode of interpretation from which developed the cento—the earliest specimens of which, as is well known, are Alexandrian though it rapidly spread throughout the Mediterranean world. Far be it from me to deny other contributory factors; but the principal impetus came from *anastrophe*. It is, after all, a small step from getting at the meaning of a text—or rather, the meaning you want from it—by mixing its various parts

---

64. On a daring attempt by a Rabbi around A.D. 100 to demonstrate the arbitrariness of the argument *a fortiori*, see Daube, *The Jewish Journal of Sociology* 3 (1961), 18 ff. [*TL*, 195–99].

to the avowed creation of a new text by such a mixture; and little more is involved in the step from *anastrophe* to cento. In a sense, except that it was not poetry, King Ptolemy Philadelphos composed the first cento when he made up Sosibios with the help of Soter and so on. He knew—as did all concerned in the affair—that he was concocting a fresh name not really intended by the others.

As a matter of fact even this small step from getting at the meaning of a text to the avowed creation of a new one was not fully taken by the cento-ists for a long, long time—something like a thousand years: the Greek and Roman centos are nearly all of them to some extent interpretations of the authors they use.[65] Homer, in connection with whose work *anastrophe* was introduced, was also the first quarry for the centoists and remained the foremost one for centuries. His admirers credited him with supernatural insight into matters physical and spiritual, past and future, and where his surface text would not yield the appropriate message, they postulated any number of layers beneath it, cryptogram beneath cryptogram, accessible, they trusted, to the earnest student. Among Latin authors, Virgil obtained this role. Once again, it is a way of looking at a text familiar from Scrip-tural exegesis, Jewish, Christian and Islamic. But we find it outside this territory—and not only in antiquity. Nietzsche, Lenin, Freud, Wittgenstein have their disciples for whom they are all-knowing and who will manage to prove that there is no advance not anticipated by the master: the latter is always held to have taught what counts as truth at the present moment. In the first thousand years of its existence; the cento was an instrument in this endeavor to read back recent experiences and discoveries into Homer, Virgil and two or three others possessed of supreme wisdom.

Take Falconia Proba of the middle of the fourth century A.D. While a heathen, she wrote a national cento on Homer. This is lost, but doubtless the notion was that, in some sense, the seer had in fact hinted at the events in the Roman world. After her conversion, she added a theological cento on Virgil, which is preserved; and it is clear that up to a point she conceived

---

65. The same is true of Jonah's psalm (Jonah 2:3 ff.) consisting of lines from other psalms which here assume a different meaning—surely held to be implied in the original, so that the displacement only brings out a hitherto unrecognized facet. It is, fundamen-tally, interpretation.

of herself as unearthing a deeper, Christian strand in that poet who was in any case widely reputed among the faithful to have had a vision of the truth. In her Preface she informs us: "I shall declare Virgil to have sung the pious offices of Christ."[66] It would be a mistake to think that it was only his famous Fourth Eclogue, with its prophecy of a prince of peace, which caused the belief in his Christian sentiments. It facilitated this belief, but his Christian fans would have held it anyway. Non-Christian ones saw in him a preacher of ethics versus sensuality and academic culture[67] or a mighty magician[68] or anything else he ought to have been. Homer never wrote a Fourth Eclogue, yet he too was turned into a Christian or whatever appealed to the particular devotee.[69] The Byzantine Empress Eudokia, wife of Theodosius II who in 438 promulgated the Theodosian Code, composed a cento on Homer recounting the life of Jesus. There is a reason, incidentally, for the relatively high number of women centoists. A serious, major cento requires much leisure, endless patience, an eye for minute correspondences, a liking for fitting things together neatly. It has distinct affinity with elaborate needlework. The modern literary occupation comparable is translation.

It is highly probable that Theodosius's plans for a legislative compilation were influenced by the cento. It certainly affected the manner in which, some hundred years later, Justinian for his great work picked and joined together excerpts from the products of a bygone age.[70] The Church,

---

66. *Vergilium cecinisse loquar pia munera Christi.* Another writer, after reciting a cento on Virgil in praise of the Church, *De ecclesia*, was acclaimed as "a younger Virgil," *Maro iunior: Anthologia Latina* 16a. He at once improvised a cento in which he declined the attribute. One line is revealing as to that group's attitude to Virgil: "For he will ever be god and master to me," *namque erit ille mihi semper deus, semper magister.*

67. Hence a cento by a relation of Tertullian—around A.D. 200—which translates into Latin a Greek work *The Picture*, attributed to Cebes.

68. Hence Hosidius Geta's tragedy *Medea* in the form of a Virgillian cento—also dating from about A.D. 200. No cause for surprise: the Bible, Homer, and Virgil were much employed as oracles in antiquity—the first passage you hit on was your answer. In passing: this use of just any fragment from any context as containing the solution to your problem reflects the very same approach that underlies *anastrophe* and the interpretative cento.

69. The fifth-century allegorical exegesis by Demo is a good example.

70. It is worth noting, in view of his treatment of his sources, that the Byzantine

it should be remarked, furnished precedents for this procedure, themselves cento-like in nature. I am thinking of attempts like Tatian's *Diatessaron*, of the latter half of the second century, to make one comprehensive, harmonious, definitive gospel out of the canonical four.

To be sure, things did not all move in one direction. There were those who disapproved of the cento, and there were those who turned it to frivolous use. Those who disapproved did so partly because they looked critically even on sages like Homer, partly because they did not agree that a text could be expounded by juggling its parts. You may recall that Ptolemy Philadelphos from the outset rejected *anastrophe*, interpretation by transposition; his quasi-cento when he constructed a receipt from Sosibius was palpably not meant to interpret the four other names on which he drew but, on the contrary, was meant by its absurdity to demonstrate the foolishness of the method. The very designation cento, apparently from Greek *kentone* or *kentron*, "patchwork," "harlequin's dress," must be due to the opposition.[71] Both Tertullian[72] and Jerome despised the genre. For the latter, Proba's efforts to baptize Virgil were futile: "Nor can we in this way name Virgil, without Christ, a Christian."[73]

In course of time, the playful cento, for the fun of it, with no intent to bring to light a hidden aspect of the original, came to be cultivated. It is prevalent in the Middle Ages, but its beginnings are early. Valentinian I, in the second half of the fourth century, composed a wedding cento on Virgil and challenged Ausonius, then tutor of his son, to emulate him. Ausonius tells us how he submitted a product not so accomplished as to provoke the Emperor's jealousy nor so dull, as to be dismissed with contempt.[74] Later

---

centoists were not above making little adjustments in the wording of the texts on which they built; cf. note 62 supra.

71. See Crusius, "Cento" in *Pauly-Wissowa, Real-Encyclopaedie Der Klassischen Altertumswissenschaften* 3 (1899), 1930. The Rabbinic term for anastrophe is *seres*, the commonest sense of which is "to castrate." It also may have been first coined by detractors.

72. *De praescr. haeret.* 39, referring to his relative's work; cf. note 67 supra.

73. Ep. 53.7 ff., *ac non sic etiam Maronem sine Christo possumus dicere Christianum.*

74. Of Napoleon's chess games which are recorded I am convinced that quite a few were advisedly lost by his opponents, who open brilliantly but then commit a timely blunder.

he revised it, and it is this revision which has survived. It is, of course, a *jeu d'esprit.* And yet, even so, the interpretative element is not quite absent: author and public feel that in some sense it is Virgil who is speaking. Ausonius is aware that some "will be angry because the dignity of Virgil's song is lowered by such a jocular theme;"[75] in a special introduction to the chapter on the first nuptial intercourse he claims to blush twice over, once for himself and once for Virgil "whom I make shameless;"[76] and in his concluding apology he points out that the original Virgil himself is not altogether free from dubious passages.[77] Significantly, too, among various comparisons by which Ausonius illumines the nature of the cento are the myths of Dionysos and Hippolytos, both torn to shreds but reconstituted from these shreds,[78] the former by the Maenads, the latter by the divine physician Aesculapius. An astonishing anticipation, by the way, of the centos our modern transplanters are getting into the habit of making with our bodies.

Today the genre has died out. The reason is simple. To enjoy a cento fully, the audience must know the original not only in a general way, but absolutely by heart, word for word. As each little unit of the cento comes up, they must be able to spot exactly from which discussion or scene of the original it is taken; the pleasure lies in savoring what the centoist has done with it, how he has slightly or greatly or monstrously twisted the meaning towards his end. Owing to our fundamentally changed approach to literature compared with earlier generations, we no longer possess this word-perfect intimacy with great writers. Hence a cento would fall flat. We still have a good general acquaintance with some authors, and, of course, a few

75. Preface: *Piget enim Vergiliani carminis dignitatem tam ioculari dehonestasse materia.*

76. Parecbasis: *ut bis erubescamus qui et Vergilium faciamus impudentem.* He ends by warning puritan readers to proceed no further and leave the rest for the curious: *hic iam legendi modum Ponite, cetera curiosis relinquite.* The translator of the Loeb Classical Library, White, has followed this advice and refrained from rendering the offensive section. See Ausonius 1.387 ff. (trans. White, Loeb Classical Library [1961]).

77. The *Purim Gemara* is comparable: on the Feast of Esther young Talmudic scholars amuse themselves by mock interpretations of Scripture, on occasion distinctly obscene. No examples here to be given: this area is the last preserve of oral tradition. I am only marginally less squeamish than Mr. White of the preceding footnote.

78. The Latin verb is *reformare.*

selected passages we may even have by heart. Parody, therefore, is still feasible: an imitation of Hiawatha or Gertrude Stein or Thomas Mann.

Unlike parody, the cento is based on verbal identity with the original. In fact, so long as this requirement is fulfilled, mood, tone, style may be totally independent. Listen to this exclamation: "Those are pearls? Thy father lies something rich! Now I hear nothing of him." This is a cento on "Full fathom five" from *The Tempest*. It would never do for a parody. Though the various clauses are straight out of that moving dirge, not a vestige of its spirit remains—not even by way of mock reversal. (A psychoanalyst, it is true, might judge less negatively). By contrast, parody can be effective without employing a single word of the model. For a parody, "Peach Melba—Apple Tart, which shall be ordered?" is near enough to "To be or not to be": it would not do for a cento.

Perhaps, after all, there is one tiny corner where the cento lingers on: the Ph.D. thesis. But the Committee is not supposed to notice. Let us call it a camouflaged cento.

The Three Quotations from Homer in Digest 18.1.1.1

In the opening fragment of Digest 18.1, Paul tells us that Sabinus and Cassius had not required a money price in sale. So long as you could distinguish buyer and seller, they had contended, the mere fact that the buyer paid with goods made no difference, but such a *permutatio* was sale. Sabinus had appealed to the authority of Homer, who says:[1] "From there (i.e., from the ships sent by Euneus from Lemnos) the long-haired Achaeans procured wine, some for bronze, some for gleaming iron, some for hides, some for whole cattle and some for slaves."

As these verses do not contain the term "sale" at all, they are generally regarded as pointless; and it is held that all Sabinus can have meant to prove by them was that other things than money might be used for trading—a platitude for which he need not have searched the ancient books.[2] This, however, is doing him an injustice. As a matter of fact, he knew very well why he adduced just this passage. The word χαλκῷ, here rendered as "for bronze," was rendered as *aere* by the Romans. Paul, in the very fragment under discussion, says that the Greeks obtained wine *aere ferro hominibusque*.[3] One of the meanings of *aes*, as indeed of χαλκός, was "money."

[*Cambridge Law Journal* 10 (1949), 213–15]

1. *Iliad* 7.472–475.

2. See C. F. von Glück, *Ausführliche Erläuterung der Pandecten nach Hellfeld* 16, 2nd ed. (1868), 4 f. The view was shared by Professor Buckland in his lectures.

3. The same rendering may be found in T. Mommsen and P. Krueger, ed., *Corpus Juris Civilis* [Stereotype edition], 1 (1928), 263 n. 2. See also C. Labbé, ed., *Cyrilli, Philoxeni aliorumque veterum auctorum Glossaria* [1679], in *Thesaurus Graecae Linguae* 8 (1825), 181 f., 194; and for various other examples of the identification, *TLL* 1 (1900), cols. 1071 ff.

(One may think, for example, of *aes alienum*.) It was, therefore, possible to ascribe to χαλκῷ in the passage quoted the sense of "for money," instead of "for bronze." Sabinus translated: "They procured wine, some for money, some for gleaming iron," etc. His point was that acquisition for money and acquisition for goods were here put on the same level. Homer treated them as a single institution, at least where, as in this case, it was clear which was the thing sold (the wine offered by Euneus) and which that given as price. That was exactly what he wished to do in Roman law.

This explanation of his argument is confirmed by Paul's criticism of it. He points out, rightly, that the verses in question speak exclusively of plain barter. In other words, though the word χαλκῷ, *aere*, is employed, in this context it denotes, not "for money," but "for bronze." In support, Paul refers to another passage from the *Iliad*:[4] "Then Zeus deprived Glaucus of his wits, and he made exchange of armour with Diomedes, son of Tydeus."

Now as these two verses stand in the Digest, they are utterly irrelevant, speaking neither for Paul nor for Sabinus. But when we look up the original, it is immediately clear that we must add the first two words of the next verse, χρύσεα χαλκείων, when the quotation becomes intelligible. The mad thing Glaucus did was to let go his precious suit of armour for Diomedes' plain one, "giving golden for bronze." These verses, Paul maintains, show that χαλκός and its derivatives, when used by Homer in connection with such transactions, refer not to money but to objects of bronze. The case of Diomedes and Glaucus, where χαλκείων occurs, is manifestly one of *permutatio*; consequently, Paul reasons, that of the Greeks getting wine, where χαλκῷ occurs, must be the same. They procured wine "for bronze," not "for money." Sabinus is refuted; his text does not equate acquisition for money and acquisition for goods, since the latter kind of transaction alone is contemplated.

When did the two words drop out, the absence of which renders the second quotation meaningless? Hardly before Paul or through him, for everything in this fragment suggests that, though he may be copying an earlier source, he fully understands what it is about. Possibly through carelessness of the compilers, and possibly even later. There is nothing surprising in a

4. *Iliad* 6.234–235.

slip of this sort. It was very usual, when citing a text from a well-known author, to put only the opening words,[5] in this case perhaps: "Then Zeus deprived Glaucus." A scribe writing out the whole might easily stop a little too early, so that "giving golden for bronze" would no longer appear.

Paul goes on to remark that there is an expression in Homer on which Sabinus might have based himself with far more justification:[6] "He bought with his wealth."

The phrase occurs several times, and once at least it is quite clear that the "wealth" given as price consists in goods, not money, namely, where we are told of Eurycleia[7] that "Laertes had bought her with his wealth long before, when she was in her first youth, and had given for her twenty oxen." Homer, then, here speaks of "buying," even though the price is not in money. A better text for Sabinus, Paul thinks, than that which he had chosen.

Nevertheless, Paul declares a money price essential. Homer is no more of a source of law for him than Shakespeare is for us. Nor, in all probability, had Sabinus's attitude been very different in this respect. To bring in a reference to one of the great authors of the olden times was an elegant thing to do—that was the main consideration. Still, writers like Cicero and Quintilian do state[8] that a certain persuasive force attaches to the opinions of illustrious poets.

The way in which some of these passages are torn from their contexts, or in which one passage is interpreted by reference to another which has nothing to do with it, is highly reminiscent of the treatment of Old Testament material in the New Testament and Talmud. It is not proposed here to go into this problem, beyond remarking that, in this as in other matters, the similarity is probably due to the influence of the rhetorical schools, which was much the same throughout the civilized Mediterranean world.[9]

5. In Gaius 3.141, the Veronese text as usual omits the Greek quotation, *Iliad* 7.472–475 (extant in *Institutes* 3.23.2). But even in the MS which the scribe had before him, only the beginning seems to have been given, since he still puts *et reliqua*. See F. Kniep, *Gai Institutionum. Commentarius Tertius §§ 88–225* (1917), 27 n. 9, 28 n. 1.

6. *Odyssey* 1.430, 14.115, 452.

7. *Odyssey* 1.430–431.

8. Cicero, *Topica* 20.78; Quintintilian, *Institutio oratoria* 5.11.36, 40.

9. See the writer's discussion of F. Schulz's *Roman Legal Science*, in *Journal of Roman Studies* 38 (1948), 115 f.

Index of Sources

283

50.17.167 pr.: 249
50.17.202: 46
Institutes
2.1.37: 90
2.2: 94
3.23.2: 281
4.6.14: 170
4.7.7: 149, 176
Novels
74.4: 129
117: 110
117.6: 125
136.4: 82

Corpus Inscriptionum Latinarum
VI. 2,8862: 46
VI. 12,133: 46

Gaius
1.5: 62
1.46: 234, 255, 257
1.85, 91: 187
1.114: 245
1.160: 187
1.200: 148
2.79: 56
3.90: 83
3.129: 145
3.141: 281
4.4: 170, 171
4.19: 82
4.48: 85

Gaii Epitome 1.2.2: 256

Lex Aquilia: 192, 193

Lex Julia municipalis 116 ff.: 32

Lex Papia Poppaea: 244

Lex Rhodia de iactu: 19

Lex Tarentina 29 ff.: 234, 243

Lex Salica
1.1: 29
6.1, 50.4: 33
Supplement to *Lex Salica*, Capitulare
6.1: 29, 33

Lex Ursonensis
33.3. col. 1.1.22: 80
95.19ff.: 32
132.4. col. 3.11.25, 29: 80

Novellae Marciani
4.1 (Code 5.5.7. pr., 1): 112
4.3.2 (Code 5.5.7.2): 108, 112, 114, 126

Pauli Excerpta
111: 31
291: 31, 32

Tabula Heracleensis
104 f.: 110
110 f., 112 f., 122 f.: 109
123: 109, 110

Theodosian Code
4.6.3 (Code 5.27.1): 108, 109, 112, 114, 126
9.40.2 (Code 9.47.17): 131
16.5.9 pr.: 198

Twelve Tables
II 2: 30, 32

CLASSICAL AUTHORS

Metamorphoses
  4.602: 138
  5.529–30: 138
  5.564–67: 138
  14.71: 170

Pap. Berlin 13426: 139

Plato
  Crito 12.50E ff.: 227
  Gorgias
    484C: 271
    523 ff.: 9
  Laws
    4.721A: 270
    4.722A: 262
  Protagoras 352D: 223
  Theaetetus 151C: 136

Plautus
  The Captives
    2.3.6.366: 83
    828: 198
  Casina 403: 198
  Curculio
    30: 197
    622, 695: 196, 197
  Menaechmi
    1.2.2: 171
    5.9.93 ff., 1153 ff.: 97
  Miles gloriosus
    1416: 196, 197
    1417: 197, 198
  The Rope 2.4.21 f, 433 f.: 83
  Trinummus 212–13, 390: 198

Pliny the Younger, Letter to Trajan
  10.96 f.: 131

Pliny the Elder
  Natural History
    18.4.17: 220
    35.7.20: 240
    36.19.34.142: 31
  Panegyric 26.5: 237

Plutarch
  Moralia
    265D (*Quaestiones Romanae* 6): 60
    483F (*De fraterno amore*): 134
    535D (*On Compliancy* 17): 24
    602B (*On Exile* 7): 235
    745E (*Quaestiones conviviales*
      9.14.6): 62
    *That the Stoics Make More Para-
      doxical Assertions than the Poets*
      4: 11

Polybius, *Histories* 10.17.9: 216

Procopius
  Anecdota
    2.17: 107
    6.17: 114
    9.30: 116
    9.47 ff.: 108
    17.5 f.: 126
  De aedificiis
    1.9.1 ff.: 126
    1.9.2 f.: 127

Quintilian, *Institutio Oratoria*
  5.10.23: 177
  5.10.27: 177
  5.10.47: 176
  5.11.36, 40: 281
  6.1.50: 44
  6.3.74: 44

LATER SOURCES

Ball v. Ball 2 Simon 35 (1827): 134

Bürgerliches Gesetzbuch 250: 56

*Cantiere San Rocco v. Clyde Ship-
   building Co.* 1923 S.C. (H.L.) 105: 2

Code Napoléon art. 2279: 262

Fibrosa Case [1942] 2 AH E.R 122: 18

Goethe, *Faust* I: 228

Law Reform (Contributory Negligence)
   Act, 1945: 18

Law Reform (Frustrated Contracts)
   Act, 1943, 2, 18

Maritime Conventions Act, 1911: 18–19

Shakespeare
   Hamlet 3.2.242: 62
   Merchant of Venice 5.1.64 f.: 62
   Titus Andronicus 1.1.218: 25

Strindberg, *The Father*: 134

Subject Index

www.ingramcontent.com/pod-product-compliance
Lightning Source LLC
Chambersburg PA
CBHW020405100426

42812CB00001B/211